HISTORY OF SOCIALISM
IN THE UNITED STATES

BY

MORRIS HILLQUIT

AUTHOR OF "SOCIALISM IN THEORY AND PRACTICE"

with a new Introduction by

ALBERT FRIED

AUTHOR OF "SOCIALISM IN AMERICA" AND "THE JEFFERSONIAN
AND HAMILTONIAN TRADITIONS IN AMERICAN POLITICS"

———

*FIFTH REVISED AND
ENLARGED EDITION*

DOVER PUBLICATIONS, INC.
NEW YORK

11-14-72

This Dover edition, first published in 1971, is an unabridged and unaltered republication of the fifth revised and enlarged edition (1910) of the work originally published by the Funk & Wagnalls Company, New York and London, in 1903. A new Introduction has been written specially for the present edition by Albert Fried.

International Standard Book Number: 0-486-22767-7
Library of Congress Catalog Card Number: 73-152418

Manufactured in the United States of America
Dover Publications, Inc.
180 Varick Street
New York, N. Y. 10014

INTRODUCTION

TO THE DOVER EDITION

MORRIS HILLQUIT'S *History of Socialism in the United States* is an exploratory voyage into the shadowy recesses of the American past. It might prove as edifying to us as it did to the audience for whom he wrote it nearly seventy years ago. How much do we know about the Shakers, the Oneida Perfectionists, the foreign millenarian sects, the Owenites, Fourierists, and Icarians, the German Lassalleans and Marxists, the North American Federation of the First International, the Socialist Labor Party, the Anarcho-Communists, the Bellamyite Nationalists, the Christian Socialists, and the Socialist Party of America? Yet reading about them—now so remote, so exotic—as they pass in review through the pages of Hillquit's *History*, we are forcibly reminded that cupidity and possessive individualism have not alone defined our national ethic, that the ideal of fraternal cooperation is in fact deeply rooted in our soil. New Leftists and youthful communitarians of our time need only consult Hillquit's *History* to realize how quintessentially American they are, how persistent has been the tradition they embody.

The *History* may be read solely as a descriptive account of nineteenth-century communitarian and socialist movements. Hillquit does not discourage such a reading; unfailingly lucid and fair, he gives each movement its ample due. But his intention is to trace a pattern, discern a tendency, that would explain why all but one of them failed. And they failed, according to Hillquit, because they were at odds with, or were flights from, reality—the sudden, catastrophic transformation of an agricultural and rural society to an industrial and urban one. In the first half of the nineteenth century many Americans—hundreds of thousands, perhaps —responded to the rise of a money economy, with its attendant evils of selfishness, impersonality, conflict, and change, by seeking to restore the gemeinschaft principle; that is, by creating small communities, religious or secular (i.e., millenarian or utopian,) consecrated to harmony, solidarity, and happiness; imperishable communities in a world that had grown hopelessly deliquescent, where nothing could be taken for granted any more. These noble experiments were doomed from the start. "The communists," Hillquit writes, "could not create a society all-sufficient in itself; they were forced into constant dealings with the outside world, and were subjected to the laws of the competitive system both as producers and consumers." Most of them disappeared very shortly after their birth, leaving behind hardly a trace. Those that survived ended up as the fossilized remains of a bygone age.

The socialists of the second half of the nineteenth century, Hillquit maintains, presented a contrary problem. They were *in advance* of reality, or at least of the prevailing consciousness of reality. The socialists who emigrated from Germany between the 1840's and '80's offered a correct analysis of conditions in this country, but it was an analysis which Americans did not fully comprehend and whose implications, in any case, they rejected. These socialists contended that only one force on earth could stop the plutocrats from ravaging the land and expropriating its institutions: namely, the working class, organized, militant, ready to "expropriate the expropriators," ready to wage combat in behalf of the cooperative commonwealth. The German socialists divided over whether the combat should be peaceful or violent; if peaceful, whether by political or economic means; if violent, by individual or collective action. Very few native-born Americans paid any heed to the socialists, most of whom spoke in a foreign tongue and engaged in controversies that were arcane and unintelligible.

By the mid-1890's a change of mood had come over the country. At the beginning of the decade a number of middle-class groups expressed their abhorrence of predatory capitalism by joining one or another moral crusade: Nationalist, Christian Socialist, Fabian Socialist. To be sure, these died out in the ensuing commotion: the Populist upsurge, the 1893 Depression, the massive labor unrest (culminating in the great Pullman strike), and the radical realignment of political parties. McKinley's landslide election in 1896 emphatically demonstrated that the middle class wanted law and order above all things, however strongly it felt about the trusts and the polarization of American life. But the election also demonstrated that socialism, the only rational alternative to the present system, might at last get a hearing from a substantial segment of the public, if offered in palatable form. The only organized socialist movement, however, was the Socialist Labor Party, now under the stern tutelage of Daniel De Leon. An inflexibly orthodox Marxist, De Leon affirmed, in one blazing polemic after another, that capitalism must soon collapse and usher in the commonwealth of the future, a political system corresponding to industrial departments under the direction of workers. He also insisted that the Party rank and file, on pain of expulsion, follow him unswervingly in all matters of theory and policy. De Leon's authoritarian leadership and doctrinaire views condemned the SLP to impotent propheticism, and it went the way of all previous sects.

Hillquit's *History*, then, is a journey of successive failures, from Mother Ann to Daniel De Leon. But at journey's end it holds out the prospect that the past might be redeemed. The final section of the book, a sort of transfiguration, is devoted to the emergence of a new socialist movement, begun in 1897 under Eugene V. Debs's inspiration and eventuating four years later as the Socialist Party of America. Here at last, Hillquit tells us, is an authentic American socialism, inclusive in its appeal to every disaffected group in the country, yet it is a socialism resting on a "scientific"—i.e., Marxist—analysis of political economy. To Hillquit's mind, the Socialist Party represents that unity of practicality and idealism that all the socialisms of the past longed for but could not attain.

Hillquit artfully conceals from the readers his role as an actor in the drama he records. His *History*, in fact, could be considered a veiled tribute to his own achievement as a prime mover, in many ways *the* prime mover, of the Socialist Party of America. At the "Unity Convention" of 1901, he was instrumental in drawing together the contending factions, revolutionary and reformist, under a compromise program. Subsequently, whenever a serious conflict arose within the Party, Hillquit, a successful lawyer, could be counted on to suggest the right formula, the precise quid pro quo, on which all sides could agree. He served as the Party's Henry Clay, its Great Pacificator, in its halcyon years before World War I. And like Clay he operated on two levels: behind the scenes, in the Party's inner councils, as a tireless administrator and strategist; and, through his outpouring of books and articles, his frequent speeches and debates, as an enormously effective propagandist of socialist ideas. If the Party had an official theoretician it was Hillquit; for he above all others defined its philosophy, its direction, the relation between its means and ends.

Personal experience had taught him how to hope realistically, how to work "constructively," for socialism. In 1886, at the age of seventeen, as Morris Hillkowitz, he came to America from Riga in Latvian Russia, a rather assimilated, or enlightened, Jew, knowing Russian and German but no Yiddish. When he threw himself into the struggle to organize the Lower East Side Jewish unions (the United Hebrew Trades) he had to learn Yiddish from Abraham Cahan (the future editor of the *Jewish Daily Forward*). Meanwhile, Hillquit joined the Socialist Labor Party and rose to some prominence in the New York City branch. As an orthodox Marxist he assumed that an insoluble "contradiction" existed between the industrial mode of production and the capitalist mode of social relations. That is, like De Leon and the other orthodox Marxists of the time— among them such giants of international socialism as Engels (who died in 1895), Kautsky, Plekhanov, Adler, and Labriola—Hillquit conceived industrial technology to have an irresistible logic, or momentum, that was driving the whole of society toward the center, organizing everything into larger and more highly concentrated units of production, simultaneously cleaving society into two classes, owners and workers, the latter possessing nothing but their labor power. If industrialism was rational, progressive, and civilizing, the capitalist form of management was irrational, retrograde, and barbaric, incapable of handling the technology it had called forth. For as capitalist productivity and wealth increased, so did the poverty and frequency of breakdowns; and so, inevitably, would the working class take matters into their own hands and overcome the "contradiction" by abolishing private property, making industry serve society, bringing about a true democracy in the place of the present factitious one.

Thanks to De Leon's disastrous policies, Hillquit soon discovered that mastering the laws of history was less difficult than applying them to the brute facts of the everyday world. In the early 1890's, De Leon tried to capture ("bore-from-within") first the American Federation of Labor and then the fading Knights of Labor. Failing in both, he set up a rival union (the Socialist Trade and Labor Alliance), entirely subordinate to the SLP. Defending this kind of "dual unionism" (always considered lèse majesté by organized labor), De Leon argued that the leaders of the AFL and the Knights were really "labor fakirs," or "lieutenants of capitalism," that only an SLP-sponsored union could be trusted to organize workers on an industry-wide basis, in political opposition to the power of the trustified corporations and the state. To large groups of SLP dissidents, resentful of De Leon's highhandedness and dogmatism, this was the last straw; they found intolerable an act which, in the name of socialism, threatened to destroy the existing trade unions, bad as they were. Cahan and many of the Lower East Side Jews left the Party in 1897 and affiliated with the new Social Democracy that Debs had just launched in Chicago. Two years later Hillquit led another group out of the SLP. This fusion of ex-SLPers and Debsian Social Democrats brought forth the Socialist Party of America.

Though Hillquit changed parties, he remained an orthodox Marxist. Only it was a Marxism that would no longer sacrifice the here and now, the daily struggles going on in the workshops and streets, for an indeterminate future; a

Marxism that would seek a more effective method of spanning the temporal gap, of resolving the tension between means and ends. He was still certain that industrial technology was the guarantor of the workers' republic. He still looked forward to the crisis that was gestating in the womb of capitalism, awaiting the midwifery of socialism. All the more reason, he now felt, why the Socialist Party should, without compunction, conduct itself like any other American party and openly solicit support from the public at large; from those who, socialist or not, could no longer abide the other parties. Hillquit, then, expected the Socialist Party to be two things at once: pragmatic, interest-oriented, an eager participant in the hurly-burly of "bourgeois" politics; and also a vanguard movement, representing the most advanced consciousness of society, committed to the root-and-branch reconstruction of American life. The Socialist Party was to be both a party of the masses and a party of the elect.

It rapidly became what Hillquit hoped it would be. By 1912—a mere nine years after the first edition of the *History* —it was a force to reckon with. Debs, running a fourth time for the presidency, won almost a million votes, or six percent of the total cast. Hundreds of socialists were elected to local offices, as councilmen, mayors, state legislators, and, in one instance, to Congress as well. Membership rose to over 100,000 (and each member, theoretically, was a witness, a proselytizer). The number of socialist publications ran into the hundreds, some achieving spectacular circulations (the *Appeal to Reason*, a weekly, had as many as three-quarters of a million subscribers). The Party's following was extremely diverse and heterogeneous—and distinctly non-proletarian. It came from the small farmers of the far West, groaning under the weight of competition from the large agricultural concentrations; from elements of the small-town middle class outraged by the pervasive corruption and hypocrisy and greed; from various foreign-born groups who favored a kind of ethnic pluralism for America (the Socialist Party made special provisions for the foreign-born affiliates, permitting each considerable group autonomy within the organization); from a high percentage—perhaps as many as a third—of the skilled workers who belonged to the AFL; and, not least, from the bearers of the public conscience: social reformers of every stripe, muckrakers, intellectuals (among them such well-known writers as Upton Sinclair, Jack London, and Ernest Poole), and non-conformists in general who saw the Party as the legatee of the country's revolutionary past.

While the Party prospered and grew, Hillquit and the other Marxist tacticians who dominated its inner councils—the vanguard of the vanguard, as it were—strove to keep it on its appointed course, making certain that it succumbed neither to sectarianism on the left nor "opportunism" on the right. The Party's relations with organized labor—that is, the AFL—was a case in point. Like De Leon, the Party regarded Samuel Gompers and the rest of the AFL leadership as "lieutenants of capitalism" (especially after Gompers joined the Civic Federation, established by Mark Hanna and other big-business statesmen to ensure industrial tranquility), and regarded the craft unions of the AFL as enclaves of privilege comprising the upper stratum of the industrial proletariat. Yet the Party had no intention of repeating De Leon's mistake. Against the urging of some of its radicals (Debs among them) it refused to sanction dual unionism, particularly since the Party had so many adherents within the AFL itself. The Party's strategy, accordingly, was to work within the AFL for the overthrow of Gompers and, ultimately, for the alliance of socialism and the unions. Hillquit and the other Socialist hierarchs had good reason to believe that this strategy would prove as successful as the Party's pursuit of votes and office.

But in the briefest of periods, within three years, the Socialist Party of America lay shattered in body and spirit. The "causes" of its destruction are well known and need not be elaborated on here. By officially opposing America's entry into the First World War the Party lost a large number of "patriotic" followers, especially native-born and working-class; socialism ceased thereafter to count for anything in the AFL. The government's cruel repression, moreover, sent the Party underground for the duration. When it surfaced in 1918 it confronted a struggle to the death between its left-wing faction, the revolutionary apostles of the Bolsheviks, and the Old Guard, chief among them Hillquit, who insisted on maintaining the Party's traditional democratic and legalistic character. The Old Guard won out, and the left wing departed to form the Communist Party. The break-up of American Socialism proved fatal to its chances. Since the shocks of 1917-19, neither the Socialists nor the Communists nor their several offshoots have been able to take advantage of the tremendous vicissitudes that the country has passed through: the Great Depression, the rise of Fascism, the Cold War, the turbulence, foreign and domestic, of the 1960's. Today, American socialism no longer exists as a coherent political force.

It would be appropriate, perhaps, to criticize Hillquit and the leaders of the pre-War Socialist Party by the same unsentimental standard that they applied to other socialisms. They failed; they therefore stand condemned by the test of "reality." Certainly Hillquit and the others were egregiously naïve in believing that industrialism was itself a force for progress and civilization in the world, that the "contradiction" between industrialism and capitalism must lead to socialism. But Hillquit's naïveté was the naïveté of all socialists at the time, including Lenin, who never imagined that socialism could be secured in pre-industrial Russia, who looked to the West to complete the revolution begun in his own country. For that matter, who in the pre-War era except a handful of "pessimists"—Sorel, Freud, Weber, and Pareto, for example—did not impute a moral value to technology? And even if, by some historical anomaly, the leaders of American socialism at the time had been pessimists too, what could they have done, being a tiny and beleaguered minority at most?

In a sense reality failed them. Force of circumstances, not the policies or ideology of Hillquit, explains the demise of American socialism. The War and the Bolshevik Revolution, neither of which could have been foreseen, simply overwhelmed it, nipped it in the bud. Those socialist parties that had the time to build sturdy organizations before 1914 managed to survive. How they survived, what disasters befell them—and the world as a whole—as a result of their division into socialists and communists, is another tale. Yet, whatever else one may say about the communist parties of France and Italy, and the socialist parties there and in the rest of Europe, they offer real and viable alternatives to the liberal and conservative defenders of the status quo. But the United States lacks such an alternative because the one time it had a chance to take hold, events conspired to crush it. History does not repeat itself, except as farce.

To the end of his days Hillquit remained a leader of the small Socialist Party of America. A life of bruising conflicts and frustrated hopes left him impenitent; he had no apologies. "I am a Socialist because I cannot be anything else," he wrote just before his death in 1934.

> I cannot accept the ugly world of capitalism, with its brutal struggles and needless suffering, its archaic and irrational economic structure, its cruel social contrasts, its moral callousness and spiritual degradation.
>
> If there were no organized Socialist movement or Socialist party, if I were alone, all alone in the whole country and the whole world, I could not help opposing capitalism and pleading for a better and saner order, pleading for Socialism.
>
> By violating my conscience, I might have made peace with the existing order of things and found a comfortable place among the beneficiaries of the system. I might have joined one of the political parties of power and plunder and perhaps attained to a position of influence and "honor." I might have devoted my life to the acquisition of wealth and possibly accumulated a large fortune. But my apparent success would have been dismal failure. I should have been deprived of all the joys of life that only an inspiring social ideal can impart, of the pleasure and comradeship of the best minds and noblest hearts in all lands, and, above all, of my own self-respect.

> Having chosen and followed the unpopular course of a Socialist propagandist, I am entirely at peace with myself. I have nothing to regret, nothing to apologize for.*

As for the *History of Socialism in the United States,* it speaks for itself. For us, reading it today, it is not what Hillquit intended it to be in 1903 or 1910: an assessment of a tradition about to be renewed and transcended. For us, the *History* is a "classic," hardly surpassed as an account of an inheritance now neglected or forgotten.

ALBERT FRIED

Loose Leaves from a Busy Life (New York: 1934), p. 331.

PREFACE TO REVISED EDITION

SINCE the first appearance of this book (October, 1903), four editions of it have been printed without any change in the text. But now, when my publishers are about to send it out into the world for the fifth time, I feel that the task of subjecting it to a thorough revision can no longer be delayed.

There are several reasons why such revision should be undertaken at this time. The last six years have been years of uncommon interest and eventfulness for the socialist movement of this country, and no history of the movement can claim to be complete without at least a brief record of these events. The task of bringing the narrative down to date has made necessary the addition of an entirely new and somewhat extended chapter.

An attempt has also been made in this edition to analyze the character of the American socialist movement and to forecast its probable future. When the "History of Socialism in the United States" was first written, socialism was only beginning to gain a foothold in this country, and the organized socialist movement was barely in its formative stage. The Socialist Party, which, to-day represents the bulk of all organized socialist activities in the United States, was only two years old. Its following was small, and its policy was somewhat unsettled. During the last six years, the party has almost doubled the number of its voters and trebled its enrolled membership. It has largely extended and perfected its organization, and has evolved more fixt and efficient methods of action. Since its organization in 1901, the Socialist Party has held three conventions and has passed through two national political campaigns. Its mission and place in the politics of the country have become more definitely settled. And as American socialism is gradually unfolding itself and revealing its nature, aims and methods, the future of the movement and its probable effects on the life and destinies of the nation are becoming the subjects of legitimate inquiry. For, after all, the history of socialism in the United States is as yet by no means a closed book. Notwithstanding its many picturesque chapters, it must on the whole be regarded as a mere prelude. What will follow that mysterious prelude? Will it be a tuneful opera, a farce-comedy or a stormy drama? This is a question of deep concern to all thinking Americans, and especially to the toiling masses of the people, to whom the message of Socialism addresses itself in the first instance. I have endeavored to answer that question without passion or bias in the light of the past course of the development of the socialist movement at home and abroad.

Besides adding these new chapters, I have found it necessary to make many minor changes in the text of the first edition. In attempting to write a "History of Socialism in the United States," I ventured into a practically new and hitherto uncultivated field, and the book has not escaped the faults of most pioneer works of this kind—a number of inaccurate statements and some important omissions. These I have attempted to correct and to supply with the aid of the many friendly and helpful criticisms of the first edition of this book and of several new and valuable works on separate phases of the American socialist and labor movement which have appeared within the last years.

I realize keenly that the work is still by far not perfect or even complete. But I consider the importance of the subject and the favorable reception of the first edition of the book, a sufficient justification for the publication of this revised edition.

MORRIS HILLQUIT.

New York, November, 1909.

PREFACE TO FIRST EDITION

WHEN John Humphrey Noyes published his "History of American Socialisms" (1870), the modern socialist movement was almost unknown in this country. The "socialisms" described by Noyes are merely the social experiments of the early schools of communism. Most of these experiments have since passed out of existence, and those still surviving can not be considered part of contemporaneous socialism. Socialism to-day is a vastly different movement from what it was in the days of Noyes. The numerous isolated communities, with their multiform socialisms of various hues and shades, have given way to one organized and uniform socialist movement of national scope.

The growth of the socialist movement in the United States has become an object of interest to all students of social problems. Many books have been written in recent years on the theories of socialism, but its history has received very scant attention. In 1890 A. Sartorius von Waltershausen published a scholarly work on Modern Socialism in the United States,[1] which contains much valuable material on the history of the movement during the period of 1850 to 1890. One year later S. Cognetti de Martiis published a book under a similar title.[2] The author dealt with the earlier stages of the socialist movement as well as with its more modern phases, but contributed little new information on the subject. Neither work can at this date be regarded as a complete history of the socialist movement in America, and, moreover, both were written in foreign languages, and are for this reason inaccessible to the majority of American readers. Of writers in the English language

[1] "Der Moderne Sozialismus in den Vereinigten Staaten von Amerika."
[2] "Il Socialismo Negli Stati Uniti."

Prof. R. T. Ely was the only one to attempt a concise and intelligent history of American socialism,[3] but Mr. Ely's book was written in 1886, and the subject was only incidental to the thesis of his work.

A knowledge of the history of socialism is, however, indispensable for an intelligent appreciation of the movement. The circumstances of its origin and the manner of its growth furnish the only trustworthy key to its present condition and significance, and to the tendencies of its future development.

In preparing this work I have endeavored to fill a gap in the literature of the subject, and I now present it to the public in the hope that it may contribute in some degree to a better understanding of a movement which is fast becoming an important factor in the social and political life of our country.

MORRIS HILLQUIT.

New York, October, 1903.

[3] "The Labor Movement in America."

CONTENTS

PART I

Early Socialism

CHAPTER I

SECTARIAN COMMUNITIES

6 CONTENTS

CHAPTER IV

THE ICARIAN COMMUNITIES

PART II

The Modern Movement

CHAPTER I

ANTE-BELLUM PERIOD

CHAPTER II

THE PERIOD OF ORGANIZATION

CHAPTER III

THE PERIOD OF THE SOCIALIST LABOR PARTY

CHAPTER IV

THE SOCIALIST PARTY

CHAPTER V

PRESENT-DAY SOCIALISM

HISTORY OF SOCIALISM
IN THE UNITED STATES

GENERAL INTRODUCTION

GENERAL INTRODUCTION

THE nineteenth century was marked by a period of industrial revolution unprecedented in history. The small manufacturing of preceding ages was swept away by the gigantic factory system of modern times. The railroad,
telegraph, and steamboat tore down all geographical barriers, and united the entire civilized world into one great
international market, while the huge machine and the
power of steam and electricity increased the productivity
of labor a hundredfold, and created a fabulous mass of
wealth.

But this process of transformation brought in its wake a
number of new social problems.

While a comparatively small number of men fell heir to
all the benefits of the process, the greater part of the population often reaped from the rich harvest nothing but suf-
fering and privation.

The invention of new and perfected machinery reduced
many skilled mechanics to the ranks of common laborers,
and deprived many more of work and wages permanently,
or at least during the long and tedious process of "read-
justment."

The planless mode of production and reckless competition
among the captains of industry produced alternately seasons of feverish activity and intense work, and seasons of
enforced idleness, which assumed alarming proportions
during the oft-recurring periods of industrial depression.

The luxury, splendor, and refinement of the possessing
classes found their counterpart in the destitution, misery,
and ignorance of the working classes. Social contrasts became more glaring than in any other period in history.

These evils of modern civilization engaged the attention
of the most earnest social philosophers and reformers of

the last century, and numerous remedial systems and theories were suggested by them. The most radical of these, the theory which discerns the root of all evils in competitive industry and wage labor, and advocates the reconstruction of our entire economic system on the basis of cooperative production, received the name Socialism.

Socialism, like most other theories and movements, passed through many stages of development before it reached its modern aspect. In its first phases, it was a humanitarian rather than a political movement. The early socialists did not analyze the new system of production and did not penetrate into its historical significance or tendencies. The evils of the system appeared to them as arbitrary deviations from the "eternal principles" of "natural law," justice, and reason, and the social system itself as a clumsy and malicious contrivance of the dominant powers in society.

True to their theory that social systems are made and unmade by the deliberate acts of men, they usually invented a more or less fantastic scheme of social organization supposed to be free from the abuses of modern civilization, and invited humanity at large to adopt it.

The scheme was, as a rule, unfolded by its author by means of a description of a fictitious country with a mode of life and form of government expressive of his own ideas of justice and reason. The favorite form of description was a novel. The happy country thus described was the Utopia (Greek for Nowhere), hence the designation of the author as "utopian."

That these theories should have frequently led in practise to the organization of communistic societies as social experiments, was only natural and logical.

The utopian socialists knew of no reason why their plans of social organization should not work in a more limited sphere just as satisfactorily as on a national scale, and they fondly hoped that they would gradually convert the entire world to their system by a practical demonstration of its feasibility and benefits in a miniature society.

Utopian socialism was quite in accord with the idealistic philosophy of the French Encyclopedists, and lasted as long as that philosophy maintained its sway.

The middle of the last century, however, witnessed a great change in all domains of human thought. Speculation gave way to research, and positivism invaded all fields of science, ruthlessly destroying old ideals and radically revolutionizing former views and methods.

At the same time the mysteries and intricacies of the modern system of production were gradually unfolding themselves, and the adepts of the young social science began to feel that their theories and systems required a thorough revision.

This great task was accomplished toward the end of the forties of the last century chiefly through the efforts of Karl Marx, the principal founder of modern socialist thought. Marx did for sociology what Darwin did later for biology: he took it out from the domain of vague speculation and placed it on the more solid basis of analysis, or, to borrow an expression from Professor Sombart,[1] he introduced realism into sociology.

The social theories of Karl Marx and the socialist movement based on them are styled Modern or Scientific socialism in contradistinction to Utopian socialism.

Modern socialism proceeds upon the theory that the social and political structure of society at any given time and place is not the result of the free and arbitrary choice of men, but the legitimate outcome of a definite process of historical development, and that the underlying foundation of such structure is at all times the economic basis upon which society is organized.

As a logical sequence from these premises, it follows that a form of society will not be changed at any given time unless its economic development has made it ripe for the change, and that the future of human society must be looked for, not in the ingenious schemes or inventions of

[1] Werner Sombart, "Socialism and the Social Movement of the Nineteenth Century," 1898.

any social philosopher, but in the tendencies of economic development.

Contemporary socialism thus differs from the early utopian phase of the movement in many substantial points. It does not base its hopes exclusively on the good-will or intelligence of men, but also and very largely on the modern tendency towards the socialization of industries. It does not offer a fantastic scheme of a perfect social structure, but advances a realistic theory of gradual social progress. It does not address itself indiscriminately to mankind at large, but appeals primarily to the working class, as the class most directly interested in the proposed social change. It does not experiment in miniature social communities, but directs its efforts toward the industrial and political organization of the working class, so as gradually to enable it to assume the direction of the economic and political affairs of society.

Both aspects of the movement have been well represented in the United States, and we will treat of them separately, devoting the first part of this work to an account of utopian socialism and communistic experiments, and the second part to the history of modern socialism.

PART I

EARLY SOCIALISM

INTRODUCTION

UTOPIAN SOCIALISM AND COMMUNISTIC EXPERIMENTS

WE noted in the General Introduction that the theories of utopian socialism frequently led to experiments in communistic settlements, and we may add here that these theories gained more or less popularity in the United States as the scheme was associated with such experiments. Thus the system of the great French utopian, Henri Saint-Simon, which had for its principal aim the organization of national and international industry on a scientific basis, and was a universal social philosophy not admitting of experiments on a miniature scale, found practically no following in the United States. The philosophy of Robert Owen, in which communities are not made an essential factor, but play an important part as preparatory schools for the communistic *régime,* gained a considerable foothold in the United States, altho it did not attain the same degree of strength or exercise the same measure of influence on social thought as it did in the country of its birth, England. On the other hand, the system of the French utopian, Charles Fourier, which was based principally upon miniature social organizations, developed more strength in this country than it did in France, while the purely experimental Icarian movement, altho originating in France, found its entire practical application in the United States.

The causes which contributed to make this country the chief theater of experiments of the utopian socialists of all nations were many.

The social experimenters as a rule hoped that their settlements would gradually develop into complete societies with a higher order of civilization. For that purpose they

23

needed large tracts of cheap land in places removed from the corrupting influences of modern life, and America abounded in such lands at the beginning and in the middle of the nineteenth century.

Besides the industrial and agricultural possibilities of the young and growing country, its political liberty and freedom of conscience had an irresistible charm for these pioneers of a new order of things.

The number of communistic and semi-communistic colonies founded in this country during the nineteenth century is largely a matter of speculation. Noyes,[1] writing in 1869, gives an account of about sixty communities exclusive of the Shaker societies. In 1875 Nordhoff[2] enumerated eighteen Shaker societies embracing fifty-eight separate "families" or communes, and twelve other, chiefly religious, communities, which, however, included three of those mentioned by Noyes; and three years later Mr. Hinds[3] recorded sixteen new communities, partly in existence and partly in the process of formation. Mr. Shaw,[4] in 1884, asserted that in the course of his researches he had come across at least fifty communities organized since 1870, and Alexander Kent,[5] writing in 1901, described twenty-five new communities and brotherhoods that had been established in our own days.

[1] "History of American Socialisms," by John Humphrey Noyes.
[2] "The Communistic Societies of the United States," by Charles Nordhoff.
[3] "American Communities," by William A. Hinds. The greater portion of the first part of this book was already written when a second revised and enlarged edition of Mr. Hinds' work appeared from the press of Charles H. Kerr & Company, Chicago. The new edition includes an account of the Owenite and Fourieristic experiments which were not touched upon in the first edition; it traces the history of the most important religious communities, as well as that of the Icarian communities, to recent dates, adds more than twenty new communities to those described by previous authors, and is now altogether the most elaborate and complete account of American communities.
[4] "Icaria, a Chapter in the History of Communism," by Albert Shaw, Ph. D.
[5] "Cooperative Communities in the United States," by Rev. Alexander Kent, in Bulletin of Department of Labor, No. 35, July, 1901.

Basing our estimates on the fragmentary accounts of these authors, we may safely assume that several hundred communities existed in different parts of the United States during the last century, and that the number of persons who at one time or another participated in the experiments ran into hundreds of thousands.

The history of these communities is as varied as their classification with reference to their origin and particular objects, but here we are concerned only with those which formed part of a general movement directly or indirectly connected with a distinct school of utopian socialism. These we may divide into the following four leading groups:

1. SECTARIAN COMMUNITIES

This group is comprised of the Shakers, the Perfectionists, and several communities organized by German immigrants. Their primary object was in all cases the free and unhampered exercise of their particular religious beliefs. Their communism was only a secondary feature, introduced in some instances as part of the religious system, and in others as a measure to preserve the integrity of the sect and to remove its members from the influences of the infidel world.

They had no general theories of social reconstruction; they made no propaganda for communism, and established their settlements, not as an object-lesson for their neighbors, but as a retreat for themselves. They are usually styled *Religious Communities* in the literature of the subject, but we hardly think this designation expressive of their aims and character. What distinguishes them from other communities is not the fact that they were religious, for so were many communities of the other groups, but the fact that their religious beliefs and practises were of a peculiar and sectarian nature.

These communities are the earliest in point of time, the strongest in point of numbers, and some of them still survive. But in the history of the socialist movement they played only a very secondary part, and for this reason we will limit ourselves to a brief account of the most important and typical of them.

2. The Owenite Communities

This was a group of communities founded either by Owen directly or under the influence of his agitation. They were the first communities organized in this country in furtherance of a general social theory and as a means of propaganda. Only twelve of the group have been rescued from oblivion, altho in all likelihood many more existed. The period covered by these experiments is that from the year 1825 to the year 1830.

3. The Fourierist Communities

These communities were organized by American followers of Charles Fourier. In their plan of organization they strove to approach as closely as possible the ideal of the industrial communities designated in Fourier's system as ''Phalanxes'' and most of them styled themselves Phalanxes.

Fourierism was the first socialist system to attain the dignity of a national movement in the United States. The movement lasted about a decade, from 1840 to 1850, and produced over forty social experiments in different parts of the country.

4. The Icarian Communities

The Icarian settlements were a series of experiments growing out from a single enterprise of the Frenchman Etienne Cabet, and altho we meet them in five different States, at different times and under different names, they must be considered as one community.

The original community, ''Icaria,'' was founded in 1848, and its numerous offshoots, formed by a constant process of schisms and migrations, prolonged its existence for almost half a century.

The Icarian movement developed some strength in the fifties of the last century, but was of little significance after that period. Altho conducted on American soil, the experiment was confined almost exclusively to Frenchmen, and had little influence on the modern socialist movement.

Chapter I

SECTARIAN COMMUNITIES

I.—THE SHAKERS

AMONG the sectarian communities of the United States, the Society of the Shakers is one of the oldest. The first Shaker settlement was established at Watervliet, New York, in 1776. The founder of the movement, and first "leader" of the society, was "Mother" Ann Lee, an illiterate Englishwoman, who, with a handful of followers, came to this country in 1774 to escape religious persecution at home.

Ann Lee died in 1784, and was succeeded by James Whitaker, Joseph Meacham, and Lucy Wright, under whose administration the society made great gains in members and wealth, and branched out into a number of communities. What strengthened the movement most was the epidemic revivals of the close of the eighteenth and the beginning of the nineteenth centuries, and especially the unparalleled religious excitement which developed in Kentucky in 1800 and lasted several years.

The Shaker societies seem to have reached their zenith in the second quarter of the last century, when their combined membership exceeded 5,000. In 1874 Nordhoff reports the total Shaker population of this country as 2,415; these figures were reduced to 1,728 in 1890, according to census returns. Scarcely more than 500 survive at present.

The Shakers are divided into three classes or orders:

1. THE NOVITIATE.—These are communicants of the Shaker church, officially styled the "Millennial Church" or "United Society of Believers," but they live outside of the society and manage their own temporal affairs.

2. THE JUNIORS.—These are members on probation. They reside within the society and temporarily relinquish

29

their individual property, but they may return to the world and resume their property at any time.

3.   THE SENIORS, OR CHURCH ORDER.—This order consists of persons who have absolutely parted with their property and irrevocably devoted themselves to the service of the Shaker church.

The unit of organization of the Shaker society is the "family." This consists of men and women living together, and ranging in numbers from a very few to a hundred and more. They maintain common households, and as a rule conduct one or more industries in addition to agricultural pursuits.

The spiritual interests of the family are administered by "elders," and the temporal affairs by "deacons."

Several families, usually four, constitute a "society."

The central government is vested in an executive board styled the "ministry" or "bishopric," and consisting of two elder brothers and two elder sisters; the head of the ministry is called the "leading elder" or "leading character." The ministry appoints the deacons, and in conjunction with them the "caretakers," or foremen, of the various branches of industry.

The leading elder fills vacancies in the ministry, and designates his own successor. Each officer of the society, spiritual or temporal, takes orders from his immediate superior, and women are represented on all administrative bodies in the same manner as men.

The principal tenet of their peculiar creed is, that God is a dual being, male and female, Jesus representing the male element, and Ann Lee the female element. Man, created in the image of God, was originally also dual. The separation of sexes took place when Adam asked for a companion, and God, yielding to the request, cut out Eve from his body. This was the first sin committed by man. The Shakers, therefore, regard marriage as appertaining to a lower order of existence, and are strict celibatarians.

The religious history of mankind they divide into four cycles, each having a separate heaven and hell. The first includes the period from Adam to Noah, the second embraces the Jews until the advent of Jesus, the third extends to the period of Ann Lee. The fourth, or "heaven of last dispensation," is now in process of formation and will include all Shakers.

They profess to hold communion with the spirit world, and the revelations received by them from the spirits are generally heralded by violent contortions of their bodies. It is this peculiar feature which earned for them first the appellation of "Shaking Quakers," and then of "Shakers."

The Shakers lead a well-ordered and healthful mode of life. They retire at about nine o'clock and rise at five. They breakfast at six, dine at twelve, and sup at six. Their diet is simple but sufficient. Their favorite dishes are vegetables and fruit, and many discard meat altogether. They eat in a general dining-hall, the men and the women sitting at separate tables.

Their dormitories, dining-halls, and shops are scrupulously clean, and the strictest order prevails everywhere.

Their amusements are few and of a very quiet order. Instrumental music is looked upon with disfavor, reading is restricted to useful and instructive topics. Singing of hymns and discourses in the assembly-room are frequent, and lately they have begun to indulge in quiet outdoor sports, such as picnics, croquet, and tennis.

The communism of the Shakers is part of their religious system, but it extends to the family only. There is no community of property in the Shaker society as a whole; one family may possess great wealth, while another may be comparatively poor.

The Shakers are at present divided into fourteen societies, located in the States of Maine, New Hampshire, Massachusetts, Connecticut, New York, Ohio, Kentucky and Florida, and their aggregate wealth is estimated in millions, their landed possessions alone amounting to over 100,000 acres.

II.—THE HARMONY SOCIETY

WITHIN a few miles of Pittsburg, in the State of Pennsylvania, lies a little village, consisting of about 100 dwelling-houses. Until a few years ago it was owned jointly by a few old men of puritanical habits, who exercised rigid supervision over the mode of life of the inhabitants.

The name of the place was Economy, and the few village autocrats were the last survivors of an erstwhile hustling and prosperous community.

The community, officially called the "Harmony Society," was more popularly known as the "Rappist Community," and had an eventful history, covering a period of almost a full century.

Its founder, George Rapp, was the leader of a religious sect in Würtemberg denominated "Separatists." The peculiar beliefs of the sect provoked the persecution of the clergy and government, and in 1804, Rapp, with about 600 sturdy adherents, left Germany and came to this country by way of Baltimore and Philadelphia. The main body of immigrants were farmers and mechanics, but there were also among them men of liberal education, and one of them, Frederick Reichert, an adopted son of George Rapp, possest considerable artistic taste and great administrative talent.

The first community established by them was "Harmony," in Lycoming County, Pennsylvania, and within a few years they erected a number of dwelling-houses, a church, a schoolhouse, some mills and workshops, and cleared several hundred acres of land.

But despite their apparent prosperity, they came to the conclusion that the site of the settlement had not been well chosen. In 1814 they sold their land with all the improvements for $100,000, and removed to Posey County, Indiana, where they purchased a tract of 30,000 acres.

Their new home was soon improved and built up, and became an important business center for the surrounding country. They grew in wealth and power, and received large accessions of members from Germany, until in 1824 their community was said to comprise about 1,000 persons.

In that year they removed again. Malarial fevers infesting their settlement had caused them to look for a purchaser for some time, and when at last they found one in the person of Robert Owen, they bought the property at Economy, and took possession of it at once.

How rapidly they developed their new village, appears from an account by the Duke of Saxe-Weimar, who visited them in 1826. He was full of praise of the neatness and good order of the village, of the beauty of the houses, the excellent arrangement of the shops and factories, and the apparent happiness of the settlers.

The peaceful course of their lives was only once seriously disturbed. In 1831 a "Count Maximilian de Leon" arrived at Economy in gorgeous attire and surrounded by a suite of followers. He pretended to be in accord with the religious views of the settlers, and announced his desire to join them.

The simple-minded people welcomed him most cordially, and admitted him to their society without any investigation. "Count de Leon," whose real name was Bernhard Müller, and who was an adventurer, soon began to undermine the beliefs of the Harmonists, and to advocate worldly pleasures. By smooth insinuating manners he gained the support of many members, and when a separation became inevitable, and the adherents of each faction were counted, it was found the 500 members had remained true to "Father" Rapp, while 250 declared for the "Count." The minority party received the sum of $105,000 for their share in the common property, and, with De Leon at their head, removed to Phillipsburg, where they attempted to establish a community of their own. But their leader forsook them, escaping with their funds to Alexandria, on the Red River, where he died of cholera in 1833. The seceders then disbanded.

The Economists meanwhile had recovered their prosperity very rapidly. At the outbreak of the civil war they had about half a million dollars in cash, which, for better safety, they buried in their yards until the war was over.

The Harmonists had not been celibatarians at the outset of their career, but in 1807, during a strong "revival of religion," the men and women of one accord determined to dissolve their marriage ties, and henceforward "no more marriages were contracted in Harmony, and no more children were born."

Outside of their celibacy, the Harmonists were by no means ascetics: they enjoyed a good meal and a glass of good beer, and in the earlier stages of their history, when the members were more numerous and youthful, they led a gay and cheerful life.

Their communism, like that of the Shakers, was part of their religious system, and was limited to the members of their own community and church. When their own population was large and their pursuits were few, they employed no hired labor, but as their numbers dwindled down and their industries developed, the wage-workers at times outnumbered their members ten to one.

In the beginning of the present century the community had practically evolved into a limited partnership of capitalists owning lands, oil-wells, and stocks in railroad, banking and mining corporations. They admitted no new members and had no children, and as the original members gradually died out, the community disintegrated. In 1904 it was formally dissolved, and its property divided among its few survivors.

III.—ZOAR

THE community of Zoar, like that of Economy, was founded by Separatist emigrants from Würtemberg.

For a number of years the founders of the sect carried on an obstinate feud with the government of their country, whose enmity they had provoked by their dissenting religious doctrines, but principally by their refusal to serve in the army and to educate their children in the public schools. They were fined and sent to prison, and driven from village to village, until they determined to look to the hospitable shores of the United States for a refuge from the persecutions of their intolerant fatherland. The generous assistance of some wealthy English Quakers enabled them to pay their passage, and in 1817 the first detachment of the ·society, about 200 in number, arrived in Philadelphia, headed by their chosen leader, Joseph Bäumeler.

Immediately upon their arrival they purchased several thousand acres of land in Tuscarawas County, Ohio, and went to work clearing much of the land and erecting a number of log houses for the members of the community, many of whom had remained behind working for neighboring farmers. This village thus founded by them they called Zoar.

The land, for which only a small cash payment had been made, was purchased in the name of Joseph Bäumeler, with the understanding that a parcel was to be assigned to each member, to be worked and the cost paid off by him individually.

They had no intention of forming a communistic society. But they had a number of old and feeble members among them who found it difficult to make their farms pay by their own efforts, and it soon became apparent that their members would be compelled to scatter, and that the enterprise would fail unless it was reorganized on a different foundation.

In April, 1819, after a thorough discussion of the situation, they resolved accordingly to establish a community of goods and efforts, and from that time on they prospered. They organized blacksmith's, carpenter's and joiner's shops, kept cattle, and earned a little money from work done for neighboring farmers.

The building of a canal through their land in 1827 was a piece of rare good fortune to them. They obtained a contract to do part of the work for the sum of $21,000, and secured a market for many of their products. Within a short time they lifted the mortgage on their property, and purchased additional lands.

Much of their early success the Zoarites undoubtedly owed to the wise administration of their leader, Joseph Bäumeler. Bäumeler, who in later years spelled his name Bimeler, was a man of little education, but of great natural gifts. He was the temporal as well as the spiritual head of the community. He had the general supervision of its affairs, attended to all its dealings with the outside world, and on Sundays delivered discourses to the Zoarites on religion and all other conceivable topics. Many of these discourses were collected and printed after his death. They make three ponderous octavo volumes, and were highly treasured by his followers.

The Zoarites prohibited marriage at first, but after ten or twelve years of celibate life they came to the conclusion that it was not good for man to be alone, and revoked the prohibition.

It is related that this change of sentiment on the question of marriage was caused by the fact that Joseph Bimeler, at a rather advanced age, fell in love with a pretty maiden who had been assigned by the community to wait on him. But be this as it may, the fact is that the leader of Zoar was one of the first to make use of the new privilege.

In 1832 the society was incorporated under the laws of Ohio, adopting the name of ''The Society of Separatists of Zoar.''

Under their constitution the government of the society's affairs was vested in three trustees, who appointed the superintendents of their different industries, and assigned each member to a certain kind of work, always taking into consideration the inclinations and aptitudes of the member.

They had a standing arbitration committee of five, to whom all disputes within the community were referred, and annual village meetings at which all members of legal age, female as well as male, had a vote.

The highest point in their development seems to have been reached shortly after their incorporation, when their membership exceeded 500. In 1874, according to Nordhoff, they still had about 300 members, and owned property worth over a million dollars.

As long as the community was poor and struggling hard for existence, perfect harmony prevailed among the members, but when it had acquired considerable wealth, temptation came in and efforts were made from time to time by discontented members to bring about a dissolution of the community and a division of its property. Thus in 1851, and again in 1862, suits for partition were brought in the Ohio courts by former members, but the courts upheld the community, and dismissed the suits.

The movement for a dissolution of the community continued, however, and in 1895 it acquired much strength from the support of Levi Bimeler, a descendant of the venerated founder of Zoar, and himself an influential member of the community. The discussion continued for three years, and at times waxed very warm and acrimonious, until, at the annual village meeting of 1898, the motion to dissolve was finally carried.

Three members were by general agreement elected commissioners to effect an equitable division. The amount awarded to each member was about $1,500.

IV.—THE AMANA COMMUNITY

THE Amana Community is the strongest of the surviving communistic societies in point of numbers. The community was founded by a religious sect denominated "The True Inspiration Society," which originated in Germany in the early part of the eighteenth century. The principal dogma of their faith is that God from time to time still inspires certain persons, who thus become direct instruments of his will.

Between 1820 and 1840 a large number of believers gathered around the principal "instruments" of the society, Christian Metz and Barbara Heynemann, in a place called Armenburg, in Germany. They found employment in the factories of the neighborhood, and their material existence seemed well secured, but increasing persecution on the part of the authorities made their further stay in Germany impossible.

At this juncture Metz had two successive inspirations, one directing him to lead the entire congregation out of Germany, and the other pointing to the United States as the future home of the inspirationists.

Toward the end of 1842 Metz, accompanied by four other members of the congregation, arrived in New York, and bought about 5,000 acres of land near Buffalo. Within the next two years they were joined by no less than 600 of their brethren from Germany, and settling on the land purchased by Metz, they formed the community of Ebenezer.

Like the Zoarites, they did not contemplate at first the establishment of a communistic settlement. But among their members there were some who were accustomed to factory labor, and to whom agricultural life was distasteful. In order to retain these members, it was necessary to build workshops and factories on their land, and this could only be accomplished by their common efforts and means.

"We were commanded at this time by inspiration," relates one of their members, "to put all our means together and live in a community, and we soon saw that we could not have got on or kept together on any other plan."[1]

Their membership increased rapidly, and they soon found that their land was not sufficient for the requirements of their growing community.

Under the circumstances it is not to be wondered at that they were "commanded by inspiration to move to the West."

[1] Quoted in Nordhoff's "Communistic Societies."

In 1855 they purchased about 18,000 acres of land near Davenport, in the State of Iowa, and there established the Amana Society, which is still in existence and flourishing, having more than doubled its original population. The community at present consists of seven separate villages, with a total of about 1,800 inhabitants.[2]

The names of the villages are Amana, East Amana, Middle Amana, Amana near the Hill, West Amana, South Amana, and Homestead. They lie about a mile and a half apart, and each has its separate schoolhouse, store, tavern, shops, and factories. Each village manages its own affairs and keeps its own accounts, but the latter are sent in annually to the headquarters at Amana for verification. The foremen and elders of the village meet every day in consultation, lay out the work for the next day, and assign the members to the various branches of the work according to the requirements of the season. The central government of the community is vested in thirteen trustees elected annually by the vote of all male members. The trustees elect a president.

Each family lives in a separate house. But they have common dining-halls, usually several in each village, where the men and women eat at different tables, to ''prevent silly conversation and trifling conduct.''

To supply them with clothing, an allowance is made to every member of the community. The adult man receives from $40 to $100 per year, according as his position and occupation make necessary more or less clothing; for each adult female the allowance is from $25 to $30 a year, and for children from $5 to $10.

The village store contains all goods used by the Amanites, and members may take what they please, being charged with the price of the article until the limit of the allowance has been reached. If a balance remains in favor of

[2] ''Amana, a Study of Religious Communism,'' by Richard T. Ely, in *Harper's Monthly* for October, 1902.
''Amana, The Community of True Inspiration,'' by Bertha M. H. Shambaugh, 1908.

a member, it is carried over to his credit for the next year.

In their schools they pay equal attention to the ordinary branches of elementary education and to manual training. Children from the age of seven to fourteen attend school during the entire year; from fourteen to twenty, during the winter season only. They dress and live plainly but substantially, and enjoy five hearty meals a day. They are very easy-going in their work, and in harvest time they employ much hired help.

They do not prohibit marriage, but neither do they encourage it. It is recorded that they even once expelled from the society their great divine "instrument," Barbara Heynemann, "for having too kind an eye on the young men."

Marriage is only permitted on the consent of the trustees and after the groom has attained the age of twenty-four. Their weddings are very gloomy ceremonies, and somewhat resemble their funeral services.

V.—BETHEL AND AURORA

THE village of Bethel, in Shelby County, Missouri, and that of Aurora, near Portland, Oregon, were sister communities, both owing their existence to Dr. Keil. Keil had a rather variegated career. Born in Prussia in 1812, he followed the trade of man-milliner until he emigrated to the United States. After a brief stay in New York, he removed to Pittsburg, where he announced himself a physician, practised "magnetic cures," and profest to be the possessor of a wonderful book of prescriptions written with human blood. At the age of thirty he underwent a sudden change: he became religious, burned his book, and joined the Methodist Church, which, however, he soon abandoned, to form a sect of his own.

He gathered around him a considerable following of simple-minded people, mostly Germans and "Pennsylvania Dutch," and in 1844, he was joined by a number of the seceders from Economy who had been abandoned by the faithless "Count de Leon."

It was at that time that Keil and his followers conceived the idea of establishing a communistic settlement, and for that purpose purchased about 2,500 acres of land in Shelby County, Missouri. This was the beginning of Bethel. The settlers seem to have had very little means, but an inexhaustible store of industry and endurance. After a few years, the greater portion of their land had been put under cultivation; they built a woolen mill, a grist-mill, a sawmill, several shops, a church, and a general store. Having added over 1,500 acres to their possessions, a post-office was established for them by the Government, and within ten years their settlement developed into a town with a population of about 650 persons.

But the restless spirit of Keil impelled him to new experiments. In 1855 we find him at the head of about eighty residents of Bethel who had set out for the Pacific coast in quest of cheap and fertile land. During the next year he organized the community of Aurora in Oregon. The membership of the new settlement, partly recruited from the outside and partly augmented by immigration from Bethel, soon reached about 400. These persons acquired over 18,000 acres of land in different counties of Oregon, duplicated almost all the industries carried on in Bethel, and in addition engaged largely in the growing and drying of fruit.

The form of government and mode of life of both communities were almost identical. Keil was president of both, and was assisted in the administration of the two villages by a board of trustees. Up to 1872 all the property in Bethel and Aurora stood in the individual name of Dr. Keil, but in that year he divided the land, and gave to each adult member a title-deed to one parcel. The partition was, however, a mere formality, the management of the villages remaining purely communistic as before.

The members were allowed to choose their own occupations, and to change them at will. They had no regular hours of work, nor was any actual supervision maintained, the foremen and superintendents being developed by a process of natural selection.

The community not only tolerated, but encouraged marriage, and maintained a strict family life. Each family had a separate house, and a number of pigs and cows sufficient for its needs. Flour and other articles of food were furnished by the community in any quantity desired. All other goods contained in the general store were delivered to members on request. Accounts were kept of dealings with outsiders, but not of transactions between the community and the members.

Their life was exceedingly peaceful and their history is not marked by any stirring events. They had few accessions from the outside, but managed to care for their own members pretty well. Once in a while a member would express a desire to leave the community, and to such they would give an equitable share in property or cash, and allow him to depart.

Of all religious communities, Bethel and Aurora had the loosest form of organization; they were held together principally by the personal influence of their founder, and disintegrated soon after his death. Dr. Keil died in 1877. Bethel was dissolved in 1880, and Aurora in 1881.

VI.—THE ONEIDA COMMUNITY

THE first historian of communism in the United States was himself the founder of one of the most noteworthy of communistic societies. The Oneida Community was the creation of John Humphrey Noyes.

Noyes was born in Brattleboro, Vermont, in 1811. He was graduated from Dartmouth College and took up the study of law, but soon turned to theology, taking courses at Andover and Yale. While pursuing his theological studies he evolved the religious doctrines which later received the name of Perfectionism.

In 1834 he returned to Putney, Vermont, the residence of

his parents, and gradually gathered around him a little circle of followers. His first permanent adherents were his mother, two sisters, and a brother; then came the wives of himself and his brother and the husbands of his sisters and then several others, until in 1847 he had about forty followers.

The movement was at first purely religious, but the evolution of its doctrines, coupled with the reading of the *Harbinger* and other Fourieristic publications, gradually led it to communism, and in 1848 Mr. Noyes established a communistic settlement at Oneida, in the State of New York.

During the first years of the experiment it had to cope with great difficulties, and succeeded but poorly. Noyes and his followers, most of whom seem to have been men of means, had invested over $107,000 in the enterprise up to January 1, 1857. The first inventory of the community was taken on that day and showed a total of assets amounting to little more than $67,000, a clear loss of about $40,000.

But during that time they had gained valuable experience, and had organized their industries on an efficient and profitable basis. They manufactured steel traps, traveling bags and satchels; they preserved fruit, and engaged in the manufacture of silk. Whatever they undertook, they did carefully and thoroughly, and their products soon acquired a high reputation in the market.

Their inventory for the year 1857, showed a small net gain, but during the ten years following, their profits exceeded $180,000.

In the meantime they had bought more land and gained new members. In 1874 they owned about 900 acres and their membership consisted of about 300 persons.

They had had several communities at the start, but in 1857 they concentrated all their members in Oneida and Wallingford, Connecticut.

The Oneida Community was the only important sectarian community in the country of purely American origin.

The bulk of its members consisted of New England farmers and mechanics, but they also had among them a large number of professional men—physicians, lawyers, clergymen, teachers, etc. Their standard of culture and education was considerably above the average.

Their affairs were administered by twenty-one standing committees, and they had forty-eight heads of industrial departments. Notwithstanding the apparent complexity of the system, their government was purely democratic and worked well.

The most striking features of the Perfectionists were their religious doctrines, their views on marriage, their literature and the institution of "mutual criticism." They held that the second advent of Christ had taken place at the period of the destruction of Jerusalem, and that at that time there was a primary resurrection and judgment in the spirit world; that the final kingdom of God then began in the heavens, and that the manifestation of that kingdom in the visible world is now approaching; that a church on earth is rising to meet the approaching kingdom in the heavens; that the element of connection between these two churches is inspiration or communion with God, which leads to perfect holiness—complete salvation from sin, hence their name of Perfectionists. The following definition of Perfectionism is quoted by Nordhoff as coming from one of the believers:

"As the doctrine of temperance is total abstinence from alcoholic drinks, and the doctrine of antislavery is immediate abolition of human bondage, so the doctrine of Perfectionism is immediate and total cessation of sin."

Their communistic theories extended to persons as well as to property, and they rejected monogamous marriage just as vigorously as they rejected individual ownership of property. Their marriage system was a combination of polygamy and polyandry. They pretended to secure the propagation of children on a scientific basis, preferably pairing the young of one sex with the aged of the other. This system they styled the "complex marriage" system.

They strongly resented the charge of licentiousness, and exacted "holiness of heart" before permitting "liberty of love."

Children were left in the custody of their mothers until they were weaned, when they were placed in the general nursery under the care of special nurses. Outside observers attested that they were a healthy-looking, merry set of children.

They maintained an excellent system of schools, and sent many of their young men to college to fit them for such professional callings as were needed within the community.

For the propaganda of their ideas they published a number of books and periodicals, the most popular among which was the *Oneida Circular*. This was a weekly magazine, well edited and printed, and was published on these singular terms, as announced at the head of one of its columns:

"The Circular is sent to all applicants, whether they pay or not. It costs and is worth at least two dollars per volume. Those who want it and ought to have it are divisible into three classes, viz.: 1, those who can not afford to pay two dollars; 2, those who can afford to pay only two dollars; and 3, those who can afford to pay more than two dollars. The first ought to have it free; the second ought to pay the cost of it; and the third ought to pay enough more than the cost to make up the deficiencies of the first. This is the law of Communism."

"Mutual Criticism" was said to have been invented by Noyes in his college days, and it became a most important institution in the Oneida Community from the very beginning of its existence. It took the place of trials and punishments, and was regarded by the Perfectionists not only as a potent corrective of all moral delinquencies, but also as a cure for a number of physical ailments.

Criticism was administered in some cases without solicitation from the subject, but more often at his own request. A member would sometimes be criticized by the entire society, and sometimes by a committee selected from among those best acquainted with him.

Plainly speaking, this procedure consisted in each member of the committee giving to the person criticized a piece of his or her mind—a pretty large one as a rule—and the salutary effect of this "mutual criticism" was supposed to show itself in revealing and thereby curing hidden defects or vices.

Nordhoff, who had the good fortune of attending one of these criticisms, gives an amusing account of it, which we reproduce in substance.

One Sunday afternoon a young man, whom we will call Charles, offered himself for criticism. A committee of fifteen, Mr. Noyes among them, assembled in a room, and the procedure began by Mr. Noyes inquiring whether Charles had anything to say. Charles said he had recently been troubled by doubts, that his faith was weakening, and that he was having a hard struggle to combat the evil spirit within him. Thereupon the men and women present spoke up in turn. One man remarked that Charles had been spoiled by his good fortune, that he was somewhat conceited; another added that Charles had no regard for social proprieties, that he had recently heard him condemn a beefsteak as tough, and that he was getting into the habit of using slang. Then the women took a hand in the criticism, one remarking that Charles was haughty and supercilious, another adding that he was a "respecter of persons," and that he showed his liking for certain individuals too plainly, calling them pet names before the people, and a third criticizing his table manners. As the criticism made progress the charges accumulated. Charles was declared to have manifested signs of irreligiousness and insincerity, and a general hope was exprest that he would come to see the error of his ways and reform. During this ordeal, which lasted over half an hour, Charles sat speechless, but as the accusations multiplied, his face grew paler and big drops of perspiration stood on his forehead. The criticisms of his comrades had evidently made a strong impression on him.

These frank expressions seem not to have provoked any ill-feeling among the members. The history of the Oneida Community discloses no discords of any kind; perfect harmony reigned at all times, and only one member was ever expelled.

The community existed and thrived over thirty years, but public opinion, aroused by the clergy of the neighborhood, finally became so pronounced against the "complex marriage" system, that the Perfectionists deemed it advisable to abandon that custom.

This became the signal for the dissolution of the Oneida Community as a communistic society. Noyes himself, accompanied by a few faithful followers, removed to Canada, where he died in 1886, and the remainder of the community was incorporated in 1880 as a joint stock company under the name of "Oneida Community, Limited."

The company is now very wealthy. The industries have all been preserved. The interests of the members in the property of the corporation are represented by stock held by them. A common library, reading-room, laundry, and lawns are the only surviving features of the old communistic régime.

Chapter II

THE OWENITE PERIOD

I.—ROBERT OWEN

THE social experiments and teachings of Robert Owen played an important part in the early history of American socialism, and a brief sketch of his life and theories are essential to the proper understanding of that period.

Robert Owen was born on the 14th day of May, 1771, in the Welsh village of Newtown, the seventh child of respectable but impoverished parents. He received a rather fragmentary public-school education, and at the age of eleven was apprenticed to a London merchant. Already the boy exhibited in a marked degree qualities which in later life were to make him a leading man in two continents: an extraordinary talent for organization, an untiring industry, and a keen analytical mind, combined with broad sympathies, excellent judgment of human nature, courage, and withal a uniformly courteous demeanor.

His business career was one of phenomenal success. Within a few years he had advanced from a subordinate clerkship in London to a very responsible position with a leading Manchester trading-house. At the age of nineteen years he was engaged by one Drinkwater to superintend his spinning-mill at Manchester, in which about 500 workingmen were employed. The manner in which he terminated the employment was very characteristic of the man. Mr. Drinkwater, after a brief trial, had agreed in writing to employ Owen for three years, and to make him a partner in his business at the expiration of that time.

In the meanwhile, however, the Manchester mill-owner had been offered very advantageous terms of partnership by a wealthy and influential merchant. Owen's outstanding agreement was the only obstacle to the arrangement, and Mr. Drinkwater determined to get rid of it at any cost. He invited Owen to his office, and explaining the situation to the young superintendent, asked upon what terms he would release him from the agreement, and offered him a position under the new management at any salary he might name. Owen, who had anticipated the purpose of the interview, and had come armed with his written contract, promptly committed it to the flames, and quietly watching the precious document reducing itself to ashes, remarked that he had no desire to force his association on Mr. Drinkwater, and that he could not remain in his employ on any terms. Shortly after this episode he acquired an interest in the Charlton Twist Company, which through his efforts became very prosperous.

During all his business preoccupations, Owen did not neglect the study of social phenomena. At the period at which we have now arrived he was already imbued with a conviction which subsequently guided all his actions, and in fact determined his entire course of life—the conviction that man is the creature of surrounding circumstances, that his character is not made by him, but for him.

"Man becomes a wild, ferocious savage, a cannibal, or a highly civilized and benevolent being, according to the circumstances in which he may be placed from his birth." His logical conclusion from this reasoning was that the only way of raising the character and habits of men is by improving the conditions in which they live.

He began the practical application of this theory in his treatment of the 500 Manchester operatives consigned to his care, but the abrupt discontinuance of his connections with Mr. Drinkwater checked the experiment before it could show positive results.

Owen now yearned for a larger field, and in the beginning of 1800 found one in the Scotch village of New Lanark. At New Lanark a cotton mill had been established on the

falls of the Clyde by Mr. David Dale and Sir Richard Ark-
wright, the famous inventor, in 1784.   In 1799 the village
consisted of about 2,500 mill-hands with their families,
and Mr. Dale was its sole proprietor.   It presented the
typical aspects of a manufacturing settlement of that time.
About 500 of the employees were children recruited from
the charitable institutions of Edinburgh, and fed and
housed in a large barrack that had been erected for the
purpose.   They were sent to the mill not infrequently at
the age of six years; their working hours lasted from six in
the morning until seven in the evening, and those of them
who survived grew up to be dwarfed and deformed, physically, mentally, and morally.   The work was so hard, and
the pay so small, that none among adults but the lowest
stratum would take employment at the mills.   The village
was dirty and the population given to brutality, drunk-
enness, thievery, and sexual immorality.   Most persons
were deep in debt to the petty village usurer, tavern-keeper,
and store-keeper.

Such was New Lanark when Owen, with several business
associates, purchased from Mr. Dale the mills (village and
all) for sixty thousand pounds.

As resident manager, Owen had power to introduce
such reforms as he thought proper.   He immediately
undertook the gigantic task of remodeling the village.
One of his first acts was to banish the village storekeepers
who had been in the habit of selling to operatives inferior
articles for excessive prices, and to establish instead superior shops, where all commodities were retailed at cost.   The
gin-mills and taverns were removed to the outskirts of the
village, the streets were cleaned, and comfortable dwelling-
houses were substituted for old hovels.

He determined to receive no more pauper children, and
discontinued the parish agreements made by Mr. Dale.
For the children of employees he established a model
infant school, and facilities for education were provided for
all.

He abolished all systems of punishment for delinquent
workmen, seeking to correct their shortcomings by kind

admonition, and to crown all, he voluntarily reduced their hours of labor and increased their pay.

Every step in these reforms was attended with difficulties; the superintendents of the different branches regarded Owen as a dangerous eccentric and blocked his schemes wherever possible. What was worse, the workingmen were by no means friendly to his reforms. Years of pitiless exploitation had made them distrustful. They suspected some hostile design behind each of his measures.

In 1806 a crisis broke out in the English cotton industry in consequence of the embargo laid by the United States upon the export of raw material. The operations of all cotton-mills of the United Kingdom were suspended. Thousands of working men thus thrown out of employment were facing starvation. Owen retained all of his employees, and altho no work was done for four months, he paid them full wages, amounting to about seven thousand pounds. This generous act finally convinced the mill-hands of the sincerity of Owen's purpose. Henceforward they had full confidence in their employer, and heartily cooperated with him in all his measures of reform.

But another obstacle arose. So long as the reforms introduced by Owen did not threaten to diminish the profits of the business, his partners did not interfere with him, but when he proposed more radical innovations, involving the building and maintenance of an expensive school and nursery, they rebelled, and pointedly declared that they had associated with him for business, not for philanthropy.

On account of these dissensions, Owen was forced to change partners twice, and in 1813 was in danger of being altogether ousted by the majority shareholders of the concern from the management of New Lanark.

But the resourceful philanthropist-manufacturer was equal to the occasion. He prepared a statement of the conditions at the works of New Lanark, of his humanitarian plans in connection with them, and of his difficulties with his partners. This he published for private circulation among well-disposed capitalists, and within a short time seven men of wealth, including the famous jurist, Jeremy Bentham, exprest their willingness to invest large sums of money in the New Lanark works, on the understanding that all profits above five per cent. on their investments should be applied to the improvement of the lot of the employees.

With the funds thus secured, Owen bought out his partners, and now had an entirely free hand to carry out his favorite reforms. Within a generation New Lanark became unrecognizable. The miserable village, with a degenerate population, had become a model colony of healthy, bright, and happy men and women, and the object of admiration of thousands of visitors who came to inspect it every year.

The fame of Owen's achievements spread to all civilized countries. Among his admirers he numbered sovereigns, princes, statesmen, and prominent men in all walks of life. At one time he was one of the most popular persons in Europe.

But Owen was not satisfied with his achievements. The splendid results in New Lanark deepened his conviction that man is the product of the conditions surrounding him. He now arrived at the ultimate and logical deduction from that theory—that an equal degree of morality and happiness presupposes equality in all material conditions of life. Owen had developed from a mere philanthropist into a full-fledged communist.

This change of views brought with it a desire for the enlargement of his sphere of activity. New Lanark had become too small a field; he longed to help the entire working class, and the remainder of his life was devoted to the propaganda of his ideas in all conceivable forms.

He early recognized the importance of factory legislation, and drafted many measures for the relief and protection of factory employees, some of which, owing to his efforts, were passed by Parliament.

In 1817 Owen was invited by the "Committee of the Association for the Relief of the Manufacturing and Labouring Poor" to state his views on the cause of increasing pauperism and to propose measures of relief. In his report to the committee he developed the view that under a system of free competition the increase of productivity of labor inevitably leads to the deterioration of the condition of the working class. The introduction of improved machinery threw thousands of working men out of employment, engendering a desperate competition for the means of subsistence, which lowered the standard of the workingman's life still more. No temporary measures could check this deplorable but inevitable concomitant of modern industrial development.

As a solution of the problem, Owen proposed the establishment of industrial communities on the basis of mutual cooperation. The communities were to consist of 500 to 1,500 persons, who would themselves produce all the necessaries of life. The members were to be housed in attractive buildings surrounded by gardens. Industry was to be conducted on a large scale by the men, while the women were to do the housework and tend to the education of the children.

The plan was rejected by the committee as too radical, but, nothing daunted, Owen continued his propaganda at public meetings and by private agitation.

True utopian that he was, he addrest himself to the spirit of benevolence of the wealthy and powerful, and even submitted his plans to Czar Nicholas of Russia, and to the Congress of Sovereigns at Aachen. Of course he met with no better success than that which had attended his efforts before the committee.

Owen now determined to undertake the experiment with his own resources, and eagerly watched for a favorable opportunity. When he learned in 1824 that the Rappist settlement in Indiana was for sale, his mind was soon made up. He purchased the settlement with everything on it, and sailed for America to superintend the experiment in person.

The varied fortunes of the communities founded by Owen and his followers in the United States are described separately in the following pages. These experiments have attracted so much public attention, that the other side of

Owen's activity in this country, his personal propaganda for the theories of communism, has been too often overlooked. That propaganda has, however, had a powerful influence on many of his contemporaries.

Upon his first arrival in the United States· he exhibited elaborate models of proposed communities, and delivered addresses on his favorite topics in many large American cities. He found numerous attentive listeners among the most intelligent classes of citizens.

At Washington he delivered several lectures in the Hall of Representatives before the President, the President-elect, all the judges of the United States Supreme Court, and a great number of Senators and Congressmen.

After the failure of New Harmony, Owen made three more visits to the United States. Each was devoted to the propaganda of socialism. In 1845 he called an international socialist convention in New York, but it turned out to be a rather insignificant affair. In 1846 we find him in Albany explaining to the Constitutional Convention of New York his theory on the formation of human character.

Several Owenite communities were founded in the twenties and thirties of the last century, in different parts of England, Scotland, and Ireland, but they met with no more success than those in America.

The failures of his communistic experiments did not discourage the indomitable reformer. In 1832 we find him enthusiastically engaged in a new enterprise, the "Equitable Banks of Labor Exchange."

"The quantity of average human labor contained in a commodity determines the value of such commodity," argued Owen; "hence if all commodities were exchanged by the producers according to that standard, the capitalist would have no room in industry or commerce, and the worker would retain the full product of his labor."

To carry this idea into operation, the "Equitable Labor Exchange Bank" was founded in London on the following plan: Every producer of a useful commodity could bring it to the "bazaar" connected with the bank, and receive for it notes issued by the bank and representing a number of labor hours equivalent to those contained in his article. With these notes the holder could purchase other articles contained in the bazaar and likewise valued according to the quantity of labor consumed in its production.

The weak point of the scheme was, that the bank occupied itself exclusively with the exchange of commodities, and did not attempt to regulate their production. Anything brought to the bazaar was accepted regardless of the actual demand for it. The result was, that after a short time all useful articles disappeared from circulation, and the bazaars were stocked with goods for which there was no demand. The "Equitable Labor Exchange Bank" suspended business, and its founder lost a fortune.

Owen was past sixty at that time, but he still continued for many years his activity in behalf of the working class. Under his influence the "Association of all Classes and Nations" was organized, a society which at one time exercised a powerful influence in English politics, and whose members called themselves "Socialists" after 1839. He also presided at the first national convention of English trade-unions.

Owen died on the 17th day of November, 1858. He had reached the age of eighty-seven years. Few lives have been so useful as his. His failures were many, but his achievements were great; he was the first to introduce the infant-school system; he was the father of factory legislation, was one of the first advocates of cooperative associations, and he anticipated many of the theories and features of the modern socialist movement.

Owen left four sons all of whom became American citizens. They all achieved renown in their chosen occupations. Robert Dale Owen was at one time the foremost exponent of his father's theories in this country. In conjunction with Frances Wright he published toward the end of the twenties of the last century, a magazine under the title *Free Enquirer,* and conducted a "Hall of Science" in New York, in which lectures were delivered on all topics of social reform. In sympathy with Robert Dale Owen and Frances Wright were the two brothers, George Henry and Frederick W. Evans, young Englishmen, who landed in New York in 1820. They published successively the *Working Man's Advocate*, the *Daily Sentinel* and *Young America*, and of these publications the last mentioned at one time enjoyed considerable popularity. *Young America* printed at its head twelve demands, of which the ninth, "Equal rights for women with men in all respects," and the tenth, "Abolition of chattel slavery and of wages slavery," are particularly interesting to-day. These demands were said to have been indorsed by no less than 600 papers in different parts of the United States.

Robert Dale Owen subsequently became very prominent in American politics. He was twice elected to Congress, and drafted the act under which the Smithsonian Institution in Washington was established. As a member of the Indiana Constitutional Convention he was chiefly instrumental in the enactment of the liberal provisions for woman's rights and the introduction of the free-school system in that State. He was for six years *chargé d'affaires* of this country at Naples, and was in his day one of the ablest and noblest figures in national politics. His letter to President Lincoln is said to have been a potent factor in bringing about the President's proclamation abolishing chattel slavery. Toward the end of his life he, like his father, turned to spiritualism. He died in 1877.

George Henry Evans remained active in the field of social reforms until his death in 1870, and Frederick W. Evans joined the Shakers in 1831, and became the leading man of the Mount Lebanon Community, where he was popularly known as Elder Frederick.

The period under discussion, which extended from about 1825 to the beginning of the industrial crisis of 1837, is remarkable for the fact that it witnessed the beginnings of the modern trade-union movement in this country. Numerous trade organizations were formed in several New England cities, and many of them conducted successful strikes for better wages and more frequently for shorter work-hours. In 1827 the first local central body of organized labor on American soil was created—the Mechanics' Union of Trade

Associations of Philadelphia. Six years later a similar body, the General Trades Union, was created in New York, and in 1834 the first national body of American trade-unions was organized under the name National Trades' Union. The organization existed four years and held three general conventions.

Partly under the influence of this early labor movement and partly under the influence of Owen's teachings, a so-cialistic movement of remarkable clearness and intensity sprang up at the same time. The movement produced several keen and forceful writers on economic subjects, chief among whom were L. Byllesby, whose main work, "Sources and Effects of Unequal Wealth," was published in New York in 1826, and Thomas Skidmore, whose "The Rights of Man to Property" appeared in 1829. Both writers may be classed as "utopian" Socialists, but in the keenness of their analysis of the modern industrial system and its effects on labor they frequently approach the clearness of conception of modern socialism.

Other persons of note who played a prominent part in the movement were Dr. Orestes Augustus Brownson, the well-known author, and subsequently editor of the Boston *Quarterly Review* and of *Brownson's Quarterly Review;* Stephen Simpson and Samuel Whitcomb, Jr., both writers of note, and Seth Luther, the talented and eloquent New England mechanic, who in 1832 delivered many telling addresses in the States of Massachusetts, New Hampshire and Maine on the wrongs of labor. The movement eventually gave rise to the formation of a political Workingmen's Party in the State of New York, whose platform, among other planks, contained a demand for the "abolition of slaves, white and black." The party held a State convention in Syracuse in 1830, and nominated Ezekiel Williams for Governor. Williams received a little less than 3,000 votes in the State, but in the city of New York, where the Workingmen's Party had fused with the Whigs, it succeeded in electing to the Legislature four of its candidates, Silas M. Stilwell, Gideon Tucker, Ebenezer Ford and George Curtis. In the following four years the Working-men's Party did not engage in practical politics or was unsuccessful at the polls. Its successor, the Equal Rights Party, in 1835 elected two of its candidates to the Legislature, Thomas Hertell and Job Haskell.

In 1831 a Workingmen's Party, similar to that of New York, was organized in Massachusetts, and in the following year it changed its name to The New England Association of Farmers, Mechanics and other Workingmen.[3]

II.—NEW HARMONY

THE scene of the first Owenite experiment on American soil was a tract of land on the Wabash River in the State of Indiana. It comprised about 30,000 acres, all of which was wilderness until 1814, when the Rappists made it their home. The marvelous industry and excellent taste of the sectarian communists within a few years converted the desert into a flourishing settlement.

In 1825 "Harmony" (or "Harmonie," as the Rappists named their community) was a regularly laid-out village, with streets running at right angles to each other, a public square, several large brick buildings, and numerous dwelling-houses, mills, and factories. Owen acquired it for the sum of $150,000.

No communistic experiment was ever undertaken under more favorable auspices: the Owenite settlers found ready homes, about 3,000 acres of cultivated land, nineteen detached farms, and a number of fine orchards and vines, all in excellent condition. The hardships usually attending the first years of pioneer life of every community had been successfully overcome by predecessors, and no debt was weighing on the property.

Associated with Owen in the enterprise was William Maclure, of Philadelphia, a man of considerable wealth, a scientist and philanthropist. Mr. Maclure was the most eminent American geologist of his time, and was known as

[3] For details of this interesting phase of the movement, see Charles Sotheran's "Horace Greeley and other Pioneers of American Socialism," New York, 1892.

"The Father of American Geology;" he was also the principal founder of the Philadelphia Academy of Natural Sciences, and, for almost a quarter of a century, the president of that institution. Besides his scientific pursuits, Maclure was especially interested in educational problems. He was the first to introduce the system of Pestalozzi in the United States, and was one of the earliest advocates of industrial education. Mr. Maclure was to have charge of the schools and institutions of learning in New Harmony, and he brought with him a coterie of eminent scientists and educators. Among the former were Thomas Say, the greatest American zoologist of his time; Charles Alexander Lesneur, a famous ichthyologist and a painter of talent; and Dr. Gerard Troost, who subsequently became professor of geology in the Nashville University. Among the professional educators were Professor Neef, who had been associated with Pestalozzi at his school in Switzerland; Madame Marie D. Frotageot, and Phiquepal d'Arusmont, also Pestalozzian teachers.[4] Frances Wright took an active interest in the founding of New Harmony, and so did the four sons of Robert Owen.

No wonder then that the future of the community seemed bright to Owen. He confidently predicted that the truth of his principles and the blessings of communism would in the near future manifest themselves in the new colony, and spread "from Community to Community, from State to State, from Continent to Continent, finally overshadowing the whole earth, shedding light, fragrance and abundance, intelligence and happiness upon the sons of men," and with his characteristic enthusiasm and broadness he invited "the industrious and well-disposed of all nations" to come to "New Harmony," as he rechristened the settlement.

And they came in flocks, men of all nations, well-disposed and otherwise; in fact, no less than 800 persons responded to Owen's call within the short space of the first six weeks, and a hundred more joined soon after. It was the most

4 For particulars of that phase of Owen's social experiment, see "The New Harmony Communities," by George Browning Lockwood, Marion, Ind., 1902.

motley and incongruous crowd that ever assembled for a joint enterprise. There were, undoubtedly, among them men and women actuated by pure and noble motives, and who joined the movement with the sincere purpose of contributing by their efforts to the success of the communistic enterprise, but there were also those who had absolutely no understanding of or sympathies with Owen's ideals, who looked upon his enterprise as the folly of a wealthy eccentric, and sought to take advantage of his generosity as long as it lasted. There were men and women of all classes and vocations, habits and notions, professionals, mechanics, laborers, idlers, and adventurers.

No test of qualification was imposed on them, no inquiry as to their motives was made. This indiscriminate admission of members at the very outset marked the community with the stamp of disharmony and shiftlessness which finally caused its downfall.

During the two years of its existence as a community, New Harmony had no less than seven different forms of government or "constitutions." It was not Owen's original intention to start the colony on a purely communistic basis. "Men brought up in an irrational system of society," he argued, "can not change to a rational system without some preparation." His first constitution accordingly provided that the settlers were to be held on probationary training for three years, under the control of a "Preliminary Committee," and only after a successful service of the probationary period were they to be admitted to full membership.

The period of three years seems, however, to have appeared too long for the New Harmonites, for, in January, 1826, we find them adopting a new constitution, by which the colony was reorganized on the basis of complete communism, with a general assembly as the chief authority and a council of six as its executive organ.

The new plan somehow did not work, and the members unanimously called on Owen to assume the dictatorship of the community. Under this new form of government, the third since its existence, the settlement seemed on a fair road to success. Some order was introduced into the general chaos; the idlers disappeared, and the shops and farms presented a scene of unwonted industry.

But in April, 1826, some members, tired of the steady and systematic work, demanded a division of the villages into several independent communities. To this Owen would not agree, but, as a result of the ensuing discussion, he presented the community with a fourth constitution. This divided the members into three grades—"conditional members," "probationary members," and "persons on trial," and provided for a "nucleus" of twenty-five selected members, who had the exclusive right to admit new applicants.

Owen retained the power to reject any new applicant, and was to continue the sole head of the community for one year and so long thereafter as at least one-third of the members should think the community unfit to govern itself.

But the clamor for a division was not stifled, and by the end of May, Owen, yielding to the general demand, agreed to form four separate communities from among the members of New Harmony, each having an independent administration.

This was the fifth constitution of New Harmony, and barely three months later the settlers adopted a sixth, abolishing all officers, and appointing in their place a committee of three, invested with dictatorial powers.

The seventh and last constitution was adopted by the members of all the colonies of New Harmony at a joint meeting held September 17, 1826. By this constitution the entire administration was placed in the hands of Owen and four other members to be appointed by him every year.

But the extraordinary mutability of its form of government did not save New Harmony from internal dissensions and splits. "Religion," records Sargant,[5] Owen's biographer, "was the earliest topic of disagreement, and the evil seems to have been aggravated by visits from itinerant

[5] "Robert Owen and His Social Philosophy," by William Lucas Sargant.

preachers, whose interference, however, was checked in a characteristic manner. It was profest that free discussion of religion, and every kind of teaching, was tolerated and even sought; and, therefore, all ministers who came for the avowed purpose of preaching publicly were entertained at the tavern free of expense: but with this unusual condition, that at the conclusion of a sermon any one of the congregation might ask whatever questions he pleased. This catechising was so little liked by the subjects of it that, during many months, no preacher visited New Harmony.''

But apparently the disappearance of itinerant preachers did not wholly cure the evil. Discussions on religion, and, together with them, on the most suitable form of government, continued to disturb the peace of the settlers, and at times assumed alarming aspects.

Every new outbreak of religious controversy and every change of the constitution was accompanied by the withdrawal of some disaffected members, until two groups of members separated from the parent organization, forming independent settlements within the territory of New Harmony.

One of them, the "Macluria," was named after William Maclure. The colony was settled by about 150 of the most conservative and orthodox members of New Harmony, and was chiefly concerned with the education of the young, paying but little attention to agriculture and industrial pursuits.

The other community was named "Feiba Peven," which name, for some mysterious reason, was supposed to indicate the latitude and longitude of the place. Feiba Peven was settled principally by English farmers, who were said to be very skilful, but somewhat too fond of whisky.

Both communities maintained friendly relations with New Harmony, and, as we have seen, rejoined it in adopting the seventh constitution.

Considering the complexity of elements and the general planlessness of the community, it is not surprising that its life was of short duration.

At the beginning life in the community looked bright and happy. "Free education was provided for the children, a store supplied settlers with all necessaries, and a respectable apothecary dispensed medicines without charge," narrates A. J. McDonald, the first chronicler of the experiment,[6] but the historian does not inform us whether the expense was covered from the earnings of the settlers, or, what seems to be more likely, from Owen's pocket.

Shortly after the establishment of the community Owen went to England, leaving the new enterprise in charge of his young son William, and, upon his return in the early part of 1826, he still found New Harmony in apparently excellent condition. On July 4th of that year, the fiftieth anniversary of the Declaration of Independence, Owen delivered an address to his followers, which has since become famous for its eloquence and boldness, and from which we quote the following passage:

"I now declare to you and the world, that Man, up to this hour, has been, in all parts of the world, a slave to a Trinity of the most monstrous evils that could be combined to inflict mental and physical evil upon his whole race. I refer to Private or Individual Property, Absurd and Irrational Systems of Religion, and Marriage founded on Individual Property and some of these Irrational Systems of Religion."

The tone of his entire address is still very hopeful; he still expects his community to become a powerful factor for the removal of the abhorred Trinity of Evils.

But a few months later we find him for the first time in a somewhat doubting and criticizing mood. "Eighteen months' experience," he observes in his *Gazette*, "has proved to us that the requisite qualifications for a permanent member of the Community of Common Property are: 1, Honesty of purpose; 2, Temperance; 3, Industry; 4, Carefulness; 5, Cleanliness; 6, Desire for knowledge; 7, A conviction of the fact that the character of man is formed for, and not by, him."

The discovery came too late. The heterogeneous crowd

6 Quoted in Noyes's "History of American Socialisms."

gathered at New Harmony was already breaking up. Member after member left the community, and Owen was unable to stem the tide.

A number of individuals banded themselves together into small communities, and to those Owen assigned parcels of land on the outskirts of New Harmony. The land was leased to them for a period of 10,000 years at a nominal annual rental of fifty cents per acre, and upon condition that the lease should terminate as soon as the land should be used for any but communistic purposes. These communities were short-lived. Within the village proper communism was altogether abandoned. Private stores and shops displaced communal industries, the gin-mill made its triumphant entry, and petty competition and close-fisted bargaining reigned in the place which Owen had hoped to make the starting-point for establishing the brotherhood of all the sons of men.

III.—YELLOW SPRINGS COMMUNITY

TOWARD the end of 1824 Owen arrived in Cincinnati, and remained there a short time lecturing and exhibiting his plans of a model community. He made many converts to his ideas, foremost among them being Daniel Roe, a minister of the "New Jerusalem," or Swedenborgian Church. This church was composed of people of culture, refinement and wealth, and many of them were so fascinated by Owen's glowing accounts of the blessings of community life that they resolved to try the experiment.

About seventy-five or one hundred familes organized themselves for that purpose, and after careful consultations and investigations they purchased a tract of land at Yellow Springs, about seventy-five miles north of Cincinnati.

Here the property was held by the purchasers in trust for all members of the community; schools were established with rational methods of instruction, public lectures held, and dancing and music cultivated.

"For the first few weeks," records a member of the
community, "all entered into the new system with a will.
Service was the order of the day. Men who seldom or
never before labored with their hands, devoted themselves
to agriculture and the mechanical arts with a zeal that was
at least commendable, though not always according to
knowledge. Ministers of the Gospel guided the plow and
called swine to their corn, instead of sinners to repentance.
Merchants exchanged the yardstick for the rake and pitch-
fork. All appeared to labor cheerfully for the common
weal. Among the women there was even more apparent
self-sacrifice. Ladies who had seldom seen the inside of
their own kitchens went into that of the common eating-
house and made themselves useful among pots and kettles.
Refined young ladies who had all their lives been waited
upon, took their turns in waiting upon others at the
table."

The members of the Yellow Springs Community, like
those of Brook Farm, consisted chiefly of "chosen spirits"
—there were but few farmers or laborers among them.
Their movement was not undertaken for economic or material considerations, but from spiritual and intellectual motives. They regarded their venture somewhat in the nature
of a prolonged picnic. The charm continued just about
half a year. By the end of that time the aristocratic communists sobered down. The ministers soon found sinners
more manageable and interesting than swine, merchants
found the pitchforks not half as remunerative as the yardstick, and refined ladies tired of the coarse company of
pots and kettles. One by one they returned to their old
homes and vocations, and Yellow Springs became a beautiful but faded dream.

IV.—NASHOBA

THE most original, if not the most important, community of the Owenite cycle was Nashoba, founded in the
fall of 1825 by Frances Wright. The settlement com-

prised 2,000 acres of land on both sides of the Wolf River, about thirteen miles from Memphis, in the State of Tennessee.

Frances Wright was one of the most striking figures of the Owen movement. Born in Scotland, she early acquired renown for philanthropic works, strong intellect, and sympathies with all the progressive movements of her time. She traveled extensively in the United States, especially in the South, where she made a study of the condition of the negro. She also visited the Rappists, Shakers, and other sectarian communities, and was deeply imprest by their social theories and mode of life. She took a leading part in the early anti-slavery agitation, and was one of the first and most forcible advocates of woman's rights.

Her chief purpose in establishing the Nashoba Community was to educate negro slaves to social and economic equality with the whites. With that object in view, she purchased several negro families, and persuaded planters to lend her a few other slaves for the experiment. With these and a number of white persons of all vocations she started the community.

Her plan was to establish model schools for common use by children of whites and blacks, and to set negroes to work on the settlement, using one-half of the proceeds of their labor for their maintenance, and the other half for the accumulation of a fund to purchase their emancipation.

The management of the community was to be in the hands of some philanthropists associated in the enterprise with the founder. The first few months of the experiment were quite satisfactory, and the results achieved under her intelligent and energetic superintendence seemed very encouraging. But just when her personal presence was most needed, Miss Wright fell sick, and was compelled to undertake a voyage to Europe for the recovery of her health.

In December, 1826, she deeded the land, together with the slaves and personal property, to General Lafayette, William Maclure, Robert Owen, Robert Dale Owen, C. Colden, R. Whitby, R. Jennings, G. Flower, J. Richardson, and Camilla Wright, "to be held by them, and their associates and successors, in perpetual trust for the benefit of the negro race." Under the management of these trustees the community lasted a little over a year. The extraordinary task assumed by Miss Wright proved to be beyond the powers of her successors, and Miss Wright, who had in the meanwhile returned from Europe, was unable to arrest the steady progress of disintegration. In March, 1828, the trustees of Nashoba announced that they had for the time being deferred the attempt to organize the community on a basis of cooperative labor, and that they merely claimed for it the title of "Preliminary Social Community." Three months later the entire experiment was abandoned. The slaves were given their freedom, and removed to Haiti.

The Nashoba experiment was not the end of Frances Wright's activity. She continued to make propaganda for the cause of communism, antislavery, and woman's rights in the columns of the *New Harmony Gazette* and *The Free Enquirer*. At one time she attracted much attention by eloquent public speeches on her favorite subjects, delivered in all the principal cities of the Union. She died at Cincinnati, Ohio, December 14, 1852, at the age of fiftyseven years.

V.—OTHER OWENITE EXPERIMENTS

OF the remaining Owenite communities, one deserves special mention for the variety of its fortunes and the persistence of its members. This community appears in the history of the Owenite period three times, at different places and under different names, but in reality it is only one enterprise, started at Haverstraw, New York, and closed at Kendal, Ohio.

The Haverstraw Community was formed in 1826 by one Fay, a New York lawyer, and several other New Yorkers and Philadelphians of culture and means. They occupied one hundred and twenty acres of land at Haverstraw on the Hudson, about thirty miles from New York. The number of their members soon increased to eighty. Among them were many persons skilled in various trades and occupations, as well as some professional men, and the material condition of the colony was at all times prosperous.

A feature of the community was the establishment of a "Church of Reason," the services of which were attended by members on Sundays. Lectures on morals, philosophy, and science were delivered. These gatherings took the place of all religious ceremonies and observances. The community had a very short-lived career. The cause of its failure is said to have been dishonest management.

After the breaking up of the Haverstraw Community, the majority of the members joined the Coxsackie Community. This experiment was very similar to that of Haverstraw. The estate of Coxsackie was also situated in the State of New York, in the upper Hudson valley, about seven miles from the river. It existed less than a year, and from what we can learn, the members spent most of that time in discussing proposed constitutions.

We meet many of the members again in the Kendal Community which was located near Canton, Ohio. It was founded toward the close of 1826, and its beginning was very promising.

The members, about 150 in number, consisted of farmers, mechanics, and the inevitable "choice spirits." They conducted a woolen factory, erected a number of dwellings, and were engaged in the building of a large common hall, 170 by 33 feet in size.

They were animated by a spirit of harmony and proclaimed triumphantly that the success of their social system had been demonstrated beyond contradiction. The following passage from a letter of John Hannon,[7] who was a member of the community, accounts for its sudden end:

"Our community progressed harmoniously and prosperously so long as the members had their health, and a hope of paying for their domain. But a summer fever attacked us, and seven heads of families died, among whom were several of our most valued and useful members. At

[7] Quoted in Noyes's "History of American Socialisms."

the same time, the rich proprietors of whom we purchased our land urged us to pay; and we could not sell a part of it and give a good title, because we were not incorporated. So we were compelled to give up and disperse, losing what we had paid, which was about $7,000. But we formed friendships that were enduring, and the failure never for a moment weakened my faith in the value of communism.''

Noyes mentions four more Owenite communities, two in Indiana, one in Pennsylvania, and one in New York. But they seem to have been insignificant and short-lived, and their history is not known.

Chapter III

THE FOURIERIST PERIOD

I.—CHARLES FOURIER: HIS LIFE AND THEORIES

CHARLES FOURIER was born on the 7th day of February, 1772, at Besançon, in France.

At a very early age he evinced a strong inclination for observation and study, his favorite topics being geography, astronomy, chemistry, and physics.

The son of a wealthy merchant, he was himself destined for a mercantile career. But the boy had no love for commerce. The practises and tricks of trade were repugnant to his upright instincts; he succeeded but poorly in the "noble art of lying, or the skill to sell," as he termed it, and, altho he filled several positions in early youth, the verdict of his employers was invariably the same—"an honest young man, but not fit for business." At the age of eighteen, Fourier undertook an extended tour through France, Germany, Holland, and Belgium in the interests of his employers, and took advantage of the opportunity to study the politics of these countries, the architecture of their principal cities, and above all, the industries, social conditions, mode of life and character of their inhabitants.

In 1781 the elder Fourier died, leaving a fortune of about 200,000 francs, of which Charles received two-fifths. Only after the death of the taciturn philosopher did his friends learn that he had lost that inheritance during the siege of Lyons in 1793.

In 1812 Fourier received a small legacy from his mother, from which he derived a yearly income of 900 francs, and, supplementing this sum with occasional earnings as a curbstone broker, he abandoned mercantile pursuits and devoted himself entirely to the study of social problems.

The first known product of his pen was an essay published in 1803, in the *Bulletin de Lyon,* under the title "Triumvirat continental et paix perpetuelle sous trente ans" ("The Continental Triumvirate and Perpetual Peace Within Thirty Years"). In this essay Fourier developed the idea that it was necessary in the interests of a lasting peace to establish a universal empire in Europe. The four European powers to be considered in connection with such an empire were, in his opinion, France, Russia, Austria, and Prussia, of which, however, the latter would be defeated in a single battle. The triumvirate and lasting peace would then become possible, but should the three empires not agree, Austria would soon be absorbed, and the contest for universal dominion would lie between France and Russia, with the chances of victory in favor of the latter. The article was said to have attracted the attention of Napoleon, who warned the publishers not to print similar sentiments in the future.

In 1808 he published his first large work under the title "The Theory of the Four Movements and of the General Destinies," which was followed in 1822 by his "Treatise on Domestic and Agricultural Association, or Theory of Universal Harmony," in 1829 by the "New Industrial World," and in 1835 and 1836 by two volumes on "False Industry, and its Antidote, Natural, Attractive Industry." Of these works, the first contained a general outline of his social system, and the others were devoted to a fortification of its several points.

The social system of Fourier is the most ingenious and elaborate scheme presented by any utopian writer, and it is impossible to appreciate the movement to which it gave rise on two continents without a knowledge of its leading features.

Fourier is the apostle of social harmony. Unlike most utopians, his starting-point in the criticism of the present order of things is not the injustice of the distribution of social wealth, or the sufferings of the poor, but the anarchy and wastefulness of modern production, and the repellent conditions of labor. He does not address himself to the sentiments of man, but to their material interests. His battle-cry is not "Justice," but "Order." The general prosperity and happiness of mankind is only an incident of the universal harmony of his system, not its primary aim.

God created the universe on a uniform and harmonious plan, argues Fourier; hence there is a harmonious connection between everything existing; between organic and inorganic matter, between man and God, man and the globe, and the globe and the universe. Endowing man with certain instincts and passions, God intended the free and full exercise of these instincts and passions, and not their suppression. Hence all human passions are legitimate and useful, and an ideal state of society is such as affords to its members a full opportunity to gratify them.

Fourier thereupon proceeds to analyze the human passions, and finds them to be twelve in number, as shown in the following table, reproduced from Brisbane's "Social Destiny":

Tendencies.

Five sensitive passions	Sight Hearing Smell Taste Touch	Elegance, r i c h e s and material harmonies	Collective tendency.
Four effective passions	Friendship Love Ambition Paternity	Groups and passional harmonies	Unityism, tendency to universal unity.[1]
Three distributive or directing passions	Emulative Alternating Composite	Series and concert of masses	

Of these, the first five, if properly exercised, tend to elegance, refinement, the cultivation of all the fine arts, and to physical health and enjoyment. The four "passions" of the second group tend to establish well-balanced and harmonious social relations between man and man, and are, therefore, designated Social Passions.

[1] "Social Destiny of Man, or Association and Reorganization of Industry," by Albert Brisbane, 1840.

The three passions of the third group are of Fourier's own creation, and require some explanation. The tenth, or Emulative Spirit, called by Fourier the *Cabaliste*, is the spirit of party, intrigue, or rivalry. Exercised in a legitimate manner, as in the rivalry of groups for the excellence of their productions, it is a source of great industrial improvements and inventions. The eleventh, or Alternating Passion, called the *Papillione* in the technical language of Fourierism, is the desire for change and variety in all pursuits. Applied to industry, it would destroy the monotony of the present methods of work, and make the latter pleasant and attractive. The twelfth, or Composite Passion, is the spirit of enthusiasm begotten by a combination of two passions of different groups, as, for instance, hearing excellent music in the company of dear friends, which gratifies both the sense of hearing and sense of friendship. Applied to industry, it signifies the association of congenial persons for the performance of pleasant and attractive work.

The free play of these passions leads to the formation of Groups and Series. A Group is ''an assemblage of persons—three, seven, twelve, or more—freely and spontaneously united for any purpose, either business or pleasure. But in strict theory, we understand by Group a mass leagued together from identity of taste for the exercise of some branch of Industry, Science, or Art.'' [2]

A full Group should consist of at least seven persons, so that it could form three Subgroups, three in the center, and two in each wing. The two wings of each Group represent two opposite extremes of taste and tendencies, while the center maintains the equilibrium, and, therefore, should be the more numerous.

A number of Groups, at least five, unite into a Series. The Series is made up of Groups on the same principle upon which the latter are made up of individuals. For instance, a cattle-breeding Series is divided into as many Groups as the kinds of cattle it breeds, and each Group is

[2] The quotation is from Brisbane.

divided into Subgroups for every variety of cattle within the breed raised by the Group.

It must be observed that the Series and Groups are not formed arbitrarily by an overseer or superintendent, but by the free choice of members, and also that they are by no means fixed organizations, but each member may go from Group to Group, from Series to Series, as his inclination dictates.

The great advantages which Fourier sees in this mode of work are choice and variety of occupations, and short duration of each; choice of congenial fellow workers; division of labor and rivalry between separate Groups and Series.

To these natural advantages Fourier adds some artificial attractions, such as elegance and beauty in all exterior objects connected with industry; honorary distinctions, such as ranks, titles, and decorations; and the stimulus of music, uniforms, and emblems.

To provide a field broad enough to allow every one to exercise usefully his varied inclinations by means of Groups and Series, a large number of individuals, preferably 1,800 to 2,000, must associate together.

This association, named the Phalanx, is the social unit in the system of Fourier; it is the corner-stone of his theory, and its workings are described by him with great detail. The domain of the Phalanx occupies an area of about three square miles, and its principal edifice is the Palace. The Palace consists of a double line of continuous buildings about 2,200 feet in length and three stories in height; like the Group and Series, it is composed of a center and two wings. The center is reserved for quiet occupations; it contains the dining-halls, council-rooms, library, etc.; in one of the wings all workshops of a noisy nature are placed. The other wing contains the hotel with apartments and saloons for strangers. The storehouses, granaries, and stables are placed opposite the Palace and the space between the two forms the grand square for the holding of parades and festivities. Around the interior of the entire building winds a spacious gallery, which may be considered the street of the Phalanx. It is an elegant covered avenue, from which flights of stairs lead to every part of the building. "The inhabitants of the Palace," exclaims Fourier with enthusiasm, "can, in the height of winter, communicate with the workshops, stables, bazaars, and ballrooms without knowing whether it rains or blows, whether it is warm or cold."

Behind the Palace are the gardens and fields of the Phalanx, arranged with due regard to the nature of the soil and the sense of beauty.

In the Phalanx are no parasites, as servants, armies, fiscal agents, idlers, etc. The women are freed from their monotonous and stultifying household duties, and do useful work in a number of branches for which they are exceptionally well adapted.

All members work, and all work is done on the cooperative plan, hence the enormous economies and great wealth of the Phalanxes. Let us suppose a Phalanx consists of 400 families. Each family, living separately, would have to maintain a separate kitchen. This would take almost all of the time of 400 housewives, and the cooking would be rather indifferent in most cases. In the Phalanx all the cooking is done in one vast kitchen, with three or four fires for preparing the food for different tables at different prices; ten skilled cooks perform all the work, and the meals are infinitely better. The same applies to all other household work, as well as to farming and industrial pursuits. Instead of a hundred milkmen losing a hundred days in the city, one or two men provided with properly constructed vehicles do the work; instead of having to manage a hundred little farms, one great domain is being cultivated skilfully and scientifically; one large granary, with all the advantages of dryness, ventilation, and locality, is substituted for hundreds of inconvenient little granaries, etc.

The education of children is the object of the greatest care of the Phalanx. All children receive an equal education in the common nurseries and schools. True to the theory of the usefulness of all human passions, the Phalanx

considers it the principal duty of teachers to detect all inclinations and tendencies of the child, to develop them, and
to turn them to good account.

The classification of children according to character and
taste begins from their very birth. Sucklings are
divided into three classes: the quiet, or good-natured; the
restless, or noisy; and the turbulent, or intractable; and
separate rooms are maintained for each of the classes. The
nurseries are large, beautiful rooms, and the work of nurs-
ing is done by women who have a special inclination for it.
Mothers may personally nurse their children, if they wish.

Children are divided into seven orders according to
age, and the education and pursuits of each order are determined by the inclinations manifested at the particular
age.

At the age of three years the child is initiated into easy
and attractive industrial pursuits, such as helping in the
kitchen, and thus the energies usually wasted by children
on play and mischief are being utilized by the Phalanx,
while the child acquires an early taste for industry.

As the child advances in age and attains a higher degree
of physical development and intellectual culture, the scope
of its useful activities is enlarged. Especially noteworthy
in this respect is the organization of the "Little Hordes."

The Little Hordes are composed of children of the age of
from ten to twelve years, who take upon themselves the
performance of all dirty and disagreeable work, such as
cleaning sinks and sewers, the management of manures, etc.

The reason why this work is assigned by Fourier to
children of that age is, as he observes, that they show a
marked passion for dirt; this passion, like any other, is
given them for a useful purpose, which can best be accomplished by the organization of "Little Hordes." The Little Hordes rank as the "Militia of God" in the service of
Industrial Unity; they hold the first place in parades, and
receive the salute of supremacy.

With all that, however, the Phalanx is not a communistic organization. Seven-eighths of the members are farmers and mechanics, others being capitalists, men of

science, and artists. The property of the Phalanx is represented by shares of stock, but it is not necessary for every member to hold stock, nor need a stockholder be a member. The Phalanx keeps accounts with every member, crediting him with his services at rates fixt by the council, with due regard to his efficiency and the nature of the services. At the end of the year an inventory is taken, and the profits are divided as follows:

Five-twelfths to labor.

Four-twelfths to capital.

Three-twelfths to skill or talent.

No jealousy or antagonism is created by this division of profits, as there are no fixt classes in the Phalanx. The same member holds one or more shares in the Phalanx, does work in one or more Groups, and develops special skill in one or more branches of industry, and thus shares in all three classes of profit. On the other hand, the capitalist is either satisfied with the mere dividends on his investment, or he adds to it such income as he may earn by applying his labor or talents to any useful pursuit, while the poor man works and earns more or less according to his preference for leisure or enjoyment.

The Phalanx contains sumptuous apartments as well as modest living-rooms; it furnishes elaborate repasts as well as simple meals; it imposes no restrictions on clothing or amusements, and every member may lead a mode of life in accordance with his means and inclinations.

This, in rough outlines, is the constructive side of Fourier's system. Its author expected his system gradually to supersede the present order of things. The first Phalanx being established, others would follow in rapid succession until the entire globe would be covered with them, and Fourier, with his usual mathematical accuracy, figures out that the globe would hold exactly two millions of Phalanxes.

Here Fourier, as many utopians before and after him, is carried away by the beauties and possibilities of his own social theories, and crowns his system with a fanciful superstructure. The system of Phalanxes, he asserts, will ultimately unite the entire human race into one brotherhood, with a uniform civilization and mode of life, and with one universal language. Constantinople will be the capital of the globe and the residence of the Omniarch, the chief executive of the world. The Omniarch will be assisted in the administration of the globe by 3 Augusts, 12 Cæsarinas, 48 Empresses, 144 Kalifs, 576 Sultans, etc., altho it nowhere appears what useful functions this host of royalties are to perform.

But the most fantastic part of Fourier's system is his theory of cosmogony. Each planet, he declares, has its period of youth, maturity, decay, and death, in the same way as man. The average life of a planet is 80,000 years, of which the period of infancy lasts 5,000 years, that of ascending and descending development 35,000 years each, and that of senility 5,000 years. Within that period the human race passes through thirty-two periods. We are now in the fifth of these periods, that of Civilization. The eighth period, that of Harmony, will bring about universal happiness. The polar crown (*couronne boreal*) will then originate, and will revolutionize the physical aspect of the globe; the climate will be uniform all over the world, wild beasts will disappear, and new creatures, useful to man, will take their place; the ocean will acquire the taste of lemonade, and the world will be one huge paradise.

As we showed above, Fourier was not a communist. "No community of property can exist in the Phalanx," he declares expressly, and again and again he reiterates that a diversity of wealth and enjoyments is essential to universal harmony. Of Owen, who was his contemporary, Fourier used to speak with contempt, saying that he did not understand the principles of association. His system was a compromise, a scheme of harmony between capital and labor.

Fourier himself considers his system as absolutely infallible, and compares his "discovery of social attractions" with Newton's discovery of physical attraction. He clings to every detail of his system with the tenacity, belief, and enthusiasms of the prophet—to borrow a happy comparison made by Bebel in his lucid study of Fourier's life and theories.[3]

That the discovery was not made sooner was simply due to the fact that all previous science, as well as all previous civilization, moved on false lines.

Fourier's faith in the ultimate realization of his scheme was never shaken; he submitted his plans of a model Phalanx to scores of princes and bankers, and was never discouraged by their skepticism or derision. In one of his latest works he appealed for the means of establishing a trial Phalanx, and, during the ten years preceding his death, he went to his house at noontime with the regularity of clockwork, expecting the arrival of a philanthropic millionaire in response to his appeal.

Fourier did not live to see the short period of popularity of his theories. He died in Paris on the 10th day of October, 1837, surrounded by a very small circle of enthusiastic disciples. His tombstone bears this legend:

"Here lie the remains of Charles Fourier. The Series distribute the harmonies. The Attractions stand in relation to the destinies."

II.—FOURIERISM IN THE UNITED STATES

In the United States Fourierism was introduced by Albert Brisbane. Brisbane was born in 1809, at Batavia, N. Y., the only son of a well-to-do landowner. He received a thorough and many-sided education, and spent his early manhood in travel in the principal countries of Europe and Asia. He studied philosophy in Paris under Cousin, and in Berlin under Hegel, and in both capitals made the acquaintance of many men and women prominent in politics and in the republic of letters.

Of great influence in the formation of his character and views seems to have been the select circle of Berlin's intellectual aristocracy, which had for its gathering-point the

[3] "Charles Fourier, Sein Leben und Seine Theorien," Von A. Bebel, Stuttgart, 1890.

drawing-room of the brilliant Mme. Varnhagen von Ense.

Of a keen analytical mind and broad sympathies, Brisbane was early attracted by the humanitarian systems of the utopian socialists of that time. He first enlisted with the St. Simonian school, and devoted much of his time and means to the propagation of its principles. But the theories of the great French utopian, extravagant in many respects, did not satisfy him long, and when the movement split under the rival leadership of Enfantin and Bazard, Brisbane severed his connections with it.

A short time after that a copy of the newly published "Treatise on Domestic and Agricultural Association," by Fourier, fell into his hands. The effect of the book on the young man was magical. He read it and reread it, and the more he studied it, the higher rose his admiration for the work.

"Now for the first time," relates Brisbane,[4] "I had come across an idea which I had never met before—the idea of *dignifying* and *rendering attractive* the manual labor of mankind; labor hitherto regarded as a divine punishment inflicted on man. To introduce attraction into this sphere of commonplace, degrading toil—the dreary lot of the masses—which seemed to overwhelm man with its prosaic, benumbing, deadening influence; to elevate such labors, and invest them with dignity, was indeed a mighty revolution!"

In 1832 Brisbane went to Paris, where he remained two years studying the more intricate features of Fourier's system, partly under the personal guidance of the master, and taking active part in the Fourierist movement, which was just then beginning to be developed. Upon his return to the United States, Brisbane carried on the propaganda of his social ideas in a quiet way until 1840, when he published his "Social Destiny of Man." The work is a concise exposition of Fourier's system. About one equal half of it consists of extracts from Fourier's work, while the other

[4] "Albert Brisbane, A Mental Biography," by his wife, Redelia Brisbane, Boston, 1893.

half is devoted to the author's commentaries and illustrations, suitable to American conditions. The style of the work is popular, the exposition lucid, and the book had an immense and spontaneous success. It was read by all classes of persons interested in social problems, and may be said to have laid the foundation for the Fourierist movement in this country.

It was also instrumental in converting to the cause of Fourierism the man who subsequently became its most eloquent and influential apostle—Horace Greeley. Of this interesting episode Brisbane gives the following amusing account:

"I engaged Park Benjamin to look over the proof-sheets of 'Social Destiny of Man,' he being a practical journalist of wide experience. Talking over the subject together one day, and of the probable effect of the book on the public, he suddenly exclaimed: 'There is Horace Greeley, just damned fool enough to believe such nonsense.' 'Who is Greeley?' I asked. 'Oh, he is a young man up-stairs editing the *New Yorker.*' I took my book under my arm and off I went to Greeley. As I entered his room I said, 'Is this Mr. Greeley?' 'Yes.' 'I have a book here I would like you to read.' 'I don't know that I can now,' he replied; 'I am very busy.' 'I wish you would,' I urged; 'if you will, I will leave it.' 'Well,' he said, 'I am going to Boston to-night, and I'll take it along; perhaps I'll find time.' Greeley took the book with him and read it, and when he came back he was an enthusiastic believer in Industrial Association."

The importance of the new acquisition for the cause of Fourierism in this country soon became manifest. Two years after the episode narrated, when the *Tribune,* founded in the meantime by Greeley, had become a popular and influential metropolitan newspaper, with a daily circulation exceeding 20,000, which was very large for that time, its editor opened the columns of the paper to the teachings of Brisbane.

The arrangement was carried out in a rather original

way. One spring morning in 1842 the *Tribune* appeared
with this heading conspicuously printed at the top of one
of the columns of its front page:

"ASSOCIATION; OR, PRINCIPLES OF A TRUE ORGANIZATION
OF SOCIETY"

"This column has been purchased by the Advocates of
Association, in order to lay their principles before the pub-
lic. Its editorship is entirely distinct from that of the
Tribune."

Both sides profited by the arrangement, for while Brisbane acquired a large daily audience for the propaganda
of his theories, the *Tribune* gained an additional circle of
readers among persons interested in social problems. Brisbane edited the column until he went again to Europe, in
the summer of 1844, and he made good use of the opportunity. Theoretical articles on Fourierism, practical hints
as to the best way of organizing associations, fervid appeals to the readers, controversial arguments and accounts
of meetings, filled the space allotted to Brisbane, from day
to day.

"At first," relates Parton,[5] "they seem to have attracted
little attention, and less opposition. They were regarded
(as far as my youthful recollection serves) in the light of
articles to be skipped, and by most of the city readers of the
Tribune, I presume, they were skipped with the utmost regularity, and quite as a matter of course. Occasionally,
however, the subject was alluded to editorially, and every
such allusion was of a nature to be read. Gradually
Fourierism became one of the topics of the time. Gradually certain editors discovered that Fourierism was unchris-
tian. Gradually the cry of Mad Dog arose. Meanwhile
the articles of Mr. Brisbane were having their effect upon
the people."

Horace Greeley's services to the cause of Fourierism
were not limited to lending space in his paper. He wrote
and spoke on the subject of Association whenever and
wherever occasion presented itself; and he took an active

5 J. Parton, "Life of Horace Greeley," Boston, 1869.

and leading part in the councils and conventions of the Fourierists, and in the attempts to realize their theories by the formation of Phalanxes.

Of lasting interest is the famous discussion on Fourierism carried on between Horace Greeley and Henry J. Raymond in the columns of the *Tribune* and the *New York Courier and Enquirer.* The debate was conducted with much spirit and ability on both sides, and was afterward published as a separate pamphlet.

Next in importance to Brisbane and Greeley in the movement was Parke Godwin, associate editor of the *Evening Post,* and son-in-law of its editor-in-chief, the poet, William Cullen Bryant. His pamphlet, *Democracy, Constructive and Pacific,* which appeared in 1843, became one of the most effective weapons in the literary arsenal of Fourierism. The pamphlet contained but little more than fifty pages, but in brilliancy of style, power of argument, and soundness of views, it excelled everything else written in this country in defense of Fourierism. Parke Godwin was one of the first American socialists to divine the tendencies of the capitalist mode of production, and he came very near the modern socialist conception of the class struggle. His appeal was addrest principally to working men. Godwin also published a booklet, entitled "Popular View of the Doctrines of Charles Fourier," and a "Life of Charles Fourier."

Of equal importance with these standard works on Fourierism were the periodical magazines devoted to the cause. In October, 1843, Brisbane established the *Phalanx,* a monthly magazine edited by him, with the able cooperation of Osborne Macdaniel. It was published until the middle of 1845. When Brook Farm was converted to Fourierism, the *Phalanx* suspended publication, and its place was taken by the *Harbinger.* The *Harbinger* was a weekly magazine. It was first published at Brook Farm, but after the dissolution of the community, was transferred to New York.

Brook Farm added a new galaxy of brilliant writers to the cause of Fourierism. One of the foremost of them was the founder of the Farm, George Ripley, a man of profound scholarship and of exceptional qualities of mind and heart. He had been a Unitarian minister, but after fourteen years of work in the pulpit he came to the conclusion that his profession was incompatible with his social and ethical views, and resigned from the ministry. Having become converted to Fourierism, he devoted himself entirely to that cause. The *Harbinger*, during the four years of its existence, contained no less than 315 contributions from his pen. Charles A. Dana was another notable acquisition for the Fourierist movement. At that time he was a very young man, but sober and serious in all he undertook. His thorough training and methodical ways earned for him, among his associates, the nickname of "Professor." Dana contributed 248 articles to the *Harbinger*.

But the most prolific writer on the staff of the *Harbinger* was John S. Dwight, who heads the list of contributors with 324 articles. Dwight, who, like Ripley, had studied for the ministry, and, like the latter, voluntarily abandoned the pulpit, was a poet, a lover of music, and, a man responsive to all appeals of human sufferings.

Prominent also in the Fourierist movement of that time was William Henry Channing, a Unitarian minister famed for his eloquence.

Of other men and women of national fame whose names are identified with the movement in this country, we may mention Theodore Parker, T. W. Higginson, Henry James, James Russell Lowell, Francis G. Shaw, and Margaret Fuller, all of whom, with the exception of the one first named, were contributors to the *Harbinger*.

The *Phalanx* and the *Harbinger* were the classical organs of Fourierism, but they were not its only representatives in the field of periodical literature. In his autobiography already alluded to, Brisbane mentions a weekly magazine published by him in conjunction with Greeley before the establishment of the *Tribune*. The magazine lasted two months. Brisbane at one time succeeded in securing the editorial management of the *Chronicle*, a small daily newspaper published in New York by John Moore, and of a monthly magazine, called the *Democrat*, published by John O'Sullivan. Both papers were converted into ardent advocates of Fourierism. The Fourierists of Wisconsin published the *Gleaner*, those of Michigan issued a paper called the *Future*, and William Henry Channing published the *Present*.

Another effective factor in the spread of Fourierist doctrines in this country were the public lectures given with great frequency, by the pioneers of the movement. Brisbane, Greeley, Channing, Godwin, Dana, and a host of orators of minor renown, were ever ready to extol the beauties of Association before audiences of any dimensions and in any place within reach. Here is a characteristic notice of one of these meetings published in the *Tribune*, and quoted by Sotheran: [6]

"T. W. Whitley and H. Greeley will address such citizens of Newark as choose to hear them on the subject of 'Association,' at 7:30 o'clock this evening, at the Relief Hall, rear of J. M. Quimby's Repository."

Extended lecture tours were also undertaken at different times by leading Fourierists, notably by John Allen, John Orvis, and Charles A. Dana. These lectures and speeches, in a majority of cases, attracted crowds of eager listeners.

The time was exceptionally propitious for the reception of their doctrines. The country was just passing through one of those periodical crises which, when they occur, seem to menace the very foundation of our economic and industrial system. Production had almost ceased, hosts of working men were thrown out of employment, the misery of the population, especially in the industrial cities of the Northeast, was appalling, and vagrancy developed with alarming rapidity.

Charitable organizations and official commissions, appointed for that purpose by several municipalities and States, tried in vain to cope with the situation: it had grown beyond their control. The nation stood bewildered

[6] "Horace Greeley, and Other Pioneers of American Socialism," by Charles Sotheran, 1892.

and helpless before the mischievous workings of economic powers. The complacent social philosophy of thousands of thinking men and women was rudely shaken by the manifestations of the crisis, and scores of new social problems were forced upon their attention.

At the same time the antislavery agitation was just beginning to assume serious dimensions, and, as has happened with almost every liberating movement, it soon transcended its original aim and bounds. Denunciations of chattel slavery logically led to criticism of all other forms of social dependence. "Abolition of chattel slavery and of wage slavery" was one of the mottoes of the more radical part of the abolitionist movement. It became the key-note of the eloquent appeals of Wendell Phillips and many other popular agitators of the time.

It was at that juncture that Fourierism made its appearance in the United States. It promised to bring permanent order and harmony into industry, and mutual independence into the social relations of men. The promises were bright and alluring, and they were preached by most eloquent tongues. No wonder that the movement spread rapidly in this country.

Numerous Fourierist societies were formed in the States of Massachusetts, New York, New Jersey, Pennsylvania, Ohio, Illinois, Indiana, Wisconsin, and Michigan. In all these States conventions were held from time to time, and on the fourth day of April, 1844, a National Convention assembled at Clinton Hall, New York. It was a most noteworthy and enthusiastic gathering. George Ripley was chosen president, and among the vice-presidents were Horace Greeley, Albert Brisbane, Parke Godwin, and Charles A. Dana.

Letters of sympathy and encouragement were received from all parts of the country. Numerous resolutions were adopted, most of them dealing with the subject of organizing associations. Associations on the plan of Fourier's phalanxes were declared to be the universal remedy for all social evils, but the adherents were at the same time warned against experiments undertaken on too small a scale or with insufficient preparations.

The convention decided to form a permanent National Confederation of Associations, with the *Phalanx* as its official organ, and with a standing executive committee of eighteen. It also declared in favor of international cooperation of Associationists, and appointed Albert Brisbane a committee to confer with the Fourierists of Europe as to the best mode of mutual cooperation.

The period immediately preceding and following the National Convention may be regarded as the high-water mark in the Fourierist movement in this country. In the next chapter we shall witness its decline.

III.—FOURIERIST PHALANXES

FOURIER early foresaw the danger of hasty experiments. He declared that a Phalanx could not prove its benefits and could not be made a success, unless it had a membership of 1,500 to 2,000 persons, and a capital of about 1,000,000 francs. To the end of his life he strenuously discountenanced all trials on a smaller scale.

Brisbane modified the high standard of the master by reducing the number of persons required for the formation of a Phalanx to 400. "The most easy plan for starting an Association," he argued, "would be to induce 400 persons to unite, and take each $1,000 worth of stock, which would form a capital of $400,000. The stockholders would receive one-quarter of the total product or profits of the Association; if they preferred, they would receive a fixed interest of 8 per cent. The investment of $1,000 would yield $80 annual interest. For this sum the Association must guarantee a person a dwelling and living; and this could be done. The edifice could be built for $150,000, the interest upon which sum at 10 per cent., would be $15,000. Divide this sum by 400, the number of prospective tenants, and we have $37.50 per annum for each person as rent. Some of the apartments would consist of several rooms, and rent for about $100, so that about one-half of the rooms could be rented for $20 per annum. A person wishing to live at the cheapest rates would have $60 left after paying his rent. As the Association would raise all its fruit, grain, vegetables, cattle, etc., and as it would economize immensely in fuel, number of cooks, and everything else, it could furnish the cheapest-priced board at $60 per annum. Thus a person who invested $1,000 would be certain of a comfortable room and board for his interest, provided he lived economically. And he would have in addition whatever he might produce by his labor. He would live, besides, in an elegant edifice surrounded by beautiful fields and gardens.''

Brisbane himself and the other leading Fourierists always clung to this ideal of a large and wealthy Association, and from time to time publicly warned the hotspurs in the movement against hasty experiments with insufficient capital and members.

But very little heed was paid to the warning. The able and persistent propagandists of Associationism had created a popular enthusiasm which soon grew beyond the control of the leaders. Fourierism had taken root in the broad masses of the population, and the masses were impatient to realize, on the spot, the bright promises of the new social gospel.

Phalanxes grew, as it were, spontaneously. They were undertaken by any number of men, large or small, with any, and sometimes without any, capital, and soon covered the States in which Fourierism had taken a foothold, with a veritable network.

The history of these experiments is one monotonous record of failure. The inherent defects of Fourier's scheme of social organization appeared on the surface as soon as it was put to the test of practical application. The supposed strength of the scheme, the compromise between the interests of capital and labor, between cooperation and exploitation, was, in fact, a source of great weakness. It robbed the Phalanxes, or at least those of them which attempted to organize on the real Fourieristic plan, of that unity of interest and endeavor which is so absolutely indispensable for a social experiment of that nature, and which alone sustained all successful communities during their early trials and struggles.

But in justice to Fourierism, it must be admitted that the instances in which the experiments were undertaken on the lines laid down by Fourier or Brisbane were very few. More of the failures are attributable to extraneous factors than to the inherent defects of Fourierism. The men who undertook the experiments were, in many cases, in the testimony of Greeley, "destitute alike of capacity, public confidence, energy, and means,"—especially of means.

Instead of a capital of $400,000, one four-hundreth part of it would frequently be all an Association would manage to get together for a start. With that sum it was manifestly difficult to purchase the fertile and beautiful "domain" in the vicinity of a populated city, as recommended by the originator of the "Phalanxes."

The experimenters, as a rule, had to satisfy themselves with a small parcel of barren land in a wilderness, and that one heavily mortgaged. The distance from the city, and the scantiness of their means, relegated settlers to agricultural pursuits exclusively, altho very few of them were trained farmers. One or more miserable log huts took the place of the gorgeous social "Palace," and the "attractive industry" turned out to be a pathetic and wearisome struggle of unskilled and awkward hands against the obstinate forces of a sterile and unyielding soil. The struggle, as a rule, lasted until the first instalment on the mortgage became due, and as the mortgagee was never satisfied with the four-twelfths of the profits allotted to capital by Fourier, the "domain" was almost invariably foreclosed. The only Phalanxes that attained significance, and at one time seemed to justify an expectation of permanent success, were the North American Phalanx in New Jersey, the Brook Farm Phalanx, and The Ceresco, or Wisconsin Phalanx. Of these the first mentioned lasted fully twelve years, and the career of the two others extended over five and six years respectively. The average life of all other known Phalanxes was about fifteen months. A brief sketch of their history will be found in later chapters.

The Phalanxes were to Fourierism vastly more significant than were the social experiments of other utopian schools to their systems. For while all the other schools contemplated a social organization on a national scale, and regarded their communities as mere illustrations and miniature models of the future state, the Fourierist Phalanxes were the final state; they were to their founders not only means of propaganda, but the realization of their teaching. The peculiar feature of the Fourierist scheme is that it introduces a state of social happiness and equilibrium in instalments. Every Phalanx is a piece of that social state, realized and complete within its limits, and quite independent of the surrounding world. The Phalanxes thus naturally became the test of Fourierism, and the movement did not survive their failure.

In vain did the American apostles of Fourierism protest that the doctrines of their leader had not had a fair trial, and were in no way responsible for the disasters of the numerous social experiments undertaken in haste and carried out in defiance of the theories of Fourierism. Their protests were not heeded. To the popular mind, *Fourierism* was synonymous with *Phalanx,* and the failure of the latter was proof of the impracticability of the former. Besides, the industrial depression which had greatly assisted the movement in its formative stages, had passed, and with it, the eagerness for radical social reforms.

Fourierism as a theory retained its hold on a number of choice intellects for some time, but as a popular movement it disappeared within the same decade that saw its origin and marvelous development—the decade of 1840–1850.

The further careers of its originators and champions was of a rather varied nature. Horace Greeley continued taking an active interest in public life. His *Tribune* was a strong and indefatigable champion of the antislavery movement from the start and until the final triumph of the cause. He was elected to Congress in 1848, and in 1872 was nominated for the Presidency by the "Liberal Republican Party," and indorsed by the Democratic Party. He survived his unsuccessful campaign only a short time and died, on November 29, 1872. Thousands of the common people in all parts of the United States mourned the loss of a sincere and devoted friend. His funeral in the city of New York assumed the dimensions of a gigantic popular demonstration. Greeley remained true to the ideals of his youth to the very end.

Albert Brisbane lived until 1890. He spent much of his time in Europe, and devoted the remainder of his life to scholarly and artistic pursuits. His entire being was so absorbed by Fourierism that, when the movement ebbed away, it seemed to have taken with it all his vigor and enthusiasm. His public career was closed, and altho he witnessed the rise of the modern socialist movement at home and abroad, he remained a passive though somewhat sympathetic observer of its progress. His son Arthur Brisbane is the brilliant editor of the New York *Evening Journal*.

George Ripley devoted the remainder of his life to literary pursuits. He was a regular contributor on the staff of the *Tribune*, and, together with Charles A. Dana, edited the "American Encyclopedia." He died on July 4, 1880.

Dana also joined the staff of the *Tribune* in 1847. He was Assistant Secretary of War under Stanton during the civil war, and in 1868 he purchased the *New York Sun*. His radical social views did not survive the Fourierist movement very long, and in later years he and his paper were consistent and able defenders of everything conservative and reactionary in politics. He died in 1897.

John S. Dwight became a musical critic and published *Dwight's Journal of Music* from 1852 to 1881. He died in 1893 at the age of eighty years, a kind-hearted, noble, and enthusiastic old man, surrounded by a host of loving friends.

Parke Godwin was the last survivor of the brilliant coterie. He died in 1904 at the age of 88 years.

IV.—THE NORTH AMERICAN PHALANX

OF all the Fourierist experiments undertaken in this country, the North American came probably nearest to the ideal of a "Phalanx." It was established by a number of earnest and cultured residents of New York and Albany for the purpose of "investigating Fourier's theory of social reform as expounded by Albert Brisbane."

Before starting upon the experiment, the advice of Greeley, Brisbane, Godwin, Channing, and Ripley was sought, and Brisbane was one of the committee to select a site for the proposed Association. The place finally chosen was near Red Bank, Monmouth County, New Jersey. In September, 1843, a few families took possession of the "domain" and at once set to work erecting a temporary dwelling-house. During the next year the number of actual settlers increased to about ninety.

Within a short time the temporary dwelling-house was replaced by a three-story mansion, with a front of 150 feet and a wing of 150 feet. A grist-mill was built on a stream running through the land, and other industries were carried on in a small way. The chief pursuit of the Association was agriculture. The settlers planted two immense orchards, occupying about seventy acres, with every variety of choice fruit, and their fields and farms were kept in better order and yielded better crops than those of their neighbors. The original investment of the Association was $8,000; on the first annual settlement in 1844 its property was inventoried at $28,000, and in 1852 it had risen in round figures to $80,000.

As soon as the industrial and agricultural pursuits of the Association had sufficiently developed, production was carried on by groups and series, and in the distribution of profits Fourier's law of "equitable proportion" was adopted.

For necessary but repulsive or exhausting labor the highest rate of wages was paid; for useful but less repulsive labor the wages were smaller; and the smallest reward of all was received by those choosing agreeable pursuits.

Thus men engaged in brickmaking received ten cents an hour, those engaged in agriculture about eight cents, while the waiters and Phalanx physicians received six and one-quarter cents per hour. In addition to these wages, special rewards were paid for skill and talent displayed in any branch of industry or in the administration of the Association's affairs. Thus the chief of the building group, who had to lay out plans for work from day to day and to supervise the work, received an extra stipend of five cents a day in addition to his regular earnings. The wages of the members, computed on this complicated system, varied from six to ten cents an hour, the latter figure being regarded as the maximum.

The members were given perfect freedom to choose such occupations as they preferred, and to work as much or little as they liked. They were credited with the amount and kind of labor performed by them every day, and were paid in full every month, the profits being divided at the end of the year. The average share of labor upon such division of profits amounted to about $13 per year, while capital received about five per cent. upon the investment. It will be perceived that the earnings of the members were not large, but then the cost of living in the Phalanx was small in proportion. The rent of a pretty good-sized, comfortable room in the principal mansion was $12 per year.

Meals were, in later years, served *à la carte,* coffee being half a cent per cup, including milk; butter half a cent; meat, two cents; pie, two cents; and other dishes in proportion. In addition to this, each member paid thirty-six and a half cents per week for the use of the dining-room, and his proportion for the waiting labor and for lighting the room. The waiters marked the charges for every meal in a book kept by each member for that purpose, and settlements were made at the end of every month.

The majority of the members of the Association were people of culture and refinement. Life in the Phalanx was exceedingly pleasant, to judge from the enthusiastic accounts of a number of prominent Fourierists who frequently paid them visits. They had a small reading-room and library, they possest several musical instruments, and singing, dancing, and merrymaking were the order of the day as soon as their labors in the field or shops were over.

"I have often heard strangers remark upon the cheerfulness and elasticity of spirit which struck them on visiting Brook Farm," writes Ripley, "and I found the same thing strongly displayed in the North American Association." Neidhart, commenting upon the appearance of the members, observes: "There is a serene, earnest love about them all, indicating a determination on their part to abide the issue of the great experiment in which they are engaged. The women appeared to be a genial band, with happy, smiling countenances, full of health and spirits. Such deep and earnest eyes, it seemed to me, I had never seen before."

The education of the children was one of the first cares of the Association, equal attention being paid to their physical and intellectual development.

The North American Phalanx endured over twelve years. It was organized at a time when Fourierism was just beginning to make itself felt, and it saw the movement at its zenith and its decline. It witnessed the death of all other Phalanxes around it, and finally remained alone, a solitary monument of the movement that had given so much promise and had ebbed away so soon.

This isolated position could not be maintained very long. The material advantages of the community were small. In the first years of its existence, it was largely kept together by the sustaining influence of an enthusiasm born of a broad and live movement of which it was part. When that enthusiasm departed, it took with it the very soul of the Association. To all outward appearances the Phalanx continued its existence in all respects with the accustomed regularity, but beneath the surface the powers of dissolution were already working. Dissensions arose over matters of administration, dissatisfaction was occasionally exprest with the scanty earnings and poor prospects of the

Association, and the question of disbanding came to be only a question of time.

The dissolution of the Association was hastened by an accident. In September, 1854, the mill, built at a cost of about $12,000, was destroyed by fire. Greeley offered to lend a sum sufficient to rebuild it, and the Association assembled to deliberate upon the offer, and to decide upon the location of the new mill. In the course of the discussion some one suggested that they had better not build at all, but dissolve. The suggestion was quite unexpected and irrelevant to the matter under discussion, but it seemed to express the sentiment secretly entertained by the majority of the members, and upon the vote being put, the Association, to everybody's surprise, determined to dissolve. Thus abruptly terminated the existence of the North American Phalanx. Its property was sold at forced sale, and its shareholders were paid sixty-six cents on the dollar.

V.—BROOK FARM

BROOK FARM is the most brilliant and fascinating page in the otherwise rather monotonous and prosaic history of Fourierist experiments in America. The farm attracted the noblest minds and choicest spirits of Fourierism, and lent poetry and charm to the entire movement. But Brook Farm did not begin its career as a Fourieristic experiment.

The origin of Brook Farm must be found in a philosophical and humanitarian movement which existed in New England in the thirties of the last century, Boston being its intellectual center. The men and women whose names are most closely associated with it are George Ripley and his wife, Sophia Ripley; William Ellery Channing and his nephew, W. H. Channing; Margaret Fuller, Ralph Waldo Emerson, Henry D. Thoreau, Nathaniel Hawthorne, John S. Dwight, Elizabeth P. Peabody, and scores of others whose names have since become part of our national history.

They were idealists and enthusiasts, and ardent advocates of all social, political, and religious reforms agitated in their days. They met at irregular intervals at one another's houses and discust all possible and impossible problems of philosophy, politics, and religion, and, altho they had no formal organization among themselves, they soon came to be known to the outside world as the "Transcendental Club."

The name was originally intended as an appellation of derision, but, as has happened so often in history, it was subsequently adopted and borne with pride by the objects of the intended ridicule. How the skeptical matter-of-fact critics of the movement understood the term *Transcendentalists* was probably best exprest by the terse and witty definition of Miss Taylor, who said of them that they "dove into the infinite, soared into the illimitable, and never paid cash." The interpretation placed upon the word by the transcendentalists themselves was, on the other hand, exprest by Ripley in the following language: "We are called Transcendentalists because we believe in an order of truth that transcends the sphere of the external senses. Our leading idea is the supremacy of mind over matter."

The "Transcendental Club" existed several years. The first result of its activity was a quarter-annual magazine of high literary standard, called *The Dial*. *The Dial* was published at irregular intervals, and contained many valuable contributions from the gifted pens of the famous men and women connected with the movement.

In 1840 Ripley finally decided to make a practical application of the principles and theories advocated by the transcendentalists. He resigned from the ministry, and, encouraged by a few of the more ardent spirits of the "Club," set out to establish a community. A site was chosen in the spring of 1841 in West Roxbury, about nine miles from Boston. The place had formerly been a milk farm, and belonged to one Mr. Ellis. It consisted of about 200 acres of good land, and was extremely picturesque. The first settlers comprised about twenty persons, including

Ripley himself, his wife and sister, Dwight, Hawthorne, and William Allen. Few of the remaining members of the Transcendental Club followed Ripley to the Farm.

The official name adopted by the little colony was The Brook Farm Institute for Agriculture and Education, and the object of the Institute was formulated by its founders in their Articles of Association, as follows:

"To more effectually promote the great purposes of human culture; to establish the external relations of life on a basis of wisdom and purity; to apply the principles of justice and love to our social organization in accordance with the laws of Divine Providence; *to substitute a system of brotherly cooperation for one of selfish competition;* to secure for our children, and to those who may be entrusted to our care, the benefits of the highest physical, intellectual, and moral education which, in the present state of human knowledge, the resources at our command will permit; to institute an attractive, efficient, and productive system of industry; to prevent the exercise of worldly anxiety by the competent supply of our necessary wants; to diminish the desire of excessive accumulation by making the acquisition of individual property subservient to upright and disinterested uses; to guarantee to each other the means of physical support and of spiritual progress, and thus to impart a greater freedom, simplicity, truthfulness, refinement, and moral dignity to our mode of life."

They also agreed that the property of the community should be represented by shares of stock and that all members be provided with employment according to their abilities and tastes. There was a uniform rate of compensation for all labor; a maximum working day of ten hours; free support of children under the age of ten years, and persons over the age of seventy years, as well as those unable to work on account of sickness; and free education, medical attendance, and the use of library and bath.

The administration of the community was entrusted to four committees styled respectively the Departments of General Direction, Direction of Agriculture, Direction of Education, and Direction of Finance.

It will thus be noticed that the Brook Farmers, con-sciously or unconsciously, showed a decided leaning toward Fourierism from the start, and that their subsequent formal reorganization as a Phalanx was an easy and logical development, rather than a sudden conversion, as it has been represented by some historians of the Farm.

The principal feature of the young community was its school. This was divided into four departments—an in-fant school for children under the age of six years, a primary school for children under ten, a preparatory school for pupils intending to pursue the higher branches of study in the institution, and a six years' course to pre-pare young men for college.

A wide range of sciences and arts was taught under the skilful and loving guidance of many competent instructors, and equal attention was paid to physical and mental de-velopment. Many men, who subsequently played an im-portant part in the literary and political life of the country, owed much of their achievements to their education in the Brook Farm School. Among the most brilliant of such students were the Curtis brothers—James Burrill, who made a name for himself in the scientific world of England, where he ultimately made his home, and George William, the well-known novelist and one-time editor of *Harper's Weekly;* Francis Channing Barlow, who became a general in the civil war and later held the offices of Secretary of State and Attorney-General in the State of New York; Colonel George Duncan Wells, noted for his bravery in the civil war; and Dr. John Thomas Codman, who wrote a charming book of reminiscences of Brook Farm.[7]

In the course of the following three years the number of members grew to about seventy. The financial success of the Farm was only moderate, and the life of its members, full of toil and devoid of earthly comforts. But the Brook Farmers understood it to cover their poverty with the attractive veil of poetry, and to infuse charm and romance into their prosaic every-day occupations.

[7] "Brook Farm, Historic and Personal Memoirs," by John Thomas Codman, Boston, 1894.

After the day's work was over, it was customary for the young men to repair to the kitchen and laundry, and gallantly offer their services in dish-washing or clothes-hanging to the ladies. This done, a dance or games would be improvised in which all the young people of the Farm would participate, while the older men and women would be interested and sympathetic onlookers.

Music, excursions, and literary and scientific discussions filled out the leisure hours. All told, the Brook Farmers were a happy and congenial lot of men and women.

Life on the Farm was rendered still more attractive by the occasional visits of friends from the outside world. Among the most frequent and most welcome visitors were Margaret Fuller, both Channings, Theodore Parker, Miss Peabody, and, later on, Horace Greeley, Albert Brisbane, Parke Godwin, and other leaders in the Fourierist movement.

In the beginning of 1844, a short time after the National Convention of Associations, Brook Farm declared itself formally a Fourieristic community, and changed its name to "Brook Farm Phalanx." The transition did not effect a radical change in the plan of organization and mode of life of the settlement. But it added a new feature to it. Brook Farm became the center and fountain-head of Fourierist propaganda. Early in 1844 the publication of the *Harbinger* was transferred to the Farm, and the presence of the high-class weekly journal opened a new field of activity for the literary talents of the Brook Farmers. The editorial department was in charge of Ripley, Dana was the principal reviewer, Dwight the art critic, Orvis wrote principally on Association, Ryckman was a steady contributor, other members of the Farm contributed occasionally some articles or poems, and all took a lively interest in the magazine, discussing the merits and demerits of every article, and hailing the appearance of every new number as an event. In addition to the publication of the *Harbinger*, the Brook Farmers promoted the cause of Fourierism in various ways, and frequently sent out some of their most eloquent and efficient members to preach the blessings of Association to the outside world. The lecture tours thus undertaken by Dana, Allen, and Orvis were the most noteworthy enterprises of the Farm in that direction. The Association was now incorporated by a special act of the Massachusetts Legislature, and it was decided to build a large unitary building on the Farm.

Brook Farm was in its most prosperous phase. It had become famous throughout the length and breadth of the country. Its visitors numbered thousands every year; it was showered with applications for admission to membership, and its financial returns were slowly but gradually improving. All was activity and hope; the place was bubbling over with life and fun. But the main interest of the members was centered on the unitary Phalanx building, or "Palace," on which they had worked indefatigably over two years, and which was now nearing completion. It was expected that the large building would enable the Association to admit to membership many deserving applicants, who had so far been kept out on account of the lack of accommodations, and that the resources and working capacity of the settlement would be greatly strengthened by the accessions to the membership.

It was on a fine spring evening in 1846, amid these pleasurable expectations, that the Brook Farmers, most of whom were dancing and merrymaking as usual, were startled by the cry, "The phalanstery is on fire!"

And sure enough it was. Through some negligence of the workmen who were engaged in putting on the finishing touches, the large wooden structure had caught fire, and the heartbroken Brook Farmers gazed on in helpless terror as the flames mercilessly enveloped the object of all their labors and hopes, and rapidly reduced it to ashes. Had the loss occurred a few years earlier, when the Fourierist movement was still strong, Brook Farm might perhaps have recovered from it; but in 1846 the movement was already on the wane, the enthusiasm of its votaries was considerably dampened, and the destruction of the phalanstery proved fatal to the further existence of the Farm, in the same way as the destruction of its mill proved fatal to the existence of the North American Phalanx. The Association struggled through the following spring and summer, but in the autumn it gradually broke up. The *Harbinger* was transferred to New York, and the property of the Association was sold. The site of Brook Farm is now occupied by an orphan asylum maintained by a Lutheran church.[8]

VI.—THE WISCONSIN PHALANX, OR CERESCO

OF all Fourieristic experiments, the Wisconsin Phalanx was conducted on soundest business principles, much of its material success being due to the great administrative abilities of Warren Chase, who was its leading spirit from first to last.

The Association was organized in May, 1844, in the county of Fond du Lac. The country then was uninhabited for miles in all directions, and land was extremely cheap, selling at $1.25 per acre. The settlers paid cash for their land. It was one of the distinguishing features of the Association that it never incurred debts on its property.

The founders of the community, about twenty in number, came with teams, stock, tents, and implements of husbandry, and speedily erected a large dwelling-house and sawmill. Within a few months they were joined by their families, and in less than one year the number of resident members increased to about 180. They drew up a charter and by-laws, under which they were incorporated by the Legislature as the "Wisconsin Phalanx." They founded the township of Ceresco, which likewise was chartered by the Legislature. There were few settlers in the town outside of the members of the Phalanx, and the latter were, therefore, elected to all town offices. By the laws of the State they were required to elect, among others, three justices of the peace, but, as they had no criminals and no

8 For a complete account of the Brook Farm experiment, see Lindsay Swift, "Brook Farm, Its Members, Scholars, and Visitors," New York, 1900.

litigation of any kind, the office became purely complimentary. They regularly elected their three oldest men to fill it. They also elected one of their members to each of the two Constitutional Conventions held in Wisconsin during the period of their existence, and sent three of their members to the State Senate. One of their members ran for the office of Governor on the Free-Soil Ticket, but he received a very small vote outside of the township. They applied for and secured a post-office, and one of their members held the office of postmaster until the administration of Taylor.

They began operations with a very small capital, which gradually increased to about $33,000. They were very industrious, had over 700 acres of land under cultivation, and in one season raised over 10,000 bushels of wheat.

They never fully introduced the system of work in groups and series, but strove to fix the rewards for labor, capital, and talent as nearly in accord with the precepts of Fourierism as practicable. The average wage was six to seven cents per hour; the average cost of board was sixty to seventy-five cents per week. They were very careful in the selection of new members, and admitted none who either from insufficient means or from physical weakness was likely to become a burden on the community.

They had a free school, but intellectual pursuits and social life were rather neglected. They had no library or reading-room, and no social gatherings or entertainment of any account. All told, the Wisconsin Phalanx surpassed the other Fourierist experiments in point of material prosperity, but fell short of the average in culture and refinement.

The standing disagreement in the Association was over the subject of unitary, or isolated households. The settlement was about evenly divided on the question, and their township elections mainly turned on that issue.

The partizans of unitary households always carried by a narrow majority, and hence a common dining-room and common mansion were maintained, but the minority were

not disposed to submit, and continued to conduct their
households in separate family dwellings.

This issue together with a number of contributing
causes, of which lack of harmony and enthusiasm are to be
counted among the foremost, finally induced the Associationists to dissolve. The formal dissolution and division of
profits took place in 1850. The property yielded 108 per
cent. on the investments, the only instance where a Phalanx
dissolved without loss to its founders and stockholders.

VII.—THE PENNSYLVANIA GROUP

The northern part of the State of Pennsylvania in the
middle of the last century was a most unpropitious location
for settlers. The region was a rocky desert, with no industrial or business centers for miles in all directions; the
land was barren and cold, and thickly covered with boul-
ders. But the cheapness of the land proved an irresistible
attraction for our social experimenters, and no less than
seven Fourieristic settlements are known to have been established in that section between the years 1843 and 1845.
Of these the most noteworthy are the Sylvania Association,
the Peace Union Settlement, the Social Reform Unity, and
the Leraysville Phalanx.

The Sylvania Association was the first Fourierist Phalanx in the United States. It was founded in May, 1843,
by a number of residents of New York and Albany.
Thomas W. Whitley was its president and Horace Greeley
its treasurer. The "domain" was selected by a committee
consisting of a landscape painter, a homeopathic doctor,
and a cooper; it consisted of 2,300 acres, situated in the
township of Lackawaxen, Pike County. It contained a
dilapidated grist-mill, which was speedily repaired by the
settlers, and three two-story frame houses, which at one
time had to accommodate all of the members, who were 136
in number. Later the settlers built a large common dwelling-house, forty feet square and three stories high.

They had agreed to pay for their land $9,000, in yearly

instalments of $1,000, and made the first payment on tak-
ing possession, but when the second payment fell due they
found themselves unable to meet it, and the owner gen-
erously consented to take back the land with all improvements made by the settlers, and to release them from
further obligations. The Sylvania Association existed
about eighteen months.

The PEACE UNION SETTLEMENT was situated in Warren
County, and consisted of about 10,000 acres of land. It
was founded by Andreas Bernardus Smolnikar, an Austrian Professor of Biblical Study and Criticism, who considered it his special mission to establish universal peace on
earth. The colony consisted almost exclusively of Germans. The settlers abandoned the experiment after a brief
but fierce struggle with the stubborn soil.

The SOCIAL REFORM UNITY was established by a group
of Fourierists of Brooklyn, New York. Their domain consisted of 2,000 acres in Pike County, Pennsylvania. The
land was sold to the settlers for $1.25 per acre, but they
only paid on account of the entire purchase $100, or five
cents per acre. They prepared and printed a very elaborate constitution, of which, however, they never made use.
The barrenness of the soil, their inexperience in farming,
and their extreme poverty, caused the dissolution of the
Association within a very few months.

The LERAYSVILLE PHALANX came into existence in a
unique manner. Near the village of Leraysville, in the
county of Bradford, were seven adjoining farms; the
owners were all Swedenborgians, the most influential among
them being Dr. Lemuel C. Belding, a pastor of the Church
of New Jerusalem.

When the tide of Fourierism reached the little congregation, Dr. Belding and his friends decided to unite their
seven farms into one "domain." Amid impressive ceremonies they tore down the old division fences, and each
turned over his farm to the Phalanx, at an appraised
value, receiving shares in exchange. The seven original
founders were soon joined by additional members, among
whom were several physicians, clergymen, and lawyers, and

a number of mechanics. The beginnings of the settlement were very promising, but an antagonism soon developed between the original owners of the farms and the new-comers, and the Association was dissolved after the brief existence of eight months.

VIII.—THE NEW YORK GROUP

THE western part of the State of New York was at one time a hotbed of the Fourierist movement. There was hardly a village or hamlet in the county of Genesee, the native county of Albert Brisbane, and in the neighboring counties of Monroe and Ontario, which did not contain one or more groups of Fourierists. Brisbane devoted much of his time to propagating the principles of Association in that region; some well-attended county conventions were held in Batavia and Rochester, and Phalanxes were organized on a large scale.

Noyes describes seven experiments growing out of that movement whose history is almost identical. They were all undertaken with great enthusiasm and little preparation, were short-lived, and entailed heavy financial losses to their founders.

The most important of the New York Phalanxes were the CLARKSON PHALANX, the SODUS BAY PHALANX, the BLOOMFIELD ASSOCIATION, and the ONTARIO UNION.

The four had a common origin, their organization having been decided upon at a mass convention held in Rochester in August, 1843. They were located on the shores of Lake Ontario, within a short distance from each other, and together had over 1,000 members and more than $100,000 of invested capital. Their average life was a little less than a year.

This group of Phalanxes is noteworthy for the reason that it was the only one to form a confederation. The confederation was styled the "American Industrial Union." Its administration was vested in a council consisting of representatives of all its component Phalanxes. The council met once in May, 1844, and passed resolutions for a uniform conduct of the affairs of the Phalanxes, and for a system of exchange of products between them. But the resolutions were never acted upon.

The failure of the New York experiments created a deep and lasting prejudice against Fourierism in the region which had once been its stronghold.

IX.—THE OHIO GROUP

Noyes records the history of five Phalanxes in the State of Ohio. Of these the most important seems to have been the Trumbull Phalanx, in Trumbull County. This was founded in the early part of 1844, and lasted until the fall of 1847.

The "domain" of the Association consisted of about 1,500 acres of land, partly purchased by the founders and partly contributed by some neighboring farmers in exchange for Association stock. The land was swampy and bred ague and a variety of other diseases; the accommodations consisted of a few insignificant dwelling-houses crowded to their utmost capacity. The luxuries and comforts indulged in by the members can be easily gaged by the fact that the average cost of living was estimated at forty cents per week for every member.

In these adverse circumstances 250 men, women, and children, most of whom had given up comfortable homes, struggled on for over three and a half years with an energy and self-abnegation which excited the admiration of their contemporaries. But the hopelessness of the struggle at last dawned upon the most sanguine of them, and reluctantly they abandoned the enterprise from which they had hoped and for which they had sacrificed so much.

The Ohio Phalanx was ushered in with much flourish of trumpets, and at one time the Associationists expected great things from it. Among its founders were E. P. Grant, Van Amringe, and other lights of Fourierism, and $100,-000 was pledged for its support at an enthusiastic mass convention at which its organization was decided upon.

The Association was founded in March, 1844, on a tract

of about 2,000 acres, near Wheeling, in the county of Bel-
mont. It seems to have suffered from a superabundance
of theoretical learning and from a proportionate lack of
practical experience. During the short period of its existence it had many discussions, several splits of a more
or less grave character, and one radical reorganization.
It was finally dissolved in June, 1845.

The CLERMONT PHALANX and the INTEGRAL PHALANX
both originated in Cincinnati, and were located within
short distances from the city. Both were conducted with
the capital of their founders, and both experiments were
failures. The Integral Phalanx published a magazine under the title of *Plowshare and Pruning-Hook.* The magazine was devoted to the teachings of Fourier in general,
and to the interests of the Phalanx in particular. It was
to appear biweekly, but only two numbers of it seem to
have been printed.

The COLUMBIAN PHALANX is the name of another
Fourierist experiment in the State of Ohio. But no particulars about the existence of that Association have become
public, save that it was located in Franklin County and was
organized in 1845.

X.—OTHER FOURIERIST EXPERIMENTS

OF other Phalanxes whose records have been transmitted
to us, four were located in Michigan, and several in Iowa
and Illinois. Of these, the ALPHADELPHIA PHALANX, in
Michigan, was the most important. It lasted over a year,
and published a magazine under the title of *Tocsin.* Its
leading spirit was one Dr. Schetterly, a disciple of Brisbane.

All told, Noyes collected data of no less than forty-one
Phalanxes, of which he found accounts or mention in
McDonald's collection,[9] or in the files of the *Phalanx* and

[9] McDonald was the first historian of American Communities.
He visited most of the communistic societies in person, and wrote
down the results of his investigations and observations. After his
death Noyes secured the manuscripts. His "History of American
Socialisms" is largely based on the accounts of McDonald.

Harbinger. Many more probably existed of which no record was left. To appreciate the full extent of the movement we must bear in mind that in all France, the home of Fourierism, no more than two Phalanxes were ever attempted, and only one of them in the lifetime of Fourier.

Chapter IV

THE ICARIAN COMMUNITIES

I.—THE ORIGIN OF ICARIA

AMONG the most interesting pages in the history of American communism are those relating to the Icarian experiments. The records of patient sufferings, heroic devotion, and acrimonious feuds of these colonies cover almost half a century; they are full of interest and pathos and have been the subject of numerous monographs, pamphlets, and magazine articles.

Etienne Cabet, the founder and spiritual father of the Icarian communities, was born in Dijon, France, in 1788. He received an excellent education, studied medicine and law, and met with considerable success in the practise of the latter profession in his native town. At an early age he settled in Paris, where he affiliated himself with secret revolutionary societies, in which the capital of France abounded at that time.

In the revolution of 1830 he took a leading part as a member of the "Insurrection Committee," and upon the elevation of Louis Philippe to the throne of France, he was appointed Attorney-General for Corsica. This appointment was a shrewd move on the part of the government which thus banished the dangerous democrat from the revolutionary atmosphere of Paris under the guise of a reward for his services during the revolution. But the advisers of the "citizen-king" did not reckon with the upright instincts of Cabet. No sooner had the new Attorney-General assumed the duties of his office in Corsica, than we find him aggressively active in the ranks of the radical anti-administration party. As was to be expected, he was removed from office with due despatch, and in 1834 his townsmen of Dijon elected him as their deputy in the

lower chamber. His steadfast opposition to the administration, and his revolutionary attitude in the chamber,
again drew on him the wrath of the Government, and after
being tried on a charge of *"lèse-majesté,"* he was accorded
a choice between two years of imprisonment and five years
of exile.

Cabet chose the latter alternative, and emigrated to England. Here the busy politician for the first time found
leisure for study and meditation, and as a result of both, he
evolved a system of communism very similar to that of
Robert Owen.

Returning to France in 1839, Cabet published his views
in a work entitled "Voyage en Icarie" ("Voyage to
Icaria"). The publication of that book marked a turning-
point in his entire career. "Voyage en Icarie" is in the
form of a novel. Its very simple plot, briefly summed up,
is this: Lord Carisdall, a young English nobleman, has by
chance learned of the existence of a remote and isolated
country known as Icaria. The unusual mode of life, habits,
and form of government of the Icarians excite his lord-
ship's curiosity, and he decides to visit their country.
"Voyage en Icarie" purports to be a journal in which the
traveler records his remarkable experiences and discoveries
in the strange country.

The first part of the book contains a glowing account of
the advantages of the cooperative system of industry
among the Icarians, their varied occupations and accomplishments, comfortable mode of life, admirable system of
education, high morality, political freedom, equality of
sexes, and general happiness. The second part contains a
history of Icaria. It appears that the social order of the
country had been similar to that prevailing in the rest of
the world until 1782, when the great national hero, Icar,
after a successful revolution, established a communistic
order.

This recital gives Cabet an opportunity for a scathing
criticism of the faults of the present social structure, and
also for an outline of his favorite measures for the introduction of the new *régime*.

Prominent among those measures are the progressive income tax, abolition of the right of inheritance, state regulation of wages, national workshops, agricultural colonies, and, above all, a thorough and liberal system of education. The last part of the book is devoted to a history of the development of the idea of communism, and contains a summary of the views of almost all known writers on the subject, from Plato to the famous utopians of the early part of the nineteenth century. The plan of the novel does not differ materially from More's "Utopia" or Morelly's "Basiliade," both of which were published before Cabet's work, or from Bellamy's, Howells's, or Hertzka's utopian novels, published after it. The success of the book was extraordinary. Between the revolutions of 1830 and 1848 the masses in France were in a constant state of vague discontent seeking some definite expression, and Cabet's work, with its popular style, its strong arraignment of the existing social order, and glowing pictures of a happy brotherhood of man, was acclaimed as a new gospel. Edition after edition was published, until there were not many working men in France who had not read it.

Encouraged by the splendid reception of "Voyage en Icarie," Cabet devoted himself entirely to the propaganda of his communistic ideas, and for that purpose he published, between 1840 and 1847, the *Populaire* and the *Icarian Almanac*. Through these periodicals, the "Voyage," and other works, he gained a powerful influence among French working men, and in 1847 he was said to have no less than 400,000 adherents.

When Cabet wrote his "Voyage en Icarie" he most likely intended merely to express his general views on social problems, applicable to any country in civilization, and with no expectation of making those views the subject of an immediate social experiment. But, as the agitation for "Icarianism" grew stronger, and gave rise to much heated controversy with opponents, his enthusiastic adherents urged the necessity of founding an "Icarian" colony, in order to vindicate the truth of his theories by a practical demonstration. Accordingly, Cabet published in May,

1847, a proclamation to the French working men under the heading, "Allons en Icarie!" ("Let us go to Icaria!")

The proclamation is in the style of exultant enthusiasm characteristic of Cabet.

Recounting the hardships and persecutions to which the Icarians were subjected in France, and declaring that a revolution in their fatherland, even if successful, would not avail the workers, it unfolds a magnificent vista of the future in the Icarian settlement. Cabet believed that not less than 10,000 to 20,000 working men would immediately respond to the appeal, and that within a short time a million skilled laborers and mechanics would follow them. With such an army he expected to build immense cities and villages on the communistic plan, with large industries, schools, theaters, etc.; in short he saw in his mind's eye a veritable paradise on earth, with a happy population of equals. The document wound up with an eloquent description of the beautiful climate and fertile soil of "America."

The proclamation had a magic effect on Icarians. Cabet received from enthusiastic disciples thousands of letters containing offers of gifts for the prospective community. The offers embraced articles of household furniture, tools, clothing, pictures, guns, seeds, libraries, jewelry, money, and everything else imaginable, including, of course, a number of highly valuable inventions of all kinds which were to be tested in the new colony. A few weeks after the proclamation was issued, Cabet announced in the *Populaire* that he expected to unite more than a million cooperators for his enterprise.

It now became necessary to fix upon a more definite location for the proposed settlement, and in September, 1847, Cabet went to London to seek counsel of Robert Owen. Owen recommended Texas. Texas at that time had just been admitted to the Union, and eagerly desired to populate its vast unoccupied territory. Large grants of land were made by the new State to private concerns on condition of procuring settlers. The representatives of one of these concerns—the Peters Company—happened to be in

London in January, 1848. Cabet, learning of that fact, went to London, and on January 3, 1848, made a contract with the Peters Company by which the latter agreed to deed to him a million acres of land in Texas on condition that the colony take possession of it before July 1, 1848.

Cabet immediately announced in the columns of his *Populaire* that "after a careful examination of all available countries," he had chosen a beautiful and fertile tract of land in Texas for the proposed colony.

The first "advance-guard," consisting of sixty-nine persons, sailed from Havre in February, 1848. Their departure was preceded by a very impressive ceremony on the pier. The pioneers solemnly signed a "social contract" pledging themselves to the principles of communism; Cabet delivered a touching address on the aims and future of the movement, and, returning home, wrote in the *Populaire:* "In view of men like those in the advance-guard, I can not doubt the regeneration of the human race. . . . The 3d of February, 1848, will be an epoch-making date, for on that day one of the grandest acts in the history of the human race was accomplished—the advance-guard sailing on the ship 'Rome' has left for Icaria. . . . May the winds and waves be propitious to you, soldiers of humanity! And we, Icarians, who remain, let us prepare, without loss of time, to rejoin our friends and brothers!"

II.—TEXAS

THE "advance-guard" of the Icarians arrived at New Orleans on the 27th of March, 1848, and their disappointments began immediately. It appears that Cabet was not equal to the smart business methods of our American land agents, and that he had taken the statements of the representative of the Peters Company too literally. The Icarians had been led to believe that the lands of the Peters Company were washed by the Red River and were accessible by boat, but, on consulting the map, it appeared that "Icaria" was separated from the river by a trackless wilderness of over 250 miles.

Another disappointment not less grave, the pioneers found in the peculiar apportionment of the land. The State of Texas had divided its unoccupied territory into square sections of 640 acres (one square mile) each, and had granted to the Peters Company the alternate sections

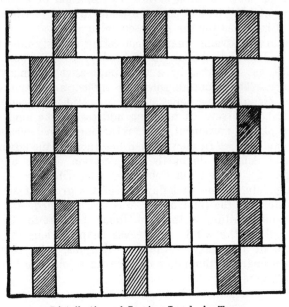

Distribution of Icarian Lands in Texas

of a certain tract of land. The Peters Company, in turn, divided its sections into half-sections of 320 acres, and transferred to the Icarians the alternate half-sections. To give the reader a clear idea of the location of the lands of our Icarian settlers, the diagram, published by Dr. Albert Shaw in his "Icaria," is here reproduced.

In this diagram the blank sections represent the land reserved by the State of Texas, the blank half-sections represent the land retained by the Peters Company, and the shaded half-sections represent the land acquired by Cabet.

The absurdity of attempting to establish a communistic colony with a central administration and a cooperative system of industry and agriculture on many scattered and disjointed parcels of land is so obvious that it needs no comment.

Nor was this all. The *Populaire* had assured the Icarians that 1,000,000 acres of land had been acquired by Cabet. Upon closer inspection it appeared that the contract of the Peters Company provided expressly that 3,125 persons, or families, should each receive 320 acres of land, provided they took actual possession, *i. e.,* built at least a log cabin on their respective parcels, before July 1, 1848. As the small advance-guard could not very well build more than about thirty log cabins within the time limit, they could not secure more than about 10,000 acres, or one-hundredth part of the promised million.

These disappointments, however, did not deter the resolute band from their course. Arrived at Shreveport, they procured a few ox-teams and one wagon, and set out on the march to Icaria. The hardships of the tedious trudge can hardly be described. Their only wagon broke down, supplies gave out, and sickness set in. At last they arrived in the promised land, a sick and weary band.

But with the energy and good cheer characteristic of the pioneer, they set to work without loss of time. A small log house and several sheds were built, and they began plowing. In the meanwhile July had arrived, and with it an epidemic of malarial fever. The weakened and overworked Icarians fell an easy prey to the disease, four of their number died, their only physician became hopelessly insane, and every man in the settlement finally was sick.

Such was the condition of affairs in September, when part of the second advance-guard, about ten in number (the second advance-guard consisted of nineteen men, instead of the promised 1,500, and part of these did not reach Icaria, having fallen sick on the way), joined them. In these circumstances the pioneers decided to abandon

Texas. To facilitate the retreat, they divided themselves into groups of two to four men, each man receiving about $6, all that was left them. After much suffering the weary party arrived in New Orleans in the winter of 1848. There they were joined by several new detachments of Icarian emigrants from France, including Cabet himself.

By this time the Icarian movement had lost much of its strength in France. The February revolution of 1848 overthrew the kingdom of Louis Philippe, and established the Second Republic. The "right to labor" was proclaimed, and "national workshops" were launched. The working men of France were full of hope for the social regeneration of their country, and the scheme to establish a great communistic state in a foreign country lost its charm for them.

The million of Icarians expected by Cabet toward the close of 1847 dwindled down to less than 500, who gathered around him in New Orleans in December, 1848, and January, 1849. The funds of the Icarians amounted at that time to about $17,000.

To go back to Texas with such meager means, and after the discouraging experience of the advance-guard, was out of the question. The Icarians resigned themselves to remaining in New Orleans until a proper location could be secured.

In the meanwhile dissensions arose among them resulting in the withdrawal of about 200 persons. The remainder, about 280 in number, finally fixt upon Nauvoo, Ill., as a place of settlement, and arrived at that town in the middle of March, 1849, having lost twenty men in transit as victims of cholera.

III.—NAUVOO

THE town of Nauvoo, in Hancock County, Illinois, was built up by Mormons under the leadership of Joseph Smith. In 1845, when the population of Chicago numbered about 8,000, Nauvoo had 15,000 inhabitants, and was the most prosperous and flourishing town in the State.

At that time the persecution of the Mormons became intense. Joseph Smith having been killed, his successor, Brigham Young, organized a general migration of his followers to Utah.

In 1849, Nauvoo, with its large stretches of cultivated land and its numerous buildings, was practically abandoned save for the solitary Mormon agent who remained in charge of the property, wistfully looking for purchasers or tenants.

The opportunity thus offered seemed to the Icarians almost providential, and they were not slow in taking advantage of it. They rented about 800 acres of land, purchased a mill, distillery, and several houses, and for the first time fortune seemed to smile on them.

The next six or seven years marked a general era of prosperity in the history of the Icarians. They had for a main building a structure about 150 feet wide, which was used as a common dining-hall, assembly-room, etc. They had, besides, a school-house, workshops, a forty-room dwelling-house, and a number of smaller houses.

They kept about 1,000 acres of rented land under cultivation, operated a flouring-mill, saw-mill, and whisky distillery, conducted tailoring, shoemaking, and carpentering shops, and acquired property estimated at about $75,000. Nor were the intellectual and ethical sides of their life neglected. In their schools the children were taught a variety of subjects and carefully trained in the principles of the Icarian philosophy. They published newspapers, pamphlets, and books in English, French and German for the propaganda of their ideas, maintained a library of over 5,000 volumes, and frequently indulged in the pleasures of theatricals, music and dances. They received many new accessions from France as well as from the United States, and their membership almost doubled during that time. The future of Icaria seemed bright with promises.

But beneath the serene surface trouble was already brewing. In February, 1850, the Icarians adopted a constitution which provided for the administration of their affairs by a board of six directors. Of these directors, the first was the president of the community, and the five others were at the head of the following departments:

1. Finance and Provisions.
2. Clothing and Lodging.
3. Education, Health, and Amusement.
4. Industry and Agriculture.
5. Printing-Office.

The acts of the board of directors were, however, subject to the approval of the General Assembly, consisting of all male members over twenty years old.

Under this constitution Cabet was elected president from year to year, and for a time he exercised his power very discreetly. But as the years rolled on, the founder of Icaria grew old, narrow, and arbitrary. His actions gave frequent cause for unpleasant friction. In these disputes, which gradually grew quite acrimonious, the members of the administration grouped themselves around Cabet, while the opposition dominated the General Assembly.

The hostilities of the two parties, now open and now concealed, continued with more or less vigor until August 3, 1856, when the final breach occurred. The immediate occasion for the rupture was the semi-annual election of directors. The three new directors chosen were opponents of Cabet. Cabet and his followers refused to recognize them.

Chaos now reigned. The belligerent factions were loud in their denunciations of each other; manifestoes, proclamations, appeals, and libels were busily published; acts of physical violence became an everyday occurrence, until the civil authorities of Nauvoo intervened, and installed the newly elected directors by force. Cabet and his party were not inclined to submit to defeat gracefully. They ceased to work, rented a separate building and did their utmost to bring about the dissolution of the community, going to the extent of petitioning the State Legislature to revoke the charter of Icaria.

In October, 1856, Cabet was formally expelled from membership in the community, and at the beginning of November he, with his faithful minority of about 180 persons, left Nauvoo for St. Louis.

A week later Etienne Cabet was no more. The father of Icaria and the originator of one of the strongest popular movements in France of the middle of the last century, succumbed to a sudden stroke of apoplexy on the eighth day of November, 1856. He died far away from the fatherland he loved so dearly, and an exile from the community on which all his thoughts and interests had been centered during the last years of his life.

IV.—CHELTENHAM

THE faithful band of 180 who had followed Cabet to St. Louis now found themselves in a pitiable plight. Bereft of their leader, with no means to speak of, and the inclement winter before them, they could not think of establishing a new colony just then.

The men, almost all of whom were skilled in one trade or another, accordingly secured work and remained in St. Louis until May, 1858, when the greater part of them, about 150 in number, migrated to Cheltenham, there to resume their interrupted community life.

Cheltenham was an estate of twenty-eight acres, lying about six miles west of St. Louis. It contained a large stone building and six small log houses. But unfortunately these advantages were more than outweighed by unfavorable features. The place was a veritable hotbed of fever; the purchase price, $25,000, was excessive, and as the cash payment had been small, the mortgage was correspondingly heavy.

But our Icarians were not discouraged. With a zeal born of enthusiasm, they went to work building up the social and industrial organization of their new colony. They set up numerous workshops, which did some remunerative work for customers in St. Louis, established a printing-office, schools, the indispensable music band and theater, and provided for periodical lecture courses and discussions.

Cabet's name lent them great prestige with Icarians in France. They were recognized by the Paris Bureau as the only genuine Icarian community, and received much financial help and moral encouragement from the fatherland. One subscription opened in Paris for their benefit netted $10,000.

Their material prosperity seemed, in 1859, to be assured, when the old and fatal issue of all Icarian communities, the form of administration, reappeared in discussions. This issue divided the Cheltenham settlers into two opposite camps. The majority, consisting mainly of the older members, believed in a single leader with dictatorial powers, while the younger men advocated a democratic form of government. The contest resulted in a complete victory for the conservative elements, whereupon the defeated minority, forty-two in number, withdrew in a body. The loss of so many able-bodied men was a blow to the young community from which it never recovered.

The industries of Cheltenham were crippled, its social life became cheerless, and members steadily withdrew, until, in 1864, the community consisted of fifteen adults of both sexes and some children.

It was a sorrowful day when the last president of the Cheltenham Community, the heroic and devoted A. Sauva, called a meeting of these last of the Mohicans, and, amid the loud sobs of the last "Popular Assembly," declared Cheltenham formally dissolved.

V.—IOWA

THE first split in the ranks of the Icarians affected the Nauvoo settlers almost as injuriously as the Cheltenham seceders.

The withdrawal of Cabet and his large following deranged their entire industrial system; their property shrank while their debts increased rapidly, and to escape certain decomposition, they decided upon a new change of locality. Nauvoo had always been regarded by the Icarians as a temporary settlement. The place was too small and too near the heart of civilization for grand social schemes. They contemplated the establishment of an' independent and highly complex communistic society on a large scale, and for that purpose they needed an immense stretch of land far away from the populated centers of the country.

With that object in view they had acquired, as early as 1852, over 3,000 acres of land in southwestern Iowa, and thither they now removed. They could not have made a worse choice.

Iowa at that time was a vast wilderness, and the land selected was in the most secluded part of the State. The settlement lay at a distance of sixty miles from the Missouri River. In 1860 the railroad now passing through the tract had not yet been built. For miles in all directions the land consisted of trackless virgin prairie, with no trace of a hamlet or any human habitation. The enormous cost of transportation made the sale of farm products to outsiders almost impossible. In addition the land was heavily mortgaged; the mortgage drew ten per cent. interest, and, as the Icarians could not pay, the debt compounded at a fearful rate.

The hardships of the early pioneer days in Iowa proved too much even for a great many of the brave and enduring Icarians; members withdrew by the wholesale, until in 1863 the number of the faithful was reduced to thirty-five, including men, women and children, and the amount of their debt exceeded $15,000.

The community seemed to face certain destruction, when the War of the Rebellion broke out. That war brought temporary relief. It enabled them to dispose of their surplus farm products at good prices, and to save up sufficient money to make a settlement with their mortgagees by which the latter accepted $5,500 in cash and 2,000 acres of land in payment of the mortgage.

The next years of the history of the Iowa Community are marked by monotonous and persevering efforts to insure material welfare. They lived in miserable huts, often lacked the most necessary articles of food and clothing, and worked themselves into a state of stupor, but the bright vision of a great and beautiful Icaria was always before their eyes, lending new vigor to their enfeebled bodies and new enthusiasm to their wearied minds.

Gradually they improved their lot. To the score of little log houses a common dining-hall and assembly-room was soon added. They purchased more land, built a grist- and saw-mill, and raised considerable live stock. With increasing prosperity the number of their members augmented, and in 1868 it had almost doubled.

The completion of the Chicago, Burlington, and Quincy Railroad gave a new impetus to their industries, and they now entered on an era of moderate prosperity.

The primitive log houses were discarded for more comfortable habitations, and a new central hall, sixty feet wide and two stories high, was erected.

With the dawn of material comfort, the attention of the community was again turned to the social and esthetic sides of life. As in Nauvoo and Cheltenham in the periods of prosperity, theatricals, music, public readings, and, above all, public discussions in the common assembly-room, became regular features in the life of the settlers.

And, as in Nauvoo and Cheltenham, public discussions eventually led to the formation of factions within the community. The hardships of pioneer life in the wilds of Iowa had naturally made the old generation conservative. Their comparative prosperity had been wrung by them from hostile surroundings in fierce and obstinate battle. It was the result of untold sacrifices and privation, and they clung to it with the love and tenderness of a fond mother. The lofty ideals which had animated their work in the early stages of their struggles gradually receded to the background; material welfare, first regarded by them as a mere means for the realization of their sublime social ideals, soon became the end. Utopian dreamers and enthusiasts developed into every-day farmers, with remnants of radical traditions reduced to a bare formula.

In marked contrast to this mental attitude stood the younger members of Icaria. Of these part had grown up in the community, but the early struggles of their fathers were to them only a pale recollection of their childhood, others who had joined more recently brought with them new ideas and a new atmosphere.

The socialist movement had seen great changes since the "Voyage en Icarie." The utopian dreams of the first half of the last century had given way to the modern socialism of Karl Marx; the International had established a firm bond of solidarity among the socialists of all great countries of Europe; the recent experiences of the Commune of Paris had given ample proof of the outbreak of active class war in Europe, while in America a strong labor movement was rapidly developing. Several of the "young party" had been members of the International, and others had fought in 1871 on the barricades of Paris.

It was under the leadership of these men principally that the young "progressive party" was formed in opposition to the "conservative party" of the old Icarians. The contest between the two parties was at first quite amicable, but gradually it assumed a more serious and threatening character.

The young men demanded a number of reforms in industrial and agricultural methods, suffrage for women, propaganda among outsiders, wholesale admissions of new members, and other radical measures; while the old pioneers were suspicious of all innovations and changes in their mode of life.

In September, 1877, the dissensions had reached such an acute point that the "young party," which was in the minority, demanded a formal separation. The demand was flatly refused by the majority, and the disaffected reformers declared war to the knife upon their opponents.

The conflict grew personal and hot, and neither party was very scrupulous in the choice of means to subdue its opponents. The party of the young finally went so far as to apply to the civil courts for a dissolution of the community. In order to secure proper legal grounds for the application, they, the "progressives," charged the Icarian community, which was incorporated as an agricultural joint-stock association, with having exceeded its powers and violated the provisions of its charter by its communistic practises.

In August, 1878, the charter of Icaria was declared forfeited by the Circuit Court, and three trustees were elected to wind up its affairs.

The Icarians never recovered from the effects of that split, altho each of the two parties made vigorous efforts to reestablish the community after its formal dissolution.

The "young party," by arrangement with the trustees and their former adversaries in the community, remained in possession of the old village, and were reincorporated under the title, "The Icarian Community." But the community somehow did not prosper, and in 1884 the young Icarians removed to Bluxome Ranch, near Cloverdale, Calif., a horticultural farm which had then recently been purchased by some of their friends. The new settlement received the name of Icaria Speranza. It never prospered, and was finally dissolved by decree of the court in 1887.

In the meantime the old party had reorganized under the name, "The New Icarian Community," with Mr. Marchand, a veteran Icarian, as president. They received as their share of the property of the former community the eastern portion of the old domain, $1,500 in cash, and eight frame cottages, which they removed bodily from the old site. They built a new assembly hall and resumed agricultural work.

With no accessions from the outside and a gradual depletion of their own ranks, caused by deaths and withdrawals of members, they struggled on until 1895, when the community was finally dissolved.

Thus ended the great Icarian movement which half a century before had made its appearance with so much flourish of trumpets, and with the bold promise of regenerating the social and economic system of the world by the mere passive proof of the blessings of brotherly community life.

OBSERVATIONS AND CONCLUSIONS

THE history of communistic experiments in the United States covers such a long period of time and furnishes such an abundance of material for analysis and induction, that it would hardly be proper to close this account without a few general observations.

What strikes us most in these experiments is the varying degree of success attained by the different groups. The sectarian or religious communities have, beyond doubt, been the most successful in point of duration and material prosperity. Most of the societies classed as sectarian have existed over half a century, and a few are still in existence with the record of a full century behind them. Some of them, as the Shakers, Oneida, and the Amana communities, have amassed fortunes, and all the others maintained themselves in comparative comfort and affluence after the brief period of pioneer days.

The careers of the "non-religious" communities, on the other hand, were, as a rule, short-lived and fraught with hardships. The average duration of the communities of the Owenite group was barely more than two years, that of the Fourierist Phalanxes, with the three notable exceptions of the North American Phalanx, the Brook Farm, and the Wisconsin Phalanx, was no longer, and the Icarian Communities were in a constant process of disintegration and reorganization. These communities, furthermore, never achieved any degree of material prosperity, and their existence was, with a few exceptions, one of abject poverty.

The glaring disparity in the fortunes of apparently similar enterprises could not fail to evoke numerous comments from students of community life. Nordhoff and others sought to explain the phenomenon by the fact that the religious societies had strong leaders, and they came to the conclusion that no community could thrive without the guidance of a strong and wise individual who knew how to gain and hold the confidence of members. Noyes and Greeley, on the other hand, advanced the theory that religion as such was the sustaining power of communities, and indispensable to the success of all communistic experiments.

On closer examination, however, both theories appear rather superficial and not in harmony with the facts. The Shakers hardly ever had a leader of great authority after the days of Ann Lee. Still their prosperity continued unabated for almost a century after the death of the prophetess, while New Harmony was a crying failure notwithstanding the leadership of a man of the intellect and executive ability of Robert Owen. Similarly, the Fourierist Phalanxes were very short-lived, altho they were, in a majority of cases, deeply religious; while the avowedly agnostic Icarians managed to maintain their existence during almost two generations.

The real reason for the comparative success of the religious communities is, however, quite obvious. In the first place, these communities were chiefly composed of German peasants, experienced farmers and men of modest needs; while the "non-religious" communities mostly consisted of heterogeneous crowds of idealists of all possible vocations, accustomed to a higher standard of life, and as a rule devoid of any knowledge of farming. What, then, is more natural than that the former should have made a better success of their "domains," or farms, than the latter?

Furthermore the religious communities were organized for religious purposes, and not for the propaganda of communism; their communism was only an incident in their existence, and whenever their material interests required, they sacrificed it without compunction of conscience. The Shakers, Harmonists, Amanites, Perfectionists, and other religious communities employed hired labor in their fields and shops, and toward the end of their existence their organizations practically ceased to be communities, and became agricultural and manufacturing corporations. Their material success was thus to a large degree due not to their communism, but to their departure from communism. In other words, the sectarian or religious communities in the long run discarded communism, and in many instances became profitable business enterprises; while the "non-religious" communities adhered to a communistic *régime* to the last, and almost uniformly had short and unsuccessful careers.

As experiments in practical communism, the American communities must consequently be admitted to have been a total failure.   And it would be idle to seek for the particular cause of the failure of each separate community as McDonald and other historians of his type have attempted to do.   The cause of failure of all communistic experiments is one—the error of the fundamental idea underlying their existence.

The founders of all communities proceeded on the theory that they could establish a little society of their own, eliminate from it all features of modern civilization which seemed objectionable to them, fashion it wholly after their own views of proper social relations, and isolate themselves from the surrounding world and its corrupting influences.

But the times for Robinson Crusoes, individual or social, have passed.   The industrial development of the last centuries has created a great economic interdependence between man and man, and nation and nation, and has made the civilized world practically one organic body.   In fact, all the marvelous achievements of our present civilization are due to the conscious or unconscious cooperation of the workers in the field and mines, on the railroads and steamships, in the factories and laboratories the world over; the individual member of society derives his power solely from participation in this great cooperative labor or its results, and no man or group of men can separate himself or themselves from it without relapsing into barbarism.

This indivisibility of the social organism was the rock upon which all communistic experiments foundered.   The communists could not create a society all-sufficient in itself; they were forced into constant dealings with the outside world, and were subjected to the laws of the competitive system both as producers and consumers.   Those of them who learned to swim with the stream, like the religious communities, adopted by degrees the main features of competitive industry, and prospered, while those who remained true to their utopian ideal perished.

Modern socialists have long discarded the idea of mending the present capitalist system by isolated patches of communism. They recognize that society is not made up of a number of independent and incoherent groups, but that it is one organic body, and it is in the progress of the whole social organization that they center their hopes and efforts.

Another and perhaps more interesting question to the student of social problems is the influence of community life upon the formation of human character.

The communities of the Owen period were too short-lived to modify the characters and habits of their members to any appreciable extent, and so were the Fourierist experiments, with the exception, perhaps, of the North American and Wisconsin Phalanxes and Brook Farm. But the Icarian communities, and, above all, the sectarian or religious communities, have lasted for several generations. And, altho the life and career of the Icarians were much disturbed by internal strife and material adversities, and the sectarian communism was not always pure and unalloyed, the two groups could not fail to produce a type of men and women with characteristics somewhat different from those of the rest of mankind.

In view of the oft repeated assertion that competition furnishes the only incentive to inventiveness and industry, it is interesting to note that the communists have, as a rule, developed these traits in a high degree. Nordhoff, who was by no means a partial observer, remarks in this connection: "No one who visits a communistic society which has been for some time in existence can fail to be struck with the amount of ingenuity, inventive skill, and business talent developed among men from whom, in the outer world, one would not expect such qualities." And again: "Nothing surprised me more than to discover the amount and variety of business and mechanical skill which is found in every commune, no matter what is the character and intelligence of its members."

It is also the unanimous testimony of all observers that the communists were, as a rule, very industrious, altho no compulsion was exercised. ''The pleasure of cooperative labor is a noticeable feature of community life when seen at its best,'' observes Ely. Hinds commenting on his personal observations of many communities, concludes that individual holding of property is not essential to industry and the vigorous prosecution of complicated business; and Nordhoff corroborates their testimony in the following passage:

''How do you manage with your lazy people?'' I asked in many places; but there are no idlers in a commune. I conclude that men are not naturally idle. Even the ''winter Shakers''—the shiftless fellows who, as cold weather approaches, seek refuge in Shaker and other communes, professing a desire to become members; who come at the beginning of winter, as a Shaker elder said to me, 'with empty stomachs and empty trunks, and go off with both full as soon as the roses begin to bloom'—even these poor creatures succumb to the systematic and orderly rules of the place, and do their share of work without shirking, until the mild spring sun tempts them to a freer life.''

But while the members of communistic societies were not idle, and did their work steadily and well, they showed no signs of the enervating hustling which mars the pleasure of work in modern civilization. They took life easily.

''Many hands make light work,'' say the Shakers, and they add that for their support it is not necessary to make work painful.

The Oneida communists had short hours of work and devoted much time to rest and recreation, and the Amana communists admitted that one hired hand did as much work in one day as a member of the commune would do in two.

The communists generally paid strict attention to the rules of hygiene, were models of cleanliness, and, almost without exception, temperate in their habits, altho the German communists did not disdain the use of good beer and wine, especially in harvest time.

Contrary to the general impression, life in communistic societies was, on the whole, not monotonous. The communists strove to introduce as much variety in their habits and occupations as possible. The Harmonists, Perfectionists, Icarians, and Shakers each changed their location several times. Of the Oneida Community, Nordhoff says: "They seem to have an almost fanatical horror of forms. Thus they change their avocations frequently; they change the order of their evening meetings and amusements with much care, and have changed even their meal hours." With the Fourierist Phalanxes, variation of employment was one of the main principles, and the same is true of almost all other communities.

They were cheerful and merry in their own quiet way; disease was a rare occurrence among them, and they are not known to have had a single case of insanity or suicide.

In those circumstances it will not be surprising to learn that the communists were among the most long-lived people in the United States.

Among the members of Amana Community there were recently two above ninety years old, and about twenty-five between eighty and ninety. Most of the Harmonists lived to be seventy and over; among Shakers ninety is not an uncommon age; the Zoarites had among them in 1877 one member ninety-five years old, and a woman of ninety-three, both of whom voluntarily continued to work, and many members past the age of seventy-five years; and in Oneida a number of members lived to be over eighty. Of the founders and leaders of the communities, Rapp reached the age of ninety years and Bäumeler and Noyes seventy-five years.

The influence of community life seems to have been as beneficial on the moral and mental development of the communists as it was on their physical condition. The Amana Community, consisting of seven different villages with a population at times exceeding 2,000, never had a lawyer. Bethel, Aurora, Wisconsin Phalanx, Brook Farm, and numerous other communities, declared with pride that they had never had a lawsuit against their communities or among their members.

Their bookkeeping was, as a rule, simple.   They did not exact any security from their managing officers; still there were no cases of defalcation.

"The communists are honest," says Nordhoff; "they like thorough and good work, and value their reputation for honesty and fair dealing.   Their neighbors always speak highly of them in this respect."

They were also noted for their hospitality, kind-heartedness, and readiness to help those who applied to them for aid.

And, finally, it must be noted that the communists invariably bestowed much attention upon the education of their children and their own culture.   Their schools, as a rule, were superior to those of the towns and villages in the neighborhood; they mostly maintained libraries and reading-rooms, held regular public discussions, and they were more cultured and refined than other men and women in the same station of life.

On the whole, the communistic mode of life proved to be more conducive to the physical, moral, and intellectual welfare of man than the individualistic *régime*.

PART II

THE MODERN MOVEMENT

INTRODUCTION

THE DEVELOPMENT OF MODERN SOCIALISM IN THE UNITED STATES

In reviewing the history of modern socialism in the United States, we encounter occasionally a seeming connecting link between that movement and its earlier utopian phases.

Thus the Icarian communities maintained close relations with the Working Men's League of Weitling in the fifties of the last century; later they took an active part in the work of the International, and their magazines, *La Revue Icarienne* and *La Jeune Icarie,* were listed as official organs of the Socialist Labor Party as late as 1879.

Alcander Longley, who was prominently connected with almost every phase of the utopian movements, reappears in about 1880 as a member of ''Section St. Louis'' of the Socialist Labor Party, vigorously advocating the principles of that party in his *Communist.* He is still alive and active to-day. Many Fourierists manifested a sympathetic interest in the development of the later-day socialism, and at least one Brook Farmer, Dr. J. Homer Doucet, of Philadelphia, was connected with the modern socialist movement.

But these instances must be regarded in the light of exceptions to the general rule, and, on the whole, it is safe to say that the early utopian theories and communistic experiments had little influence on the formation of the modern socialist movement in the United States.

The two movements are substantially different in their character and methods.

The socialist movement of the early part of the last century reflected to a large extent the immaturity of the industrial conditions of the time. It represented a blind revolt against the evils of the growing capitalist system of

135

production rather than an intelligent criticism of it. Theoretically, utopian socialism was mainly built on moral conceptions, and sought its inspiration in the teachings of Christ or in other codes of ethics. To the votaries of utopian socialism the movement seemed equally justified in the eighteenth century as in the nineteenth, and in this country as on the old continent.

Modern socialism, on the other hand, is the product of full grown capitalism, and as a rule it does not take root in any country before its industrial conditions have made it ripe for the movement.

The present socialist movement largely depends for its support upon the existence of a numerous class of workers divorced from the soil and other means of production, and permanently reduced to the ranks of wage labor. It is the result of a system of industry developed to a point where it becomes onerous upon working men, and impels them to organized resistance. In other words, the modern socialist movement presupposes the existence of the modern factory system in a high state of development, and all the social contrasts and economic struggles incidental to such a system.

And these conditions practically did not exist in any part of the United States during the first half of the last century. America has long held an exceptional position among the nations of the earth. At a time when the countries of Europe had almost exhausted every square foot of ground and all of their natural resources, the western hemisphere had boundless stretches of fertile soil waiting for the first comer to occupy. Agriculture was a comparatively easy and lucrative occupation, and the greater part of the American population consisted of independent farmers, at a time when manufacturing industries were dominant factors in Europe. The abundance of land, in drawing the greater part of the able-bodied men to the fields and pastures, furthermore left the supply of labor for the young industries far below the demand, and thus induced a comparatively high standard of wages.

Wage labor was, besides, a temporary condition rather than a permanent institution: the workingman after a time frequently succeeded in saving up sufficient money to purchase a farm, or to acquire the very simple and inexpensive tools of his trade, and to establish himself in business on his own account.

Nor were the advantages of American life confined to mere economic conditions. The great struggles and triumphs of the Revolutionary War were still fresh in the memory of the nation; the inspiring doctrines of the Declaration of Independence still rang in the ears of Americans; the "inalienable right" of men to life, liberty, and the pursuit of happiness was a living truth to them; they were proud of their political sovereignty, of their freedom of conscience, and of their liberty of speech and press. The young republic was prosperous, its future was brilliant; it had no political privileges and hardly any economic stress, and it was only natural that its citizens should have developed an unusual national optimism and complacency which caused them to frown upon any movement based on dissatisfaction with the existing order of things.

But gradually the economic conditions of the country changed. The unprecedented increase of population diminished the area of public lands from year to year; the more fertile soil became rapidly occupied, and what remained was mostly forest or barren. Land became an object of commerce and speculation, steadily rising in price and growing more and more inaccessible to the poor, who were, in consequence, compelled to turn from agriculture to industry. The foundation for a permanent class of wage-workers was thus laid.

At the same time, and as part of the same movement, modern industry made its appearance in the United States, and soon assumed marvelous dimensions. The inexhaustible resources of raw material of the country, and the enterprise and ingenuity of our inhabitants, soon conquered for us a front rank among the industrial nations. Commercial cities, factory towns, and mining-camps sprang up in all parts of the continent; railroad lines and telegraph wires soon covered it with a veritable network, and from a peaceful and contented agricultural community, the United States turned into a busy, hustling, and noisy workshop.

The industrial revolution brought in its wake a very radical change in the social relations of men. A new era was introduced in the national life of America—the era of multi-millionaires and money-kings, of unprecedented luxury and splendor, but also the era of abject poverty and dire distress.

Overt struggles between capital and labor, in the shape of strikes, lockouts, and boycotts, became more and more frequent, and were ofttimes attended by acts of violence.

The flow of workers to the industrial centers caused a congestion of population; slums and tenement-houses became as much a feature of our principal cities as their magnificent avenues and mansions.

In short, the United States, so recently the republic of relatively equal and independent citizens, became the theater of the most embittered class wars and most glaring social contrasts ever witnessed in modern times.

And these astounding social and economic changes were accomplished with incredible rapidity. In 1850 the population of the United States was but little over 23,000,000; in less than sixty years later it rose to about 85,000,000. In 1850 the wealth of the country amounted to little over $7,000,000,000, and was pretty well distributed among the population; in 1905 the "national wealth" reached $95,-000,000,000, and more than one-half of it was concentrated in the hands of 40,000 families, or one-fourth of one per cent. of the population. In 1850 fifty-five per cent. of the wealth of the United States consisted of farms; in 1900 the farms made up less than twenty-two per cent. of the wealth of the country. In 1860 the entire capital invested in manufacturing industries in the United States was little over $1,000,000,000; in the space of the following forty years it had increased more than ninefold.

In 1870 the supply of labor was too inadequate for the

demand; three decades later there was a standing army
of over 1,000,000 idle working men. In 1870 strikes and
lockouts were hardly known in America; between 1881
and 1894 the country witnessed over 14,000 contests between capital and labor, in which about 4,000,000 working
men participated.

The process of development sketched in the preceding
pages thus prepared the ground for the socialist movement
of the modern type, but a variety of circumstances rooted
in the economic and political conditions and historical
causes peculiar to this country operated to retard the progress of the movement.

In the first place, the American working men still enjoyed some actual advantages over their brethren on the
other side of the ocean. The marvelous variety of industries and the constant opening of new fields of enterprise made the United States a comparatively favorable
market for labor, and, notwithstanding the temporary industrial depression, the wages of American working men
were, on the whole, better, and their standard of life higher,
than those of European wage-workers. In the next place,
there was a great difference between the mental attitude of
the working classes of America and Europe, which is to be
accounted for by the difference in their origin and history.

European industry was developed from the small manufacture of the seventeenth and eighteenth centuries;
the master of the old time workshop grew into the capitalist of to-day, and the apprentice and helper into the
modern wage-worker. The process was slow and gradual,
and both classes had ample time to crystallize. The
European wage-workers were several generations old; they
had their class traditions and sentiments; they were "class
conscious."

Not so with the American working men. Their existence
as a class was of too recent date to have developed decided
class feelings in them; they had yet before them the example of too many men who before their very eyes rose
from the ranks of labor to the highest pinnacles of wealth

and power; they were still inclined to consider wage labor as a mere transitory condition.

Another check to the progress of the socialist movement in the United States was to be found in the political institutions of the country: the working classes of the European countries were, as a rule, depríved of some political rights enjoyed by other classes of citizens, and the common struggle for the acquisition of those rights was frequently the first cause to draw them together into a distinct political union. Universal Suffrage was the battle-cry of the German working men when they gathered around Lassalle in the early sixties, and founded the nucleus of the now powerful Social Democratic Party: "The repeal of all laws curtailing individual liberty, freedom of the press, education, coalition, and association," was one of the first demands of the French socialists upon the revival of the movement a short time after the fall of the Commune; and similarly the first struggles of the Austrian and Italian socialists were for universal suffrage, for freedom of assemblage and association, and for the right of coalition among the working class.

In the United States, however, the working men enjoyed full political equality at all times, and thus had one less motive to organize politically on a class basis.

Furthermore, the periodical appearance of radical reform parties on the political arena of the country often had the effect of side-tracking the incipient socialist movement into different channels.

All these and many more obstacles of minor import contributed to make the progress of socialism in this country a much slower and more laborious process than in most countries of Europe.

The beginnings of modern socialism appeared on this continent before the close of the first half of the nineteenth century, but it took another half a century before the movement could be said to have become acclimatized on American soil.

The history of this period of the socialist movement in the United States may, for the sake of convenience, altho somewhat arbitrarily, be divided into the following five periods:

1.   THE ANTE-BELLUM PERIOD, from about 1848 to the beginning of the civil war.   The movement of that period was confined almost exclusively to German immigrants, principally of the working class.   It was quite insignificant in breadth as well as in depth, and was almost entirely swept away by the excitement of the civil war.

2.   THE PERIOD OF ORGANIZATION, covering the decade between 1867 and 1877, and marked by a succession of socialist societies and parties, first on a local then on a national scale, culminating finally in the formation of the Socialist Labor Party.

3.   THE PERIOD OF THE SOCIALIST LABOR PARTY, extending over twenty years, and marked by a series of internal and external struggles over the question of the policy and tactics of the movement.

4.   THE ADVENT OF THE SOCIALIST PARTY, and with it the adjustment of the socialist movement to the conditions of the country, the acclimatization of socialism on American soil.

5.   PRESENT-DAY SOCIALISM, which embraces the period of the last few years.

Chapter I

ANTE-BELLUM PERIOD

I.—THE BEGINNINGS OF THE MOVEMENT

In the early part of the last century the thirty odd countries composing the German fatherland had apparently little attraction for their sons. The political condition and economic backwardness of the country caused a flow of emigration which only diminished after the formation of the Empire. It is estimated on reliable data that over 3,000,000 Germans left their fatherland during the first half of the nineteenth century. The bulk of this emigration was made up of journeymen and mechanics, but a considerable portion of it consisted of men of culture and education, of whom Germany always had a generous supply; and finally the ill-fated revolutions of 1830 and 1848 added a new and numerous element to it—that of the political refugees.

The German emigrants formed large settlements in France, England, Switzerland, and Belgium, and many of them ultimately landed on the shores of this country. Around 1830 the German population was well represented in almost every State and Territory of the Union, and was especially numerous in Pennsylvania, Ohio, New York, and Maryland.

The radicalism of these emigrants in Europe, as well as in America, fostered by the political and economic conditions of their fatherland, found additional support in the theories of French utopian socialism, and soon resulted in a widespread movement among them. They formed secret revolutionary societies and organized working-men's educational clubs for the discussion of social problems, and many of the "intellectuals" among them took an active and leading part in the movement, notably Karl Marx, Frederick Engels, and the distinguished coterie of their friends and followers.

Thus was originated the Communist Club at whose request Marx and Engels drafted the famous "Communist Manifesto." The "Manifesto" was the first complete exposition of Marxian or Scientific socialism. Contemporary socialism may be said to date from the time of the publication of that document, February, 1848, altho the movement was for a long time almost wholly confined to the *élite* among the German emigration.

The general movement among the German emigrants could not fail to find some echo in the United States. A society named "Germania" was founded in the city of New York in the early thirties for the avowed purpose of gathering together political refugees and holding them in readiness to return to the fatherland as soon as the next political revolution should break out.[1]

When the Free-Soil Party appeared on the arena of American politics, German working men were among the first to support it; they organized numerous Free-Soil clubs, and in 1846 published, in the interests of that party, a weekly magazine, called *The Tribune of the People (Volkstribun)*.

Many thousands of German immigrants were, besides, organized into debating societies, cooperative associations, gymnastic unions, and trade organizations of a somewhat rudimentary character. But the movement was rather disjointed, and did not attain any appreciable power and influence until the arrival of the famous German communist, Wilhelm Weitling.

II.—WILHELM WEITLING AND THE GENERAL WORKING-MEN'S LEAGUE

Wilhelm Weitling was born in Magdeburg in 1808 as the illegitimate child of a woman in humble circumstances. As a youth he learned the tailoring trade, and, according

[1] " In der Neuen Heimath," von Anton Eickhoff, New York, 1884.

to the custom of German journeymen in his day traveled extensively during the period of his apprenticeship.

The young man combined extraordinary mental gifts with a veritable thirst for knowledge, and during his travels he managed to master the French language and to fill many gaps in his neglected education.

He became very early in life an enthusiastic apostle of communism, and devoted himself entirely to the work of organization and propaganda among German working men sojourning abroad. He organized a number of cooperative restaurants for journeymen tailors in Paris and Switzerland, and a communistic working-men's educational society in London. He took an active part in various secret revolutionary societies which were then in vogue in Paris, and in 1846 joined the German Working-Men's Society at Brussels, of which the youthful Karl Marx and Frederick Engels were the leaders.

Weitling's first literary production to attract wide attention was a book printed by the secret revolutionary press in Paris in 1838. It was entitled, ''The World as It Is, and as It Should Be,'' and contained the first exposition of the author's communistic theories.

His best-known work, ''The Guaranties of Harmony and Freedom,'' was published four years later, and met with a decided and spontaneous success. It was widely read and commented on, and translated into French and English.

These two books, together with the ''Gospel of a Poor Sinner,'' published in 1846, compose his principal works.

In his social philosophy Weitling may be said to have been the connecting link between primitive and modern socialism. In the main he was a utopian, and his writings betray the unmistakable influence of the early French socialists. In common with all utopians, he based his philosophy exclusively on moral grounds. Misery and poverty were to him only the results of human malice, and his cry was for ''eternal justice'' and for the ''absolute liberty and equality of all mankind.'' In his criticism of the existing order, he leaned closely on Fourier, from whom he also borrowed the division of labor into the three classes of the Necessary, Useful, and Attractive, and the plan of organization of "attractive industry."

His ideal of the future state of society reminds us of the St. Simonian government of scientists. The administration of the affairs of the entire globe was to be in the hands of the three greatest authorities on "philosophical medicine," physics, and mechanics, who were to be supported by a number of subordinate committees. His state of the future was a highly centralized government, and was described by the author with the customary details. Where Weitling to some extent approached the conception of modern socialism, was in his recognition of class distinctions between employer and employee. This distinction never amounted to a conscious endorsement of the modern socialist doctrine of the "class struggle," but his views on the antagonism between the "poor" and the "wealthy" came quite close to it.

Unlike most of his predecessors and contemporaries, Weitling was not a mere critic; he was an enthusiastic preacher, an apostle of a new faith, and his writings and speeches breathed love for his fellow men and an ardent desire for their happiness.

Weitling's magnetic personality and affable manners won the hearts of his fellow workers, and his persistent persecutions by the Swiss and German governments augmented his popularity.

In the forties of the last century he was, beyond doubt, the most influential figure in the numerous colonies of German working men in Switzerland, France, Belgium, and England.

Weitling's first visit to the United States was undertaken toward the end of 1846 upon the invitation of a group of German Free Soilers to take editorial charge of the *Volkstribun*, already alluded to. But, upon his arrival, he found that the magazine had suspended publication, and when, one year later, rumors of an approaching revolution in his fatherland reached this country, he hurriedly returned to Germany. But the "glorious revolution of 1848'' was nipt in the bud in very short order, and Weitling, disappointed but not discouraged, came back to the United States in 1849. Here he found a wide and fruitful field of activity.

As already mentioned, the German immigrants had at that time formed a number of labor organizations of different kinds, but there was little organic connection and still less unity of aim and action among them. Weitling immediately undertook the task of centralizing the movement and directing it into definite channels. For this purpose he published *The Republic of the Working Men (Die Republik der Arbeiter)* a magazine which appeared monthly during the year 1850, and was converted into a weekly in April, 1851.

Under Weitling's influence also a ''Central Committee of United Trades'' was formed in New York in 1850. This was a delegated body of labor organizations, representing from 2,000 to 2,500 members. Similar bodies were organized in other cities of the Union, and a lively movement soon sprang up among German working men, especially in the East.

Mass-meetings were held, leaflets distributed, and numerous clubs organized. The movement attracted the attention of the American press, and was made the subject of much favorable and unfavorable criticism, with the result that it soon spread beyond the bounds of the purely German labor organizations, and enlisted the sympathies and cooperation of working men of other nationalities, including native Americans.

Every issue of the *Republik* of that period contains glowing reports of progress. In March, 1850, a mass meeting of negroes in New York declared itself in accord with Weitling's ideas of a ''labor-exchange bank,'' and a similar stand was taken in April of the same year by a convention of American working men in Philadelphia. On May 10th the *Republik* published a letter from Cabet, in which the famous French utopian expressed himself in favor of harmonious cooperation between the Icarian colony at Nauvoo and Weitling's movement, and in the same issue the paper reported that a number of American farmers at Weedport, New Jersey, had organized under the name of "Farmers' and Mechanics' Protective Association," for the purpose of establishing a labor-exchange bank on Weitling's plan. On the twenty-first day of September a call for a general working-men's convention, a subject long agitated by Weitling, was published in the *Republik*, and the convention was actually held in Philadelphia in October, 1850.

This was the first national convention of German working men on American soil, and is of great interest to the students of the labor movement, and especially of the socialist movement, in this country. The convention was opened on October 22d, and it completed its work on October 28th.

The basis of representation was one delegate for every one hundred organized members, and the number of members represented was 4,400. These were distributed among forty-two organizations in the following ten cities: St. Louis, Louisville, Baltimore, Pittsburg, Philadelphia, New York, Buffalo, Williamsburg, Newark and Cincinnati.

The subjects discussed at the convention were: 1. Labor-Exchange Banks. 2. Associations. 3. Political Party Organization. 4. Education and Instruction. 5. Propaganda. 6. Colonies. 7. Conventions.

The views of the delegates on these subjects were expressed in resolutions published in the *Republik* and other newspapers.

The "Exchange Bank" of Weitling was, in the main, identical with Owen's "Equitable Bank of Labor Exchange." It was to be an institution where every producer of a useful commodity could deliver his product and receive in exchange a paper certificate of an equivalent value, with which in turn he could purchase any article contained in the bank store at cost. The difference between Owen's plan and that of Weitling was that the latter included cooperative industries as an indispensable complement to the bank.

The Exchange Bank was Weitling's pet idea; through its operations he hoped gradually to displace the capitalist mode of production, and he never tired of extolling the advantages of the scheme.

The convention adopted his plan without modification, and prescribed minutely the mode of administration and practical workings of the institution.

The political views of the convention were summed up in the motto, "Equal Rights and Duties," and its platform consisted of twelve planks, almost all of them borrowed from the program of the Free-Soil Party.

The delegates also provided for a central political committee of seven in each city, who were to act in conjunction with each other in State and national elections, and they also adopted resolutions in favor of an extension of educational facilities and the organization of communistic settlements.

The delegates appointed the "Exchange Commission" of New York as the temporary executive organ of the movement, and provided for the time and manner of holding the next convention. But, singularly enough, they failed to designate an official name for the combination of organizations represented at the convention, and the body was for some time thereafter vaguely referred to as "the movement," "the association," or "the union of cities," until the name "General Working-Men's League" (*Allgemeiner Arbeiterbund*) was by common consent settled upon.

The period immediately following the Philadelphia convention marked the zenith of power and influence in Weitling's public career, and was followed by a period of rapid decline. His Exchange Banks never materialized. Altho some money was occasionally subscribed for the enterprise and some shares issued for it, the amount realized was altogether insufficient for even a very modest experiment, and Weitling reluctantly abandoned his favorite dream.

His followers made one attempt to realize his colonization scheme by founding the settlement called "Communia" in Iowa in 1849, but the attempt proved a disastrous failure and involved its originators in financial losses and unpleasant litigations over the title to the land.

In the meanwhile Weitling's methods and his self-asserting conduct provoked the antagonism of many prominent members of the League, and after a brief but intense quarrel, Weitling, irritated and disappointed, withdrew from public life.

The remainder of his years he passed as a clerk in the Bureau of Immigration in New York. Toward the close of his life his notions of the value of his own achievements became morbidly exaggerated. He wrote a book on astronomy which, he asserted, contained discoveries by far excelling those of Newton, and he also claimed to have invented many valuable devices in sewing-machines, all of which were stolen from him by men who made immense profits out of them.

His attitude of listlessness toward the succeeding phases of the labor movement was broken only once, when he appeared at a joint meeting of the New York Sections of the International on January 22, 1871. Three days later he died.

The General Working-Men's League continued in existence for some years after Weitling's withdrawal, but it never attained the significance of which its bright beginnings gave promise.

In 1853 a call for a second convention of trade organizations to be held in New York was issued, but the only trade represented in the convention was that of the typesetters.

In 1858 the League established a new weekly magazine under the title *Social Republic*, and elected as editor the well-known German revolutionist, Gustav Struve, a romantic phrasemonger of confused mind, under whose influence the League soon succumbed. To characterize the spirit and mental caliber of the League at that time, we quote the following resolutions on the obligations of its candidates for political office: [2]

[2] For these quotations and many other details of the movement of that period the author is indebted to Sorge's excellent articles on the Labor Movement in the United States. F. A. Sorge, "Die Ar-

"*Resolved,* That the following questions be asked of each candidate for office in the presence of the executive or ward officers:

"1. Are you prepared, on life and death, to break the chains which tie labor to capital, and generally to defend the rights of the poor to the best of your abilities?

"2. Are you prepared, on life and death, to maintain the absolute rights of labor before the law and to combat every injustice to immigrants through nativistic tendencies, etc.?"

Here follows a long string of similar questions, culminating in the following emphatic declaration:

"*Resolved,* That any candidate who may break his vows by acting contrary to the above principles be delivered to the judgment of the people."

The *Social Republic* suspended publication in 1860, and the General Working-Men's League was heard of no more.

Some new life was infused into the German labor movement about the middle of the fifties by the activity of Joseph Weydemeyer. Weydemeyer was a personal friend of Marx and Engels and well versed in the theories of scientific socialism. He came to New York at about the same time as Weitling. In the spring of 1852 he published a monthly magazine entitled *The Revolution,* in the second and last issue of which Marx's famous historical essay, "The 18th Brumaire of Louis Bonaparte," was printed for the first time. Weydemeyer strove to inoculate the doctrines of Marxian socialism in the Working-Men's League, and delivered many lectures on the subject in German and English before the members.

Toward 1856 Weydemeyer settled in Chicago, and remained there until the outbreak of the civil war.

beiterbewegung in den Vereinigten Staaten," 1850–1860. Neue Zeit, No. 31, 1890–1891.

For other details of Weitling's career in the United States the student is referred to the files of the *Republik der Arbeit,* and for Weitling's biography to Emil Kaler's booklet, "Wilhelm Weitling. Seine Agitation und Lehren," Göttingen-Zürich, 1887.

III.—GYMNASTIC UNIONS

OF some significance in the spread of socialist teachings during the fifties were the German Gymnastic Unions (*Turnvereine*).

At that time the importance of gymnastic exercises for the development of the human organism was beginning to be appreciated. In Prussia gymnastics had been recognized as a part of the regular school exercises by a cabinet order of June, 1842. Other countries followed the example, and, as is apt to happen with every new and inexpensive sport it was at first somewhat overdone. Gymnastics became the fashion, especially among the poorer classes, and working-men's gymnastic societies sprang up in all parts of Germany and in many other European countries.

In the United States most of these societies set apart some of their meetings for the discussion of social and political problems, an exercise which they styled "mental gymnastics." The early "Turners" were, as a rule, very radical in their political views. In 1850, the year of Weitling's convention in Philadelphia, they held a convention in the same city. It was attended by delegates from seventeen different local organizations and a National Union was formed under the name "United Gymnastic Unions of North America" (*Vereinigte Turnvereine Nordamerika's*). In 1851 the name of the organization was changed to "Socialist Gymnastic Union" (*Sozialistischer Turnerbund*).

The Turners supported politically the Free-Soil Party, but declared it to be their aim to establish a Socialist Party in the United States. Professor Ely, in his work on the American Labor Movement, already cited, and after him Sartorius von Waltershausen, the German historian of the socialist movement in the United States, ascribe considerable importance to the part played by the gymnastic unions in the early stages of modern socialism in this country, but F. A. Sorge, who has had the advantage of personal observation and recollection, disagrees with them on that point. At any rate, it does not appear that the gymnastic unions had any direct influence on the labor movement before the civil war, and after the war the Turners modified their political and social creed very considerably in the direction of conservatism, and changed the name of their national organization to North American Gymnastic Union, altho some local organizations still retain the word "Socialistic" as part of their name, and are still in sympathy with the socialist movement.

IV.—THE COMMUNIST CLUB

THE next organization of pronounced socialist tendencies to make its appearance in the United States was the Communist Club, organized in New York in 1857. But little is known of the history of that club. Its membership seems to have been composed principally of men of the middle classes who had received a good education in Germany. Their communism was based on philosophic rather than economic grounds, and their aim and views were set forth in a printed copy of their constitution, dated in October, 1857,[3] in the following language:

"The members of the Communist Club reject every religious belief, no matter in what guise it may appear, as well as all views not based upon the direct testimony of the senses. They recognize the perfect equality of all men, regardless of color and sex, and therefore they strive above all to abolish private property, inherited or accumulated, to inaugurate in its place the participation of all in the material and intellectual enjoyments of the earth. They pledge themselves with their signatures to carry out their aims in the present state of society as far as possible, and to support each other morally and materially."

Their constitution also provided for the formation of branches of the club, but none appear to have been organized. The only time the club attracted considerable attention was when it arranged a well-attended mass-meeting in 1858, in commemoration of the Paris insurrection of 1848.

[3] "Statuten des Kommunisten-Klubs in New York," New York, October, 1857.

V.—GERMAN SOCIALISTS IN THE CIVIL WAR

THE German socialists of the early period were, of course, in full accord with the abolition movement, and the abolition of chattel slavery was always one of their political demands. But as the impending contest drew nearer, the issue assumed greater practical importance. When war was finally declared it absorbed their attention to the exclusion of all other political interests.

Each of the various groups of socialist organizations then in existence furnished its full quota of soldiers for the Union army. "The Turners from every quarter," relates Professor Ely, "responded to Lincoln's call for troops, some of the unions sending more than half their numbers. In New York they organized a complete regiment in a few days, and in many places sent one or more companies. There were three companies in the First Missouri Regiment, while the Seventeenth consisted almost altogether of Turners. It is estimated that from forty to fifty per cent. of all Turners capable of bearing arms took part in the war."

The proportion of soldiers furnished by other socialist organizations probably fell below these figures, but was nevertheless quite considerable, and embraced some of the most energetic leaders of the young movement. Joseph Weydemeyer served during the war on the Union side with great distinction, and was appointed to a post of responsibility in the municipal administration of St. Louis immediately after the termination of the war.

August Willich, who in 1848 was a member of the London Communist League, together with Marx and Engels, and who had come to the United States in 1853, enlisted in the army immediately upon the outbreak of the war, and having been rapidly advanced to the ranks of lieutenant and colonel, was commissioned brigadier-general in 1862.

Robert Rosa, an ex-officer of the Prussian army and a member of the New York Communist Club, served in the

Forty-fifth New York Regiment, and advanced to the rank of major. He died in 1901.

Fritz Jacobi, one of the brightest and most promising young members of the Communist Club, enlisted in the Union army as a private. He was promoted to the rank of lieutenant, and fell in the battle of Fredericksburg.

Dr. Beust, Alois Tillbach, and many more socialists of less prominence were to be found in the ranks of the German volunteers.[4] In fact, the war had thinned the ranks of the incipient socialist organizations to such an extent as to paralyze their activity, and it was not until 1867 that the movement began to recover.

[4] For the greater part of this information the author is indebted to Mr. F. A. Sorge.

Chapter II

PERIOD OF ORGANIZATION

I.—THE INTERNATIONAL WORKING-MEN'S ASSOCIATION

THE history of the socialist movement in the United States during the period immediately following the civil war is closely linked with the career of the International Working-Men's Association. Some acquaintance with the nature and history of that association will prove valuable for a proper understanding of that period of the movement.

The International Working-Men's Association, popularly known as the International, was formally organized at St. Martin's Hall, in London, on the twenty-eighth day of September, 1864. Neither time nor place could have been chosen better for the launching of a movement which stands unparalleled in the eventful history of the nineteenth century for the boldness of its conceptions, the loftiness of its ideals, and the grandeur of its proportions.

The beginning of the sixties witnessed a most remarkable industrial, social, and political upheaval in all civilized countries of both hemispheres.

The advent of steam power and railroads had rapidly revolutionized former slow methods of production and transportation in Europe as well as in America. Home industries and small manufacturing were supplanted by gigantic factories and a system of mass production. New machines were invented, new industries created, new markets discovered, and new relations established. A fresh breeze wafted through the old countries and imbued them with new energy and vigor. The industrial progress was followed by a general political awakening and a renewal of the working-class movement.

In Germany political indifference and reaction following the defeat of the revolution of 1848 was giving way to a lively agitation for a unified fatherland, and the working men, inspired by their tireless and eloquent champion, Ferdinand Lassalle, opened a spirited campaign for universal suffrage and the rights of labor. In Italy the population, under the leadership of Garibaldi and Mazzini, was engaged in a desperate struggle against Austrian, French, and papal subjugation, and the cry for a "united republic" often drowned the demand for an "independent kingdom."

In the United States the antislavery agitation had reached its climax in the outbreak of the war; and the unfortunate Poles were winning the sympathies and admiration of Europe by gallant feats in their courageous but hopeless struggle against the autocrat of all the Russias.

In England and France the trade-union movement was rapidly developing, and had gained some substantial victories in numerous skirmishes with capital.

The whole continent of Europe was in a state of political and social unrest, and London teemed with political refugees of all nations. Almost every revolutionary movement of the time was represented in the capital of England by a more or less numerous group of men, and these refugees had frequent and friendly intercourse with each other.

On the occasion of the world's fair in 1862, several French working men, chosen by their fellow workers with the special permission of Napoleon III., were sent to London at the expense of their Government. They were cordially received by their British fellow workers and a "Festival of International Brotherhood" was arranged, at which the working men of various nationalities exchanged views and exprest the desire of seeing a lasting union established among the workers of Europe. About one year later, on July 22, 1863, the London working men arranged a public demonstration to express their sympathy with the Polish revolutionists, and several delegates of the organized French working men attended the meeting. The idea of an international union of workers was again broached.

This time the subject elicited more interest, and the organizers of the meeting decided to take immediate steps for the practical inauguration of the movement.

An address to the French working men was accordingly prepared by a committee, of which the shoemaker Odger was the leading spirit. The address was couched in strong and eloquent language, and laid special stress on the evil of international competition in the labor market. "Whenever working men of one country are sufficiently well organized to demand higher wages or shorter hours, they are met by the threat of the employer to hire cheaper foreign labor," argued the authors, "and this evil can only be removed by the international organization of the working class."

The address had a decidedly strong effect, and the French working men immediately elected a deputation to convey their answer to London.

It was for the purpose of receiving that deputation that the meeting at St. Martin's Hall, already alluded to, was called. Professor Beesly, who took a very active part in the early phases of the International, presided, and Henri L. Tolain, who headed the French deputation, read his countrymen's answer to the London address. The answer was in effect an unqualified indorsement of the stand taken by the Englishmen.

After some lively discussions, the meeting elected a committee with instructions to draft a platform and constitution of an international working-men's association, to be in force provisionally until the next convention of the association.

The committee, subsequently reinforced, consisted of fifty members. Twenty-one were Englishmen, ten were Germans, France was represented by nine members, Italy by six, Poland by two, and Switzerland by two.

The subcommittee appointed to present a constitution and declaration of principles submitted two drafts: one prepared by the famous Italian patriot Mazzini, and the other by the father of modern socialism, Karl Marx. The latter was unanimously accepted.

This provided for the continuance of the various national labor organizations affiliated with the International in their original form, and created a General Council for the administration of the international affairs of the association. The council was to be composed of delegates from the various nationalities represented in the International, and its functions were: to serve as a medium between the working men of different countries, to arbitrate all international disputes between labor organizations, to keep members informed of the progress of the labor movement in all countries, to compile and publish international labor statistics and other useful information, etc.

The International, in the forceful language of Frederick Engels, was to be "an association of working men embracing the most progressive countries of Europe and America, and concretely demonstrating the international character of the socialist movement to the working men themselves as well as to the capitalists and governments—to the solace and encouragement of the working class, and to the fear of its enemies."

The platform or declaration of principles was a brief exposition of the fundamental doctrines of modern socialism; it was never modified by the International, and has been adopted by several socialist parties as their national platform. We reproduce it here verbatim:

"In consideration: That the emancipation of the working class must be accomplished by the working class itself, that the struggle for the emancipation of the working class does not signify a struggle for class privileges and monopolies, but for equal rights and duties, and the abolition of class rule;

"That the economic dependence of the working man upon the owner of the tools of production, the sources of life, forms the basis of every kind of servitude, of social misery, of spiritual degradation, and political dependence;

"That, therefore, the economic emancipation of the working class is the great end to which every political movement must be subordinated as a simple auxiliary;

"That all exertions which, up to this time, have been

directed toward the attainment of this end have failed on account of the lack of solidarity between the various branches of labor in every land, and by reason of the absence of a brotherly bond of unity between the working classes of different countries;

"That the emancipation of labor is neither a local nor a national, but a social problem, which embraces all countries in which modern society exists, and whose solution depends upon the practical and theoretical cooperation of the most advanced countries;

"That the present awakening of the working class in the industrial countries of Europe gives rise to a new hope, but at the same time contains a solemn warning not to fall back into old errors, and demands an immediate union of the movements not yet united;

"The First International Labor Congress declares that the International Working-Men's Association, and all societies and individuals belonging to it, recognize truth, right, and morality as the basis of their conduct toward one another and their fellow men, without respect to color, creed, or nationality. This Congress regards it as the duty of man to demand the rights of a man and citizen, not only for himself, but for every one who does his duty. No rights without duties; no duties without rights."

The active career of the International embraced a period of about eight years, from 1864 to 1872, and the zenith of its power and influence was reached toward the end of the sixties. The organization was rather loose, and it is hardly possible to estimate the number of its adherents at any time with any degree of accuracy. But it was certainly the most extensive and influential labor organization of its time. It had numerous branches in France, England, Germany, Austria, Belgium, Holland, Denmark, Spain, Portugal, Italy, Switzerland, Poland, as well as in Australia and in the United States.

The European press, which had started by treating the existence of the International as a joke, soon took alarm at the growth of the organization, and instigated a crusade against this "great European menace to organized society.'' In the eyes of the frightened bourgeoisie it became a widely ramified secret society, with boundless resources at its command, actively engaged in a conspiracy to instigate an immediate political revolution in all countries of Europe. The most adventurous and fantastic accounts of the powers and doings of the International were published and circulated, and almost every great labor struggle and every political and social event of the time were laid at its door.

But the International never was a conspiratory society, and its influence on European politics and on the international labor movement was purely moral. Its main significance consisted in establishing closer and more harmonious relations between the working men of different countries, and in the deliberations of its conventions. These conventions, in which the labor organizations of the principal European countries were often represented by their ablest thinkers and most influential leaders, were six in number, and they were held at the following places and dates:

Geneva,	.	.	.	September	3 to	9, 1866.
Lausanne,	.	.	.	"	2 "	8, 1867.
Brussels,	.	.	.	"	6 "	13, 1868.
Basle,	.	.	.	"	5 "	11, 1869.
Hague,	.	.	.	"	2 "	7, 1872.
Geneva,	.	.	.	"	8 "	13, 1873.

The number of delegates at the conventions ranged from sixty to one hundred, and the subjects which engaged their attention included: Strikes, Reduction of Hours of Labor, Minimum Rate of Wages, Woman and Child Labor, Cooperative Industries, Trade-Unions, Direct Taxation, Standing Armies, Freedom of the Press, The Unemployed, Machines and their Effect, Division of Labor, The Functions of the State, Public Service, Means of Transportation and Communication, The Right to Punish, Attitude of the Working Class toward War, Ownership in Land, Grievances of Working Men, Right of Inheritance, Mutual Aid and Credit of Working Men, Political Action of the Working Class, and many other questions of interest to the labor movement. The discussions at the conventions were, as a rule, thorough and instructive, and the resolutions and declarations of the International are a most valuable contribution to the history of the development of modern socialist thought.

Karl Marx was, from the start, the leading spirit of the International, and his policy and views maintained undisputed sway in the organization until the time of the Basle convention of 1869, when an opposition to Marx and Marxism was manifested for the first time, the opposition being led by the famous apostle of revolutionary anarchism—Michael Bakounin.

Bakounin was one of the most picturesque characters produced by the stormy political atmosphere of the middle of the nineteenth century. He seems to have been as energetic, eloquent, and daring as he was ambitious, inconsistent, and changeable; and even now, several decades after his death, the most conflicting estimates of his character and motives are current. The scion of a highly aristocratic Russian family, he devoted himself early in life to the study of German philosophy. He was identified with every revolutionary movement in France, Germany, Austria, and Russia before 1848, and was placed in charge of the defense of Dresden during the Saxon revolt of 1849. Captured and condemned to death, he was saved by the successive demands of Austria and Russia for his extradition on the ground of their prior rights of execution. He was delivered to Russia and banished to Siberia, whence he made his escape, arriving in London in 1860. His restless activity was from now on divided between the agitation of Panslavism and a peculiar brand of revolutionary "anarchistic communism." In 1868 he founded the "*Alliance Internationale de la Democratie Socialiste,*" a society partly open, partly secret, with a highly centralized form of organization, having for its aim the destruction of all present forms of government and industry, and the introduction of a social system founded on autonomous cooperative agricultural and industrial associations. In 1868 the

Alliance made application for admission into the International as a body, but the application was rejected by the General Council. An intense and bitter feud between the two organizations was waged until the Hague convention of the International in 1872, when Bakounin was expelled. As a result of these disputes the Spanish, Belgian, and Jurassian federations seceded from the International and joined the Alliance. At the same time the Hague convention decided to transfer the seat of the General Council from London to New York.

The removal of the chief executive organ of the International far away from the center of the socialist and labor movement practically amounted to a suspension of the existence of the association, and such keen tacticians as Marx and the other advocates of the measure could certainly not have failed to perceive it. The step was taken deliberately.

At this stage of its career the International had practically outlived its usefulness; its principal aim had been to educate the working class of different nationalities to a uniformity of thought and action, and that object was substantially accomplished. To continue the formal organization of the International had become difficult in view of the existing political and industrial conditions of Europe, and dangerous in view of the designs on it on the part of Bakounin and his adherents.

II.—THE INTERNATIONAL AND THE NATIONAL LABOR–UNION

THE influence of the International on the labor movement in the United States was exerted through two distinct channels: the outspoken socialists, principally of foreign birth, affiliated with the association directly by means of branch organizations established in various places of the country, and the indigenous American labor movement, reached by its agitation principally through the medium of the National Labor-Union. We will describe the latter first.

Immediately after the close of the civil war a strong trade-union movement developed in the United States. New local and national organizations sprang up in almost every trade, but there was as yet no common bond between these organizations.

The subject of consolidating the forces of organized labor in the United States was frequently discust among the leaders, and the Machinists' and Blacksmiths' Union at its annual convention of 1863 finally took the initiative by appointing a committee "to request the appointment of similar committees from other national and international trade-unions to meet them fully empowered to form a national trades' assembly." But it was not until March, 1866, that a preliminary conference of a number of men prominent in the movement was held in New York for the purpose of considering the plan. The conference issued a call for a convention to be held in Baltimore in August of the same year, and the convention met accordingly. It was an earnest and enthusiastic gathering of working men, over sixty organizations being represented by delegates. Committees were appointed to present resolutions on the various topics discust at the convention, and the debates on the proposed resolutions were at times very stormy.

Of great interest in connection with these debates is the appearance on the floor of the convention of a German socialist of the Lassallean school, Edward Schlegel by name. Schlegel represented the German Working-Men's Association of Chicago, and was the first to broach the subject of the formation of an independent political labor party. His address on the subject was eloquent and persuasive. "A new party of the people must be in the minority when it first comes into action," he said among other things, "but what of that? Time and perseverance will give us victory; and if we are not willing to sacrifice time and employ perseverance, we are not deserving of victory. A new party must be formed, composed of the element of American labor. We are shy of fighting the old political parties, but should not be. If we are right, let us go ahead. The Free-Soil Party originated with a few thousand votes; but if it had not been formed, Lincoln would never have been President of the United States. . . . A political question is one that is decided at the ballot-box, and *here* must this question be met." Altho no immediate steps looking toward the formation of a political labor party were taken by the convention, the impassioned appeals of Schlegel made a deep impression on the delegates, who elected him vice-president at large in attestation of their "appreciation of his views and abilities."

The first convention of the International of Geneva took place within less than two weeks from the convention of the National Labor-Union above described. The topics discust and results arrived at by the two conventions are similar in many respects. Both conventions discust the subjects of trade-unions, strikes, woman and child labor, and cooperative industries. The stand of the National Labor-Union on these questions, altho less analytical and scientific than that of the International, was substantially in accord with it. Still more striking is the resemblance between the attitude of both bodies on the question of the reduction of the hours of labor. The resolution adopted by the National Labor-Union on that subject read as follows:

"*Resolved*, That the first and grand desideratum of the hour, in order to deliver the labor of the country from the thraldom of capital, is the enactment of a law whereby eight hours shall be made to constitute a legal day's work in every State of the American Union. We are firmly determined to use every power at our command for the achievement of this glorious aim."

The resolution of the International on the same subject was:

"The legal reduction of the hours of labor is a prerequisite without which all attempts to improve the condition of the working class and to ultimately emancipate it will fail. It is just as necessary to restore the health, physical strength, and energy of the working class—the great majority of every nation—as it is to secure to it the possibility to develop intellectually and to act socially and politically.

The convention, therefore, proposes that eight hours be made to constitute a legal day's work. The shortening of the work-day is now being generally demanded by the working men of America; we demand it for the working men of the entire world.''

But the similarity of the proceedings of the two conventions is only to be accounted for by the similarity of the conditions of the working men on both sides of the Atlantic. Otherwise there was at that time little connection between the two bodies.

The first direct mention of the International was made at the second convention of the National Labor Union held in Chicago in August, 1867. The convention was much better attended than the first, the number of delegates exceeding 200, and the interest in its proceedings was heightened by the presence of the man who was for a time destined to play the most important part in the councils of the organization—William H. Sylvis.

Sylvis's influence on the labor movement of the period under discussion was so great that a brief biographical sketch of him will not be out of place here. He was born in the village of Armagh, Pennsylvania, on the 26th day of November, 1828, as the second son of a journeyman wagon-maker. His parents were too poor to give him any education, and at the age of eleven he was hired out as a domestic and general farm-hand to a certain Mr. Pawling, who first taught him the alphabet. At the age of eighteen he learned the trade of iron molding, and in 1857 joined the Iron Molders' Union of Philadelphia, then recently organized. From that time on until his death, Sylvis was ever active in the trade-union movement. Wherever an enterprise or struggle of any magnitude was undertaken by workingmen of his trade, Sylvis was sure to be found in the front ranks of the movement. His name is identified with almost every important phase of the trade-union history of that period.

In 1859 a national convention of iron molders was called on the suggestion of Sylvis, who was also the author of the address issued by the convention to the iron molders of the United States. The address was a brief and pithy document, and very characteristic of the keenness of intellect and eloquence of style of this humble working man with no educational advantages worth mentioning.

"In all countries," he observes, "and at all times, capital has been used by those possessing it to monopolize particular branches of business, until the vast and various industrial pursuits of the world have been brought under the immediate control of a comparatively small portion of mankind."

And again:

"What position are we, the mechanics of America, to hold in society? Are we to receive an equivalent for our labor sufficient to maintain us in comparative independence and respectability, to procure the means with which to educate our children, and qualify them to play their part in the world's drama; or must we be forced to bow the suppliant knee to wealth, and earn by unprofitable toil a life too void of solace to confirm the very chains that bind us to our doom?"

Sylvis was elected successively treasurer and president of the national union, and when the organization had been considerably weakened during the war years, the arduous task of reorganizing it fell to his lot. "During this period," relates his brother,[1] "Sylvis wore clothes until they became quite threadbare, and he could wear them no longer; the shawl he wore to the day of his death was filled with little holes, burned there by the splashing of the molten iron from the ladles of molders in strange cities, whom he was beseeching to organize, and more than once he was compelled to beg a ride from place to place on an engine, because he had no money sufficient to pay his fare."

The extraordinary efforts of Sylvis were crowned by success, and within a short time the Iron Molders' National Union was one of the strongest and most prosperous labor organizations in the country. Sylvis took an active and prominent part in the formation of the National Labor-

[1] "The Life, Speeches, Labors, and Essays, of William H. Sylvis," by his Brother, James C. Sylvis, Philadelphia, 1872.

Union, but sickness prevented him from attending the first convention of that body.

In the Chicago convention of 1867 he played a leading part. He reintroduced the plan to form an independent labor party, and advocated the measure with his customary logic and vigor, but the majority of the delegates were as yet not ready for so radical a step, and the proposition was defeated by a close vote.

The establishment of official connections with the European International was also discust, and strongly advocated by the president of the union, Jessup, and by Sylvis, who had already, on a previous occasion, exprest himself on the subject in the following language: "At this hour a struggle is going on in the Old World, the result of which will be the social and political emancipation of enslaved millions. . . . Need I tell you that the interests of labor are identical throughout the world? . . . It is a matter of vital importance that an equilibrium of wages should be established throughout the world. Hence both our sympathies and interests are enlisted in favor of the great reform movement abroad. A victory to them will be a victory to us; and the news of their triumph shall be heard across the Atlantic; the working men of America will ring out shouts of triumph from Maine to California."

The convention, however, decided against formal affiliation with the International, and disposed of the subject by the adoption of the following resolution:

"Whereas, The efforts of the working classes in Europe to acquire political power, to improve their social conditions, and to emancipate themselves from the bondage under which they were and still are, are gratifying proof of the progress of justice, enlightenment, and civilization;

"Resolved, That the National Labor Convention hereby declares its sympathies, and promises its cooperation to the organized working men of Europe in their struggle against political and social injustice."

The third convention of the National Labor-Union was held in New York in August, 1868. By this time the organization had largely grown in membership, influence, and power, and a number of professional politicians had succeeded in gaining access to its councils.

But the leading spirit of the convention was Sylvis, and his pet idea—the establishment of an independent labor party—was at last realized; the National Reform Party was organized amid deafening cheers from the numerous delegates of the convention. Sylvis was elected president and it was he who drafted the platform. The document was patterned after the Declaration of Independence; it dwelt at some length upon the rights of labor, and devoted much space to the discussion of monetary reforms in the vein of Kellog and the Greenback Party, under whose influence Sylvis had come.

A wide and fruitful field of activity was now opened to Sylvis, who set himself to the task of building up the new party with his customary earnestness and vigor. Hardly a labor meeting of any significance was held anywhere in the country that did not receive a letter or circular from the indefatigable agitator and organizer.

"The organization of a new party—a working man's party—for the purpose of getting control of Congress and the several State legislatures, is a huge work, but it can and must be done." He proclaimed in one of his circulars, "We have been the tools of professional politicians of all parties long enough; let us now cut loose from all party ties, and organize a working man's party founded upon honesty, economy, and equal rights and privileges of all men."

And in another circular:

"Our people are being divided into two classes—the rich and the poor, the producers and the non-producers.

"The working people of our nation, white and black, male and female, are sinking to a condition of serfdom. Even now a slavery exists in our land worse than ever existed under the old slave system."

Since the organization of the Labor Reform Party, Sylvis had been in correspondence with leading members of the European International, and had strongly leaned in the direction of modern socialism. In a letter to the General Council at about that time he wrote:

"Our aim is a common one—it is the war between poverty and riches. Our last war has resulted in the development of an infamous moneyed aristocracy. This money power is rapidly consuming the power of the people. We are combating it, and hope to be victorious." And the General Council of the International was not slow in responding to these advances. In May, 1869, it addrest an open letter to the National Labor-Union, of which we quote the following portion:

"In our address of felicitation to Mr. Lincoln on the occasion of his reelection to the presidency of the United States, we exprest our conviction that the civil war would prove as important to the progress of the working class as the War of the Revolution had been for the progress of the bourgeoisie.

"And actually the victorious termination of the antislavery war has inaugurated a new epoch in the annals of the working class. In the United States an independent labor movement has since sprung into life, which is not being viewed with much favor by the old parties and the professional politicians."

The address was followed by a formal request to the National Labor-Union to send delegates to the next convention of the International, to be held at Basle in 1869.

Another connecting link between the National Labor-Union and the European Socialist movement was found in the German labor organizations of the United States.

Already, in 1866, a number of German trade-unions in the city of New York had organized a central body under the name "Arbeiter Union" (Working-Men's Union), and two years later the organization published a paper under the same title, *Arbeiter Union*, which gradually gained much influence in the German labor movement.

When the Labor Reform Party was organized, the *Arbeiter Union* supported it, but at the same time it published reports of the proceedings of the International, and

by degrees fell under the influence of socialism. Especially
was that the case when the editorial charge of the paper
was assumed by Dr. Adolph Douai.

Douai had had a very eventful career. Born in Alten-
burg, Germany, in 1819, he received an excellent education, and devoted himself to his chosen vocation, that of
teaching. He took an active part in the revolution of 1848,
was captured, tried, and imprisoned, and in 1852 emigrated
to Texas. He founded a small paper in San Antonio,
which was written, set, printed, and distributed by him
without any outside help, so that he was often compelled
to work 100 hours a week. The paper was devoted to the
cause of abolition, and its editor was, on that account,
often subjected to persecutions and ill treatment by the
mob. After three years of struggle, Douai was compelled
to leave San Antonio, but the negro population of Texas
always bore him a grateful memory for his devotion to
their cause, and in 1868 he received a newspaper with the
following announcement printed in bold type at the head
of the first column:

"This paper, edited and set by negroes, is being printed
on the same press from which Dr. Douai for the first time
advocated the emancipation of the negroes in Texas. Let
this serve him as a token of gratitude of the colored race
that they preserve the memory of his efforts for their freedom."

During the following ten years Douai resumed his interrupted pedagogic work in Boston, Hoboken, and New
York, until he was elected to the editorship of the *Arbeiter Union* in 1868. Later, Douai became a leading exponent of Marxian socialism in the United States, and
from 1878 to 1888 was one of the most valued members of
the editorial staff of the *New Yorker Volkszeitung*. The
Arbeiter Union, however, only marked his *début* in the
practical labor movement. His views on the labor problem
were not yet quite clear and settled.

His support of the platform of the National Labor Party
and his advocacy of the principles of the International at
one and the same time were frequently criticized as incon-

sistent. But be that as it may, his paper contributed materially to the establishment of friendly relations between the two movements, and these relations were strengthened still further when the General German Working-Men's Association affiliated with the National Labor-Union in February, 1869.

The fourth convention of the National Labor-Union and Labor Reform Party thus arrived with every prospect of a definite union being established between that body and the International, but the progress in that direction was suddenly checked by an unexpected event—on the 27th day of July, 1869, Sylvis died after a brief illness.

Ordinarily the life or death of a single individual matters little in a great social or political movement, but at a time when a young movement has reached the critical point of a parting of the ways, and the masses are uneducated and inexperienced, and easily led into any direction, the loss of a clear-minded, energetic, and honest leader becomes a great blow. And such was undoubtedly the effect of Sylvis's death on the further career of the National Labor-Union. That the International fully appreciated the loss is evidenced by the memorial of the General Council, which concluded with these words:

"That the American labor movement does not depend on the life of a single individual is certain, but not less certain is the fact that the loss sustained by the present labor convention through the death of Sylvis can not be compensated. The eyes of all were turned on Sylvis, who, as a general of the proletarian army, had an experience of ten years outside of his great abilities—and Sylvis is dead."

The premature death of its leader proved fatal to the progress of the National Labor-Union. Sylvis did not leave a single successor in the ranks of the organization of sufficient intelligence and power to inoculate in the young movement the doctrines and spirit of the International—the recognition of the distinctness of the interests of labor, and the German socialists had too little influence on the American labor movement to guide its political course.

At the fourth convention of the National Labor-Union, held in Philadelphia in August, 1869, it was decided to send an official representative to the Basle convention of the International. A. C. Cameron was elected delegate, and attended the convention where he gave grossly exaggerated accounts of the strength of the organization represented by him, but did not otherwise participate in the deliberations.

The only prominent member of the National Labor-Union who remained in active correspondence with the International after Sylvis's death was Jessup, and it was he who, at the fifth convention, held in Cincinnati in August, 1870, procured the passage of the following resolution: "The National Labor-Union declares its adherence to the principles of the International Working-Men's Association, and expects to join the said association in a short time." But the National Labor-Union never joined the International, and never developed into a genuine class-conscious working men's party.

The further fate of the Union, and with it the Labor Reform Party, was the fate common to all independent political parties formed by American trade-unions before and after it. As soon as it acquired appreciable strength, it was invaded by professional politicians, who entangled it in alliances with other political parties. Its platform was gradually watered, its class character obliterated, its identity obscured, and finally it merged into one of the dominant political parties.

The dissolution of the National Labor-Union was also accelerated by a series of ill-fated strikes, which weakened the labor movement in the United States. In January, 1871, the leaders met at Washington to discuss a plan of campaign. In view of the decreasing interest in the movement on the part of industrial workers, it was decided to enlist the sympathies of the farmers by adopting some farmers' planks in the platform. The result of the change was, that the strongest trade-unions withdrew from the National Labor-Union, and when its regular annual session was held at St. Louis in August of the same year, it was attended by only twenty-one delegates. Like crows at the scent of a corpse, the professional reformers gathered around the political corpse. In this case it was Wendell Phillips and Benjamin F. Butler who officiated at the funeral services of the erstwhile strong and promising labor organization. The platform adopted under their influence was composed of the usual stock-in-trade of the middle-class reformer. Two more attempts were made to revive the movement, conventions for that purpose being called in 1873 at Columbus and in 1874 at Rochester, but the conventions evoked no interest or enthusiasm in the working class, and the National Labor-Union passed out of existence.

Another organization of American workingmen maintaining some connection with the International was the Eight-Hour League of Boston, which under the able leadership of Ira Stewart, attained considerable influence in the seventies of the last century. In many ways Stewart was an even more noteworthy figure in the labor movement of America than William H. Sylvis. A plain workingman, with very scant education, he was early attracted to the study of the social problems of his class. He was a keen thinker and a gifted writer and speaker. Although unacquainted with the works and theories of European socialism, he evolved a social philosophy and program of labor reform very much akin to the latter. Stewart clearly recognized the evils of wage-labor, and advocated the establishment of a system of cooperative production. But the first and most effective step in that direction he saw in the introduction of a legal eight-hour workday. His ideas on the subject were most tersely expressed in a resolution drafted by him for adoption by one of the conventions of the Eight-Hour League, which read in part as follows:

"Resolved, That poverty is the great fact with which the labor movement deals;

"That cooperation in labor is the final result to be obtained;

"That a reduction in the hours of labor is the first step in labor reform; and that the emancipation of labor from the slavery and ignorance of poverty solves all of the problems that now must disturb and perplex mankind.

"That less hours mean reducing the profits and fortunes that are made on labor or its results;

"More knowledge and more capital for the laborer; the wage system gradually disappearing through higher wages."

From about 1860, when he was barely thirty years old, to the day of his death, March 13, 1883, he was restlessly, indefatigably active in the propaganda of that reform. He addrest meetings, published pamphlets, wrote newspaper articles, and caused bills for the legal limitation of the workday to be introduced in the State Legislatures of Massachusetts and other New England States and in the Congress of the United States.

It was chiefly under the influence of his activity that the eight-hour movement assumed such an important place in the struggles of the organized American workers in the seventies and eighties of the last century.

In 1869 the Boston Eight-Hour League was organized principally through the efforts of Ira Stewart, who remained the spiritual leader of the organization throughout its existence, and who was the author of most, if not all, of its official publications, declarations of principles and resolutions.

The clearest and most advanced of these resolutions was the one adopted by the League in 1876, which, among other things, declared that the continuance of the republic of the United States was seriously menaced by the existence of a class of wage-workers; that the difference between the workers and the capitalists consists in the fact that the capitalist sells the labor power of the workers to other persons as a commodity, so that the worker retains for sale only his own labor, his personality, his own self.

The capitalist class had monopolized all industries, and obtained control of all instruments of production and the raw material to such an extent, that it had become impossible for the worker to employ himself, and without employment he faced starvation.

It was also mainly through the efforts of Ira Stewart and the small band of his friends that the Massachusetts Statistical Bureau of Labor was created in June, 1869. The Bureau was the first of its kind in the country, and owing to the active cooperation of Stewart and his gifted and noble wife, it became, at least during the first years of its existence, a powerful aid to the organized labor movement, extending its influence far beyond the confines of the Bay State.

Towards 1876 Stewart made the acquaintance of some of the leaders of the International in the United States, and to the end of his days maintained friendly relations with them. He declared himself in accord with the platform and principles of the Socialist Labor Party, when the latter was founded, but criticized the practical political demands of the party on the ground that "there were too many of them."

Ira Stewart was a man of exceptional personal integrity and disinterestedness; he lived and died in extreme poverty.

Closely associated with Stewart in the propaganda of the Eight-Hour philosophy was George E. McNeill, a journalist and speaker of great ability. Upon the establishment of the Massachusetts Statistical Bureau of Labor, McNeill was made its deputy and chief manager, but his radical views and unswerving fidelity to the cause of labor soon made his position in the Bureau untenable. During the wave of independent working-class politics of 1886, he was the working-men's candidate for Mayor of Boston, and in the same year he edited and published the noteworthy book entitled: "The Labor Movement, or the Problem of To-day." He took a very active part in the formation of the American Federation of Labor, and always exerted great influence in its councils. George E. McNeill in later years called himself a Christian socialist, but was not directly connected with the organized socialist movement. He died in 1906.

III.—THE INTERNATIONAL IN THE UNITED STATES

THE first organizations directly affiliated with the International appeared in the United States about the year 1869. They were small societies in New York, Chicago, and San Francisco, composed almost exclusively of German socialists, and styled "sections" of the International.

In New York the movement was initiated in December, 1867, by a call issued for a mass meeting to be held in the Germania Assembly Rooms, on the Bowery, in January, 1868. It was signed by C. Carl, E. Eilenberg, A. Kamp, F. Krahlinger, and C. A. Petersen, all of whom were men of influence in German labor circles. The meeting was well attended. After a thorough discussion of the political situation, it was decided to organize an independent political labor party, and THE SOCIAL PARTY OF NEW YORK AND VICINITY was accordingly formed.

The party adopted a platform which was a sort of compromise between the declaration of principles of the International and the platform of the National Labor-Union, and appointed two executive boards—one an English-speaking, and the other a German-speaking—who together formed the political campaign committee of the party. The Social Party nominated an independent ticket in the elections of 1868, but its vote seems to have been very insignificant.

Immediately after this, its first and last campaign, the party dissolved, and some of its most active and intelligent members organized the "General German Labor Association" (Allgemeiner Deutscher Arbeiterverein).

This was the first strictly Marxian organization of strength and influence on American soil. The present socialist movement in this country may be said to date from the organization of that society.

"The members." relates Sorge,[2] "almost exclusively plain wage-workers of every possible trade, vied with each other in the study of the most difficult economic and political problems. Among the hundreds of members who belonged to the society from 1869 to 1874, there was hardly one who had not read his Marx ('Capital'), and more than a dozen of them had mastered the most involved passages and definitions, and were armed against any attacks of the capitalist, middle-class, radical, or reform schools."

In February, 1869, the General German Working-Men's Association was admitted to the National Labor-Union, receiving the name "Labor-Union No. 5 of New York." It was represented by delegates in the conventions of the National Labor-Union of 1869 and 1870, but withdrew from that body immediately after the latter convention.

In the fall of 1869 the society joined the International Working-Men's Association as "Section 1 of New York," and all through the career of the International it remained its strongest and most trustworthy branch in this country.

Section 1 maintained active and friendly relations with a number of trade-unions and other labor organizations in this country, and was instrumental in the formation of other sections of the International in the United States.

In 1870 a French section of the International was organized in New York, and was followed by a Bohemian section in the fall of the same year.

In 1868 a German section was created in San Francisco, and one year later the German socialists of Chicago formed their first section.

In December, 1870, the three New York sections of the International, by direction of the General Council, constituted themselves into a provisional Central Committee for the United States, and the movement began to make substantial progress. The warm reception accorded by the International to the Fenian leader, O'Donovan Rossa, upon his arrival at New York in 1871, won for the organization

[2] "Die Arbeiterbewegung in den Vereinigten Staaten, 1867-1877," von F. A. Sorge. Neue Zeit, No. 13, 1891-92.

the sympathies of many Irishmen; the fall of the Paris
Commune in the same year drove numerous radical Frenchmen to this country, where they were cordially welcomed by
the International; and finally the organization succeeded in
reaching the ranks of American labor by active support of
the numerous strikes of that year.

The most significant of these strikes was that of the an-
thracite coal miners in Pennsylvania, which lasted over six
months and involved over 30,000 men.

In these favorable circumstances the International
spread rapidly. The number of sections within about one
year grew from six to thirty or more, and the territory covered by them embraced the cities of New York, Chicago,
San Francisco, New Orleans, Newark, Springfield, Washington, and Williamsburg. The total number of enrolled
members was about 5,000, composed of Americans, Irishmen, Germans, Frenchmen, Scandinavians, and Bohemians.
"The International," says Sorge in his article already
quoted, "had at that time become the fashion." The press
devoted much space to its proceedings; its views and
methods were discust at public meetings, and even the
United States Congress paid considerable attention to its doings. Congressman Hoar, in the course of a debate on the
question of the appointment of a commission to investigate
the condition of labor, quoted extensively and with approval from some resolutions adopted by the General Council of the International.

This sudden popularity of the movement had, however,
its reverses. Reformers of all shades invaded the International, each of them endeavoring to use the organization
for the propaganda of his or her peculiar social doctrines.
Especially troublesome in this respect was one of the
American sections of New York, known as Section 12.
This was dominated by the two sisters, Victoria Woodhull
and Tennessee Claflin, women of culture and wealth, but of
rather singular notions on many subjects, which they pro-
mulgated in their magazine, *The Woodhull and Claflin
Weekly.*

Under the leadership of these ladies, Section 12, and

after it, Section 9, set up a separate "American" movement in opposition to the "aliens," and centered its activities chiefly on woman's rights, free love, etc.

"Section 12," complained the Federal Council of the International in an official document,[3] "finally proceeded on
its own hook to issue an appeal to the English-speaking
citizens of the United States for affiliation—an appeal
famous for its ludicrous attempt to saddle the International with every imaginable visionary idea of issue, except
the cause of labor, the name of which even does not seem
to agree with that section's idea of euphony, since it
is scarcely mentioned in that appeal of considerable
length."

This conduct provoked the dissatisfaction of the older
sections. Section 1 demanded the suspension of Section 12,
and was supported in that demand by the majority of the
German and Irish sections. The American, two German,
and the majority of the French sections, grouped themselves around Section 12, and as a result, the organization
of the International was divided, Section 1 and its adherents forming an independent Federal Council.

Both sides submitted their grievances to the General
Council of the International at London, which rendered its
decision in March, 1872. By this decision Section 12 was
suspended, and the administrative boards of both factions
were directed to unite into one provisional committee until
the next national convention, which was to establish definite
regulations for the administration of the affairs of the
American sections of the International. The feud was
thus ended. Section 12 still continued for some time an
independent existence, but its doings became so ridiculous
that it lost all influence with its former supporters in the
International. The last act in the career of section 12 was
the convocation of a convention of all "male and female
beings of America," to be held at the Apollo Theater in
New York. The convention met pursuant to call, and after
discussing all possible kinds of reform, including the introduction of a universal language, wound up by nominating

[3] "Appeal to the Working Men of America," New York, 1872.

a ticket headed by Victoria Woodhull as candidate for the presidency of the United States.

The first national convention of the International was held on the 6th day of July, 1872, in the city of New York. Twenty-two sections were represented. The convention assumed the official name of NORTH AMERICAN FEDERATION OF THE INTERNATIONAL WORKING-MEN'S ASSOCIATION, and adopted a set of rules and regulations for the government of its affairs.

The executive functions of the organization were vested in a committee of nine, designated the Federal Council. The council elected for the first year consisted of three Germans, two Frenchmen, two Irishmen, one Swede, and one Italian.

The rules and regulations also provided that in every section to be formed in the future, at least three-fourths of the members should be wage-workers, and enjoined upon all sections "to entertain good relations with the trade-unions and to promote their formation."

A new impetus was given to the American movement at about the same time by the transfer of the seat of the General Council of the International from London to New York. The convention at The Hague elected to the council twelve members, of whom four were Germans, three Frenchmen, two Irishmen, one an American, one a Swede, and one an Italian. The council was headed by F. A. Sorge as general secretary. Sorge was well qualified for the duties of this responsible and delicate position. A veteran of the German revolution of 1848, and a personal friend of Marx and Engels, he had arrived in this country in 1852, and by his tact, ability, and intimate knowledge of the labor problems, soon conquered for himself a position in the front ranks of the early socialist movement in this country.

He became the leading spirit of the International in the United States, ever active in organizing new sections and in the direction of their activity. His name is prominently connected with every phase of the movement of that period. In the later periods of the movement, Sorge took no active part. He died in Hoboken, N. J., in 1907.

During the year following the events above described, the history of the International was devoid of any significant incidents. Some old sections disbanded, and new ones were organized, but on the whole the organization remained stationary, if not somewhat stagnant.

Toward the close of the next year it was again brought prominently before the public in connection with the general labor troubles of the country.

The collapse of the Northern Pacific in 1873 caused an almost unprecedented financial and industrial panic in the United States. The destitution of the population in all industrial centers grew alarming, especially during the winter season, and it was estimated that in the State of New York alone over 180,000 working men were without means of subsistence. A lively agitation for the relief of the unemployed was begun. In the city of New York the German socialists stood at the head of the movement. The *Arbeiter-Zeitung*, official organ of the International, published a plan for the relief of the unemployed which consisted of the following three measures:

1. Employment of the unemployed on public works.

2. Advances of money or food for at least one week to all who stand in need of it.

3. Suspension of all laws for the dispossession of delinquent tenants.

A joint mass-meeting was subsequently held at the Cooper Institute by several sections of the International and some American trade-unions, and an executive committee was chosen with instructions to take such further steps in the movement as it should deem expedient. Under the management of this committee, a number of public meetings were held, and a petition for relief was addrest to the mayor.

As a culminating point in the agitation, a gigantic demonstration in the form of a procession of unemployed was arranged to be held on the 13th day of January, 1874. It was the original plan of the committee that the parade should disband in front of the City Hall, but this was prohibited by the authorities, and Tompkins Square was chosen as the next best place for the purpose.

At the appointed time the parade was formed. Crowds of working men from all parts of the city fell in line during its progress, and by the time it reached its destination it had swelled to an immense procession.

There was no sign of impending trouble; the procession was orderly and peaceful. The mayor of the city was expected to address the assembled crowds and to suggest measures of relief. No sooner had the paraders reached Tompkins Square than a large force of policemen, without provocation or warning, charged the crowd with drawn clubs, striking right and left, and during the ensuing melée hundreds of working men were seriously injured. Several arrests were made, and the "offenders" were heavily punished for resisting the police. The Tompkins Square incident caused much bitter feeling among the working men of New York.

A demonstration of similar dimensions took place at almost the same time in Chicago. That city was just recovering from the horrors of the famous conflagration, when the panic of 1873 threw it anew into a state of indescribable destitution.

A movement for the relief of the unemployed, similar to that in New York, was organized by the Chicago sections of the International in conjunction with a few other labor organizations. On the 21st day of December, 1873, the leaders of the movement arranged a mass-meeting, in which over 5,000 persons are said to have participated. Speeches were made in five languages, and a committee of eight was chosen to submit the demands of the meeting to the City Council. To insure greater attention on the part of the city fathers, it was decided to give the delegation a mass escort of unemployed working men.

On the next day Chicago witnessed a most remarkable and unexpected spectacle. Early in the evening masses of working men assembled at the appointed place and formed themselves into lines. All Chicago seemed to be on its feet, and when the procession, headed by the committee of eight, started for its destination, over 20,000 persons were in line. There seemed to be no commander or leader, but perfect order prevailed in the ranks, and the whole procession looked more like a well-drilled and disciplined military body than a heterogeneous crowd of working men gathered at random.

The demonstration had its effect on the City Council: the latter promised to do all in its power to comply with the requests of the unemployed, and invited the delegation to a conference on the subject on the following day. The promises were not kept, and the demonstration led to no practical results, but out of the movement grew a new socialist party—THE LABOR PARTY OF ILLINOIS, with a membership of over 2,000.

Similar occurrences took place in other cities of the Union, notably in Philadelphia, Cincinnati, St. Louis, Louisville, and Newark. Members of the International took an active part in the agitation and demonstrations of the unemployed in those cities.

On the 11th day of April, 1874, the second national convention of the American sections of the International was held at Philadelphia. It did not assemble in very auspicious circumstances. The events in the labor movement just described had given rise to sharp controversies as to the policy to be pursued in the future by the International. A large number of members, and among them some of the most active, advocated a greater degree of attention to the labor movement at home than abroad, and a more liberal interpretation of the rules and regulations of the International, so as to permit of cooperation with elements in the labor movement that could not be classed as socialistic in a strict interpretation of the term; the older and more influential members, on the other hand, insisted on the preservation of the old principles and methods of the International in all their purity.

The result of these controversies in Chicago was the formation of a rival socialist party, the Labor Party of Illinois mentioned above. In New York several sections withdrew from the organization for the same cause, and a few months later organized the Social Democratic Work-ing-Men's Party of North America.

In these circumstances, the attendance at the Phila-delphia convention was, as might have been expected, rather poor. Only twenty-three sections sent delegates. It was proposed to transfer the seat of the Federal Council to Philadelphia or Baltimore, but neither of the two cities was willing to accept the proffered honor, and the convention wound up by abolishing the office altogether, and vesting its functions in the General Council of the International.

To prevent any abuse of power by the council, a Control Committee was appointed, with authority to investigate and pass upon any grievances against the official acts of that body. The attitude of the International toward po-litical action in the United States was defined in the fol-lowing resolution:

"Considering that the emancipation of the working classes must be conquered by the working men themselves,

"The Congress of the North American Federation has resolved:

"The North American Federation rejects all cooperation and connection with the political parties formed by the possessing classes, whether they call themselves Republicans or Democrats, or Independents or Liberals, or Patrons of Industry or Patrons of Husbandry (Grangers), or Reform-ers, or whatever name they may adopt. Consequently, no member of the Federation can belong any longer to such a party.

"The political action of the Federation confines itself generally to the endeavor to obtain legislative acts in the interest of the working class proper, and always in a man-ner to distinguish and separate the working-men's party from all the political parties of the possessing classes.

"The Federation will not enter into a political cam-paign or election movement before being strong enough to exercise a perceptible influence, and then, in the first place, on the field of the municipality, town or city (commune), whence this political movement may be transferred to the large communities (counties, States, United States), according to circumstances, and always in conformity with the Congress Resolutions.''

The convention of 1874 failed to adjust the International to the existing conditions of the American labor movement, and, despite the apparent harmony of its proceedings, did not succeed in quelling the dissensions within its ranks.

After a short time a controversy arose over the editorial management of the *Arbeiter-Zeitung,* the official organ of the International, established in 1873. Sorge and his adherents exprest dissatisfaction with the manner in which the paper was conducted, and offered some improvements. C. Carl, the editor of the paper, resented the criticism. The controversy grew heated and personal.

Section 1 of New York, heretofore the strongest organization in the International, sided with Carl, and, claiming the paper as its own, appointed a guard of ten men to protect its property against the General Council of the International.

The latter retorted promptly by suspending the section. The matter was subsequently brought before the courts, the *Arbeiter-Zeitung* suspended publication, and the split in the ranks of the International became general.

But if the progress of the International in the United States was unsatisfactory, it was still more so in Europe. Since the seat of the General Council was transferred from London to New York, the existence of the association in Europe was only nominal.

In 1875 it was decided to dispense with the International convention planned to be held that year. ''The condition of our association has steadily grown worse since the Geneva convention,'' complains the new General Council in a circular issued on that occasion. ''More or less regular communications were had only with Zurich and London, and loose connections were maintained with Germany, Austria, and Hungary. Of all former federations, the North American is the only one to survive, and the existence of even this one is greatly impaired by internal dissensions. In most European countries, as France, Austria,

Italy, Spain, Germany, Denmark, and others, our members and adherents are being persecuted to such a degree that even the most devoted of them have grown somewhat timid, and were compelled to abandon direct connections with us."

The last convention of the International Working-Men's Association was held in Philadelphia on the 15th day of July, 1876. The convention stood in sad contrast to the reunions of the International in the period of its bloom: it was composed of ten delegates from the United States, and one, A. Otto-Walster, who was supposed to represent a group of members in Germany.

To continue the nominal existence of the erstwhile powerful international organization of labor in such circumstances was not to be thought of; the organization had to be formally dissolved, and the delegates at once proceeded to the performance of the sad duty.

The General Council of the International was abolished, and the records and documents of the organization were entrusted to F. A. Sorge and C. Speyer, to be turned over by them to any new international labor-union that should be formed in the future.   Before adjourning, the convention adopted the following proclamation:

"Fellow Working Men:

"The International convention at Philadelphia has abolished the General Council of the International Working-Men's Association, and the external bond of the organization exists no more.

" 'The International is dead!' the bourgeoisie of all countries will again exclaim, and with ridicule and joy it will point to the proceedings of this convention as documentary proof of the defeat of the labor movement of the world. Let us not be influenced by the cry of our enemies!   We have abandoned the organization of the International for reasons arising from the present political situation of Europe, but as a compensation for it we see the principles of the organization recognized and defended by the progressive working men of the entire civilized world.   Let us give our fellow-workers in Europe a little time to strengthen their national affairs, and they will surely soon be in a position to remove the barriers between themselves and the working men of other parts of the world.

"Comrades! you have embraced the principles of the International with heart and love; you will find means to extend the circle of its adherents even without an organization. You will make new champions who will work for the realization of the aims of our association. The comrades in America promise you that they will faithfully guard and cherish the acquisitions of the International in this country until more favorable conditions will again bring together the working men of all countries to common struggle, and the cry will resound again louder than ever:

" 'Proletarians of all countries, unite!' "

The prediction of the last convention of the International came true. Thirteen years later the first of a series of brilliant international socialist conventions was held at Paris. It was attended by 395 delegates from twenty countries in Europe and America.

IV.—THE FORMATION OF THE SOCIALIST LABOR PARTY

In the last chapter we had occasion to take passing notice of the formation of the SOCIAL DEMOCRATIC WORKING-MEN'S PARTY OF NORTH AMERICA. This party was formally organized on the 4th day of July, 1874, by several sections of the International which had withdrawn from the organization earlier in the year, in conjunction with some radical labor organizations of New York, Williamsburg, Newark, and Philadelphia. The founders of the new party were in the main German Socialists of the Lassallean school. They attached greater importance to practical politics than did the adherents of the International. The party adopted a terse platform and declaration of principles which, as revised one year later, read as follows:

"The Social Democratic Working-Men's Party seeks to establish a free state founded upon labor. Each member of the party promises to uphold, to the best of his ability, the following principles:

"1. Abolishment of the present unjust political and social conditions.

"2. Discontinuance of all class rule and class privileges.

"3. Abolition of the working men's dependence upon the capitalist by introduction of cooperative labor in place of the wage system, so that every laborer will get the full value of his work.

"4. Obtaining possession of the political power as a prerequisite for the solution of the labor question.

"5. United struggle, united organization of all working men, and strict subordination of the individual under the laws framed for the general welfare.

"6. Sympathy with the working men of all countries who strive to attain the same object."

The administration was vested in an executive board of five members and a "control committee" of nine. The first secretary of the board was A. Strasser, a cigar maker of New York, a man of great tact and energy, who played an important part in the socialist movement of this country during the period under consideration, but later devoted himself exclusively to the trade-union movement.

As the International lost ground in the United States, the Social Democratic Party, in a measure, gained strength and influence.

Its second convention, held in Philadelphia on July 4th, 5th, and 6th, 1875, was well attended. A number of new members had joined the party, among them some very active organizers and gifted propagandists, such as P. J. McGuire, afterward for a number of years General Secretary of the United Brotherhood of Carpenters; Albert R. Parsons, who subsequently turned anarchist and played a conspicuous part in the Chicago tragedy of 1886; and G. A. Schilling, an eloquent speaker and a man of considerable influence in Chicago labor circles. The party also, at about that time, published an English weekly in New York under the title *The Socialist*.

The most important act of the second convention of the Social Democratic Working-Men's Party was the passing of a resolution instructing the executive board to use its good offices to bring about a union of all socialist organizations in the country.

In the fall of 1875 several conferences of such organizations were accordingly held in the city of New York. These conferences were composed of J. P. McDonnell and D. Kronberg, members of the ''United Workers,'' an independent organization of English-speaking socialists, at one time affiliated with the International; A. Strasser, McGregor, J. G. Speyer, and Hansen, representing the Social Democratic Working-Men's Party; while the German-speaking sections of the International were represented by Sorge, Bertrand, Leib, and Hesse, and the French section by the famous Icarian and Communard, A. Sauva.

No definite results were reached by the conferences. In the meanwhile the scattered remnants of the National Labor-Union gathered themselves together in a last attempt to revive their movement. Upon the initiative of John Davis, editor of the *National Tribune*, and at one time presidential candidate of the N. L. U., a national convention was called for the purpose of forming a new political labor party. The convention was to be held at Pittsburg on the 17th day of April, 1876. The socialists of the United States saw in this proposed convention a good opportunity for strengthening their movement, and representatives of their various parties and organizations by agreement assembled at Pittsburg on the eve of the convention.

The convention of the National Labor-Union was composed of 106 delegates of the most heterogeneous political complexion, and was easily captured by the socialists, some twenty in number, who spoke and acted as a unit, had well-defined views, and knew how to express them.

The victory had no practical significance, as the convention adjourned without accomplishing anything, but it proved fruitful for the socialist movement in another direction—the various socialist groups assembled at Pittsburg agreed upon a plan of union, and arranged to hold a convention in the near future for the purpose of putting the plan into practical execution. The convention was held in

Philadelphia from the 19th until the 22d day of July, 1876.

The composition and strength of the convention were as follows: The North American Federation of the International Working-Men's Association, with a membership of 635, represented by F. A. Sorge and Otto Weydemeyer; the Social Democratic Working-Men's Party of North America which claimed a membership of 1,500, represented by A. Strasser, P. J. McGuire, and A. Gabriel; the Labor Party of Illinois, with a membership of 593, represented by C. Conzett; and the Socio-Political Labor-Union of Cincinnati, represented by Charles Braun, who claimed for his organization a membership of 250.

Representatives from the Free German Community of Philadelphia, the Slavonian Socio-Political Labor-Union of Cincinnati, and the Labor-Union of Milwaukee, were refused seats in the convention, on the ground that their respective organizations had not been represented in the Pittsburg conference. The work of the convention was begun by formally consolidating the several organizations into one party, under the name of the WORKING-MEN'S PARTY OF THE UNITED STATES.

At the head of the new party was placed a national executive committee of seven, subject to the control of a "board of supervision" consisting of five members. The headquarters of the national committee was placed in Chicago, that of the board of supervision in New Haven.

The *Socialist* and *Sozial Demokrat*, heretofore published by the Social Democratic Working-Men's Party, were declared official organs of the new party, and their names changed to *Labor Standard* and *Arbeiterstimme* (Voice of the Working Men) respectively. The *Vorbote* (Harbinger), published in Chicago by the Labor Party of Illinois, was continued under the same name and also made an official party organ.

J. P. McDonnell was elected editor of the *Labor Standard*, and C. Conzett editor of the *Vorbote*. The *Arbeiterstimme* was left under its former editorial management. A. Douai was made assistant editor of all three papers.

The platform adopted by the Working-Men's Party of

the United States was a scientific and somewhat abstract exposition of the cardinal points of Marxian socialism.

In December, 1877, at the second convention of the Working-Men's Party, held at Newark, N. J., the name of the party was changed to SOCIALIST LABOR PARTY OF NORTH AMERICA.

Chapter III

THE SOCIALIST LABOR PARTY

I.—THE PLACE OF THE SOCIALIST LABOR PARTY IN THE SOCIALIST MOVEMENT

THE Socialist Labor Party became the dominant factor in the socialist movement of this country and so remained for more than twenty years. Its varied career forms one of the most intricate and interesting chapters in the history of American socialism.

At first glance its history appears as a series of incoherent events, ill-considered political experiments, sudden changes of policy, incongruous alliances, internal and external strife, and as a succession of unaccountable ups and downs, with no perceptible progress or gain. But the confusion is only apparent. On closer analysis we find a logical thread running all through the seemingly devious course of the party, and a good reason for almost every one of its seemingly planless moves.

The difficulties which beset its path were extraordinary. As one of the first socialist parties organized in this country on a national scale, it had to cope with the usual adversities which attend every radical reform movement at the outset of its career—weakness and diffidence in its own ranks, hostility and ridicule from the outside.

But apart from these natural obstacles, the Socialist Labor Party suffered from one great disadvantage peculiarly its own. In Europe the socialist movement sprang up in the midst of the native population and adjusted itself to the economic and political conditions of each country quite mechanically and without effort. But in the United States the situation was altogether different. It is estimated that no more than ten per cent. of the members of the Socialist

Labor Party, during the period described, were native Americans. All the rest, including the most active and influential leaders, were men of foreign birth, insufficiently acquainted with the institutions, customs, and habits of the country of their adoption, and frequently ignorant of its very language.

In these circumstances the pioneers of the movement soon realized the hopelessness of their task to effect radical social and economic changes in this country by their own efforts, and henceforward they considered it their special mission to acclimatize the movement and to leave its further development to the American working men. The endeavor to "Americanize" the socialist movement is the main keynote of the activity of the Socialist Labor Party throughout its entire career.

That the movement could not become "Americanized" before the great masses of the population, and especially the working men, were reached by the propaganda of socialism, was too obvious to admit of dispute: the great question was, how to reach them most effectively. This question was at all times the subject of the most animated discussions and heated controversies within the party, it shaped its policy, determined its actions, and was at the bottom of most of its struggles.

Surveying the field of American institutions, the founders of the Socialist Labor Party discovered two principal avenues through which they could expect to approach the native working men with the greatest chances of success— the trade-unions and political activity.

On the continent of Europe, socialism had in some cases preceded and to a certain degree created the trade-union movement; in other cases both movements had developed simultaneously and were regarded as a necessary complement to each other. On the whole the trade-unions were in full accord with the socialist movement.

In the United States the trade-union movement made its appearance before the socialist movement; the Socialist Labor Party found it just entering on the period of its bloom.

In 1878 the first general assembly of the Knights of Labor was held, and the period of phenomenal growth of the order began. Three years later the Federation of Trade and Labor Unions, which subsequently developed into the American Federation of Labor, was organized.

In these two bodies, as well as in the numerous unaffiliated national and local trade-unions, hundreds of thousands of American working men were organized during the next few years. Their platforms were often radical, and in many instances inclined decidedly toward socialism. In their meetings and conventions they discust social problems, with particular reference to the relations of capital to labor, and in their oft-recurring strikes they were trained in active battle against capital. No wonder then that the socialists saw in the trade-unions their natural allies, and that they strove to bring the two movements into close touch with each other.

At almost every one of its conventions the Socialist Labor Party proclaimed its sympathy with the objects and methods of the labor-unions, and called upon its members to join the organizations of their trade; in a number of instances the party sought direct representation in the central bodies of organized labor; its official organs supported the trade-unions, and in many important strikes the socialists were found on the side of the strikers, aiding, counseling, and at times directing them in their contests. But notwithstanding these efforts, the influence of the Socialist Labor Party on the trade-union movement was rather insignificant. The socialists were as yet numerically too weak to permeate the much-ramified labor movement and to shape its course as they had hoped to do, and voices were at times raised within the party protesting against work in the unions as a waste of time.

These protests grew especially loud during the periods of industrial depression, when the efficiency of the trade-unions was greatly impaired. At such times the party would not infrequently assume an attitude of indifference, sometimes even hostility, to the trade-unions. Again, whenever the trade-union movement advanced anew owing to a wave of prosperity, the party would center its hopes on it again.

Hardly less varying were the fortunes of the party in the field of politics. Politics were at all times regarded by the socialists as an essential part of their movement. The issues of socialism are political in their nature; the conquest of the political machinery is regarded by them as a necessary prerequisite to the realization of their social ideal; they believe in the efficiency of legislative measures to correct economic abuses, and finally they regard political campaigns as great educating factors and as excellent opportunities for the dissemination of new social theories among the people.

At the time of the organization of the Socialist Labor Party the socialists in Germany had been in the political arena about ten years, and had succeeded in uniting almost half a million voters under their banner. In the United States, with its more democratic form of government and the greater importance and frequency of elections, the opportunities seemed to be still more tempting. But how to go about it? On this question the camp for a number of years was divided. One group, consisting principally of the native American element within the party and a number of former Lassalleans, advocated at all times, active and independent politics, while others pointed at the weakness of the party and its poor chances of success as an independent political factor, and advised either to abstain from politics altogether until such time as the party should be strong enough to make a respectable showing at the polls, or to cooperate with other existing reform parties and endeavor to infuse into the latter as much of the doctrines of socialism as possible. According to the political and economic situation of the country at any given time, either the one view or the other gained ascendancy in the councils of the party.

A series of labor troubles due to a period of industrial depression would create a sentiment favorable to radical reform politics, and then the party would either nominate its own candidates, or, if a reform party had sprung up as a result of such sentiment, cooperate with it. In several places and at several times, the Socialist Labor Party, alone or in conjunction with its political allies, succeeded in polling a comparatively large vote, but it had no means of following up and retaining its gains. A new wave of prosperity would strike the country, the spirit of discontent would subside, and the socialist votes would disappear.

In these unpropitious circumstances, it is not to be wondered at that even the sturdiest and most optimistic among the socialists at times succumbed to discouragement, while those of the weaker clay either withdrew from public life altogether, or sought a quieter haven in the ranks of the trade-union movement or the old political parties.

It was at the period of the greatest depression in the socialist camp that the movement of practical anarchism sprang up in the United States. Anarchism, with its negation of all theories of gradual social progress, its ridicule of reform measures, and its gospel of violence—anarchism, ofttimes the philosophy of despair—had a peculiar fascination for the discouraged and disgruntled socialist of that period. The new doctrine threatened to make deep inroads into the ranks of the Socialist Labor Party, and to wipe out whatever progress the young organization had made, by discrediting it in the eyes of American working men. The Socialist Labor Party now had the additional task of combating anarchism, and for several years its efforts were diverted from the work of furthering its own movement to maintaining the struggle with the new foe.

The struggle was carried on relentlessly on both sides, and terminated only when anarchism had lost all influence on the labor movement in the United States.

The manifold experiments, disappointments and struggles of the Socialist Labor Party, and the frequent changes of policy and methods involved in or consequent upon them, naturally could not pass without producing effects on the relations of the members among themselves. Every new experiment gave rise to a heated controversy as to its expediency, every new failure was a fruitful source of discussion as to its causes. Discussions were carried on with the earnestness characteristic of all adherents of a new faith or doctrine. At times these internal disputes filled the columns of the party papers for months and all other party work was temporarily lost sight of; at times the controversies were conducted with unnecessary bitterness and assumed a personal character; and at times the differences transcended the bounds of mere controversies and developed into splits, on several occasions rending the party in twain.

The assertion has, therefore, repeatedly been made, that the men of the Socialist Labor Party were a set of querulous individuals who wasted their time in mutual recriminations and accomplished little for their cause. Nothing can be more unjust.

When the founders of the Socialist Labor Party assumed the task of acclimatizing the socialist movement in this country, they undertook an enterprise of extraordinary difficulty and tremendous proportions.

For almost a generation they plodded at their self-imposed task in the face of adversities which have no parallel in the history of the socialist movement in any other country. Their internal strifes were only the natural echo of great struggles with hostile surroundings, and may easily be pardoned; their courage, perseverance, and devotion to the cause can not fail to arouse admiration.

In the socialist movement they performed a great mission. Through their trials and failures they evolved working methods of socialist activity, and through their ceaseless propaganda they prepared the ground for a genuine American movement of socialism.

The party had the misfortune of surviving the period of its usefulness. Its remnants brought in a shrill note of dissonance to the movement, but that does not alter the fact that the men of the Socialist Labor Party did the pioneer work of modern socialism in this country. The present socialist movement owes its existence largely to their efforts.

II.—CAREER OF THE SOCIALIST LABOR PARTY

1. EARLY TRIUMPHS AND REVERSES

THE Socialist Labor Party began its career under rather favorable auspices. The extraordinary industrial activity which was developed after the close of the civil war was succeeded by the great financial panic of 1873. The acute stage of the panic subsided after a few months, but the industrial depression continued for fully five years and caused an unprecedented degree of destitution. In the large cities cases of death from starvation, not only of single individuals but of entire families, were reported. During the winter of 1877, police stations were filled every night with crowds of working men and their families seeking shelter from the cold of the streets. Police courts were besieged by men, women, and children imploring to be committed to the workhouse. The number of the unemployed in the United States was estimated at no less than three millions. At the same time the wages of those who had employment were reduced from year to year. In 1877 they were so low that the working men rebelled, and a series of strikes broke out. The movement was quite spontaneous; it was an outbreak of despair rather than a planned and deliberate undertaking; but the time was ill-chosen, the masses were unorganized and undisciplined, and the strikes were almost uniformly unsuccessful.

The most significant of these strikes, in point of size and the bitterness with which it was fought, was that of the railway employees. The construction of railroads had become a favorite form of investment and financial speculation immediately after the civil war. Between 1867 and 1877 about 25,000 miles of new railway tracks were laid, and in the latter year the railroads of the country were capitalized for about $500,000,000. Roads were frequently built on mere expectation of future development of the country, and without reference to the actual requirement of traffic. When the panic of 1873 set in, the railroads, therefore, were more affected by it than any other industry, and the men to suffer most were the employees. Between 1873 and 1877 the wages of railroad workers were reduced in the average by about twenty-five per cent. and in June 1877, the principal lines announced another reduction of ten per cent.

It was to resist this last reduction that the strike was declared. The first clash occurred at Martinsburg, West Virginia, on the 16th day of July, but the movement soon became general, and in less than two weeks it had spread over seventeen States.

The first men to quit work were the machinists and switchmen of the Baltimore and Ohio Railroad. They were immediately joined by the locomotive engineers and other employees. The management of the road soon succeeded in filling the places of the strikers, but when the new men attempted to move the cars, they were prevented by force. Two companies of the State militia sent by the Governor were powerless to cope with the situation, and regular troops to the number of 250, sent by President Hayes to the seat of the battle, had no better success.

No serious disorders, however, occurred in West Virginia, but in Maryland, where the strike had broken out at the same time, a company of militia was greeted by the strikers and their sympathizers with hooting and shouts of derision, which soon turned into an active attack. Missiles were hurled at the militiamen, who retorted by opening a fusillade on the crowd, killing ten men and wounding many more. The shooting precipitated a riot; the militia was overpowered, rails were torn out, and cars burned.

On the same day, July 19th, a series of disorders began along the system of the Pennsylvania Railroad. There the movement was started by the switchmen, who struck against the introduction of the "double-heading" system. In the course of the day the switchmen were joined by employees of the road in all other branches of the service. The strikers now demanded not only the abolition of the "double-heading" system, but the recall of the last ten per cent. reduction of wages.

Toward the evening all freight traffic in Pittsburg was blocked. Large crowds of strikers paraded the streets and were rapidly reenforced by multitudes of the unemployed and the dissatisfied among the labor population. The demeanor of the masses grew more threatening from hour to hour; the local militia which was called into requisition by the sheriff having refused to interfere, 600 militiamen were obtained from Philadelphia. The arrival of the latter only served to increase the excitement of the crowd. A brief but fierce battle between the hostile camps ensued. The defeated militiamen retired to the company's engine-room, where they barricaded themselves against the onslaughts of the strikers. There they passed a very uncomfortable night amidst the threatening shouts of the infuriated mob and the sound of bullets whizzing past the windows. Early on the next morning they left Pittsburg and never halted on their retreat until they reached Claremont, a point about twelve miles distant from the city.

The crowds were now undisputed masters of the situation, and their long-pent-up hatred against the railroad company, intensified and inflamed by the recent battle with the militia, vented itself in a wild crusade of destruction of the company's property. One thousand six hundred cars and one hundred and twenty locomotives are said to have been demolished in one day.

Disorders of a more or less serious nature also occurred in different parts of New York, New Jersey, Pennsylvania, Ohio, Indiana, Illinois, Missouri, and other States.

In Reading, Pennsylvania, a large force of militia was ordered out to combat the strikers, but here something quite unexpected occurred. Most of the companies were composed of working men, who openly fraternized with the strikers, distributed their munitions among them, and threatened to turn their arms against all hostile militiamen. One company, however, recruited almost exclusively from the possessing classes, and led by a reckless officer, opened fire on the crowd, killing thirteen persons and wounding twenty-two. The effect of this unjustifiable act was to arouse the strikers and their sympathizers to fury; the noisy but peaceful crowd turned into a wild and dangerous mob. Freight trains were derailed, cars demolished, and bridges burned. The hostile militiamen were maltreated, and the majority of them managed to make their escape from the city only by changing their military uniforms for civil attire.

Most singular of all were the occurrences at St. Louis, where the excitement communicated itself to all classes of the labor population. Traffic on the bridge between East and West St. Louis was stopped. All communication between the Eastern and Western States was thus interrupted. Slaughter-houses and factories were closed, and the strikers took full possession of the city. The socialists called a mass-meeting which was attended by thousands, and at which an "executive committee" was elected to protect the interests of the working men. Nobody ever knew who that executive committee really was. It seems to have been a rather loose body composed of whomsoever chanced to come in and take part in its deliberations. It had no definite plan of action and limited its activity to tying up all the industries of the city.

But such was the general excitement that the mysterious committee maintained undisputed sway of the city for an entire week. Only when the general fear and excitement had somewhat subsided, did the city administration, aided by the "leading citizens" of St. Louis, rouse itself to some activity. A vigilance committee was formed in opposition to the executive committee, and finally the former, aided by the entire police force and several companies of militia, surrounded the headquarters of the executive committee at Shuler's Hall, and forced the rebels to capitulate. Seventy-five persons were arrested in the raid, but all of them had to be released, as they appeared to be mere idlers and curiosity seekers in no way connected with the insurrection. Of the much-feared "executive committee" no trace was found.

The socialists of the United States had no part in the instigation of the labor troubles of 1877, but; on the other hand, they did not neglect the opportunity to propagate their theories among the excited masses. They did not overestimate the significance of the strikes, and realized at the very outset that the movement was only a passing phase in the struggle between capital and labor. They were opposed to unnecessary acts of violence, and at the numerous mass-meetings called by them, they dwelt almost uniformly on the futility of planless revolts, and the necessity of organized and intelligent action by the working class.

In Philadelphia the party decided to hold two mass-meetings "to discuss in a quiet and moderate manner the pending dispute between capital and labor, to express sympathy with the strikers, but to declare energetically against any destruction of property."

The socialists of New Jersey held several mass-meetings in Newark and Paterson. In Brooklyn a mass-meeting of 2,000 working men, called by the local socialists, declared in favor of the public ownership of railroads. In New York large mass-meetings were held under the auspices of the party in Tompkins Square and in the Cooper Institute. At the former fully 12,000 persons congregated. John Swinton addrest the meeting in English, and Alexander Jonas and Otto Walther in German. A resolution of sympathy with the strikers was adopted, which wound up with the declaration that it had become necessary "to form a political party with a platform based upon the natural rights of the working men, and with the aim of enacting legislation against the monopolies which oppress the people."

In Chicago the strike movement was conducted under the direct supervision of the party's National Executive Committee, which had been organized immediately after the convention of 1876. Chief among the Chicago agitators were the party's national secretary, Phillip Van Patten, the chairman of the city committee, Schilling, and Albert R. Parsons.

But the activity of the party was by no means limited to agitation during the strike. Many labor troubles and the general destitution of the period had made the minds of the working class more receptive to the teachings of socialism than ever before, and the socialists sought to take advantage of the situation by every means at their command. In all great industrial centers demonstrations were arranged, proclamations issued, street corner meetings held, and some of the most eloquent speakers of the party—McGuire, Parsons, Sotheran, Savary, and many others—undertook extended and systematic lecture tours through the country. Socialist newspapers appeared in all parts of the United States and in many languages. Between 1876 and 1877 no less than twenty-four newspapers, directly or indirectly supporting the party, were established. Of these, eight were in the English language, among them one a daily, the *Star* in St. Louis, and seven weeklies; *The Labor Standard* in New York, the *Working-Men's Ballot* and *The Echo* in Boston, *The Social Democrat* in Milwaukee, the *Emancipator* in Cincinnati, *The Socialist* in Detroit, and *The Times* in Indianapolis. The German press was represented by fourteen newspapers, of which no less than seven were dailies—the *Chicago Sozialist* and *Chicago Volkszeitung*, the *Volksstimme des Westens* in St. Louis, *Die Neue Zeit* in Louisville, the *Philadelphia Tageblatt*, the *Vorwaerts* in Newark, and the *Ohio Volkszeitung* in Cincinnati; one, the *Chicago Arbeiter-Zeitung*, appeared three times a week; and six—the *Arbeiterstimme* of New York, *Arbeiter von Ohio* and *Freiheitsbanner* of Cincinnati, *Neue Zeit* and *Vorbote* of Chicago, and *Vorwaerts* of Milwaukee—appeared weekly. The Bohemians had a weekly under the title *Delnicke Listy*, which was published in Cleveland, and the Scandinavian members published a Swedish weekly in Chicago under the title *Den Nye Tid*.

The energetic activity of the party, aided by the favorable conditions of the time, bore fruit; the organization grew rapidly in numbers and influence.

On the 26th day of December, 1877, the first national convention was opened in Newark, New Jersey, thirty-one sections being represented by thirty-eight delegates. The seat of the national executive committee was transferred from Chicago to Cincinnati, and Van Patten was reelected national secretary. The main changes effected by the convention were those relating to political action. The Unity Convention of 1876 had considered the principal mission of the newly organized party to be one of education and propaganda, and its platform and constitution were framed in accordance with that conception. The platform emphasized the superiority of the economic struggle over politics, and the constitution contained no provisions as to the political action of the party or its subdivisions. A separate resolution adopted on the subject expressly called ''upon the members of the party, and all working men generally, for the time being to refrain from participation in elections, and to turn their backs upon the ballot-box.''

But the situation had greatly changed within that year. The rapid growth of the party, and its unexpected success at the ballot-box, had demonstrated to the socialists the importance and possibilities of politics, and had created a reaction in favor of it. The party was reconstructed on the lines of a political organization, and its platform and constitution were remodeled to meet the requirements of the new situation. It was this convention which, as already stated, changed the party name from WORKING-MEN'S PARTY OF THE UNITED STATES to SOCIALIST LABOR PARTY.

The growth of the party continued unabated during the next year. In the beginning of 1879 the party consisted of about one hundred separate ''sections'' in twenty-five different States, with a total enrolled membership of about 10,000. At the same time another change in the industrial conditions of the country was already preparing. The period of industrial depression had gradually passed away, and was succeeded by an era of prosperity. The factories of the country reopened their doors, new industries sprang up, the demand for labor increased, and wages rose. The general dissatisfaction which had made the working men so responsive to the appeals of socialism during the preceding two or three years rapidly subsided, and the socialist agitators found only scanty and indifferent audiences where they had formerly met enthusiastic throngs. "The plundered toilers," said Van Patten, "are rapidly being drawn back to their old paths, and are closing their ears to the appeals of reason. They are selling their birthright for a mess of pottage by rejecting the prospect of future emancipation in their greed for the trifling gains of the present."

The party was young and inexperienced at that time, and its hold on its own membership rather weak. With the returning wave of prosperity it disintegrated rapidly, and the efforts of its leaders to stem the tide of disorganization were of little avail. Its membership fell off, its sections disbanded, and its press succumbed for lack of readers. Of the eight English party papers reported as existing at the Newark convention of 1877, not one survived in 1879. A new party organ in the English language, under the title of *The National Socialist*, was established in May, 1878, and was with great sacrifices kept alive a little over one year. Of the German papers the *Philadelphia Tageblatt* and the *Arbeiter-Zeitung* and *Vorbote* of Chicago, were the only ones to escape the general wreck.

In the beginning of 1878 the party press received, however, a notable reenforcement by the establishment of the *New Yorker Volkszeitung*, a daily newspaper in the German language, devoted to the interests of the socialist and trade-union movement. The paper was edited with exceptional ability by a staff of the most efficient and experienced journalists in the American socialist movement, including in its numbers Alexander Jonas, Dr. Douai, and S. E. Schewitsch, a Russian of noble birth, who had received his education in Germany and England, and was an eloquent speaker and brilliant writer. On the death of Dr. Douai, a more than competent substitute was found in Hermann Schlueter, a veteran in the socialist movement of both hemispheres, who still stands at the head of the *Volkszeitung's* editorial management.

The *Volkszeitung* from the very day of its appearance assumed a position of leadership among the socialist press of this country. Its good judgment has helped the party to sail safely through many a crisis since the early days in its career.

On the 26th day of December, 1879, the second national convention of the Socialist Labor Party was opened at Allegheny City, Pa. Twenty sections were represented by twenty-four delegates. The total number of members of the party was not officially stated at the convention, but it certainly was distressingly small. According to a subsequent report submitted by McGuire at the International Socialist Conference held at Chur, Switzerland, in 1881, it was about 2,600, but in the estimate of A. Strasser it was only 1,500.[1]

The report of the national secretary on the work of the Executive Committee and the condition of the party was rather cheerless. The convention decided to recommend that a daily socialist paper under the title *Union* be established in the city of New York; it divided the territory of the United States into four geographical "agitation districts" for the purpose of socialist propaganda, made some minor changes in the constitution, and devoted the greater part of its deliberations to the questions of the participation of the party in the presidential election of 1880. On the whole the Allegheny convention accomplished little toward raising the drooping spirit of the movement.

Toward the end of 1880 and the beginning of 1881 the movement received some reenforcements from the arrival of several parties of political refugees from Germany. These were mostly men who had been active in the movement in their fatherland, and who for that reason had been exiled by the German government during the crusade against socialists inaugurated by the anti-socialist laws of

[1] See Sartorius von Waltershausen, p. 162.

1878. They were warmly welcomed by their comrades, and a number of public meetings were held for their reception.

In August, 1880, the Social Democratic Party of Germany, at its convention in Castle Wyden, decided to send a deputation to the United States for the purpose of informing the German-American working men of the condition of the party under the anti-socialist law, and collecting funds for the approaching elections to the German Diet. F. W. Fritsche and Louis Viereck, two socialist deputies and popular speakers, were selected for that purpose, and they arrived in the United States in February, 1881. They were warmly received not only by the party but by a number of trade-unions and other labor organizations. They spoke at large mass-meetings before enthusiastic audiences in New York, Boston, Newark, Philadelphia, Milwaukee, Chicago, and other cities. As a rule their meetings were made the occasion for the general propaganda of socialism, and English addresses were frequently interspersed with German speeches. Thus the tour of the German deputies, altho undertaken for a different purpose, had the effect of reviving the local socialist movement.

But the revival was temporary. As soon as the two German agitators left this country, the newly acquired members fell gradually off, and the party relapsed into its previous state of inaction. In December, 1881, the third convention of the party met in the city of New York. Seventeen sections were represented by about twenty delegates, most of whom had come from New York and Brooklyn either as representatives of the local sections or as proxies for other sections. No business of importance was transacted, and the national secretary regretfully stated that the majority of the socialists in the United States were outside of the party.

The struggles of the Socialist Labor Party grew harder and harder: the social contentment and the political indifference of the masses seemed impregnable. No new converts were made, while the old party members, growing disheartened, dropped out in large numbers.

What made the position of the party still more precarious, was the new and threatening apparition which at that period loomed upon the horizon of the American labor movement—the apparition of anarchism.

2. STRUGGLES WITH ANARCHISM

Socialism and anarchism proceed equally from a criticism of the present organization of society, and are in accord in condemning existing social and economic institutions. But there the similarity between the two social theories ends; in most other aspects they are diametrically opposed to each other.

Socialism implies the supremacy of the social body over the individual, while anarchism strives to emancipate the individual from the bonds of society. These divergent conceptions of the respective rights and functions of society and the individual account for most of the differences in the two schools.

While the socialist does not regard modern human society as an organism in the biological sense of the term, he considers it a highly organized body, indissolubly connected with the individual members of which it is composed. The individual is to the socialist above all a member of society, performing different functions for the benefit of society as a whole, and in turn deriving his main strength and well-being from his connection with it. The socialist finds fault with the present state of society because it is characterized by the absence of a proper social equilibrium; his ideal of human civilization is the cooperative commonwealth—*i. e.*, that state of society in which social life and industry are organized on a rational and scientific basis, exacting from each individual his proper share of usefulness in his own sphere, and guaranteeing to each an opportunity to enjoy and to develop all of his faculties.

The anarchist, on the other hand, considers society as a mere aggregation of individuals. He sees the highest state of development in the sovereignty of the individual, and considers all social restraints upon untrammeled personal liberty as injurious and reactionary elements in human civilization. He regards the State as an arbitrary contrivance to curb the individual liberty of the citizen, and abhors all government and laws as so many unnecessary checks upon the free exercise of the individual will. The anarchist finds fault with the present state of society, not so much because it is insufficiently organized for the general public welfare, as because it is too much organized. His ideal state is one consisting of a multitude of autonomous groups of individuals freely and loosely organized for the purpose of production and exchange, somewhat on the plan of the Fourieristic Phalanxes. The anarchist is opposed to a systematic regulation of production and industry, he relies on the natural results of the free play of demand and supply. He is opposed to all forms of social restrictions, and he confidently predicts that all crime will disappear and that proper relations of man to man will be established automatically as soon as the present artificial social and governmental institutions shall be abolished. The anarchist abhors majority rule as the worst form of tyranny, and points to the fact that the most useful innovations in the history of our race have as a rule been introduced after hard battles with the majority.

The opposite tactics and methods of procedure of the socialists and anarchists are only the results of the practical application of antagonistic social philosophies.

Conceiving society as an organized body, the socialist recognizes that its development is gradual and subject to certain laws. He does not admit the possibility of a radical social transformation unless such a transformation is prepared by a series of social and industrial evolutions and a corresponding gradual change in the social and political views of men. It is the system not the individuals, that he combats. His hope of social regeneration is based primarily upon the tendencies of development of modern industry as he sees them, and he expects the realization of his ideal to be brought about by the concerted efforts of the greater portion of the population. He believes the work-

ing class will be the prime factor in the social transformation for the reason that the benefits of such transforma
tion appeal more directly to the interests of that class,
hence his energies are bent upon the task of preparing
the working men for the rôle to be played by them.

He seeks to develop the consciousness of their class interests by the oral and written propaganda of the views
and theories of socialism. In the industrial organizations
and struggles of the working men he sees a manifestation
of discontent with the present industrial system, he encour-
ages them, and seeks to imbue them with the spirit and
philosophy of socialism. In politics the socialist perceives
a powerful agent for molding, expressing, and enforcing
popular demands, and hence he advocates political action
by the working class on socialist lines. The watchwords of
socialism are education and organization, and its weapons
the propaganda, cooperation with the trade-unions, and the
ballot-box.

From the point of view of the revolutionary anarchist's
philosophy, however, these methods of procedure are altogether unnecessarily tedious and slow. He believes the
world is ready for the most radical revolutions at all times.
All that is required for their successful accomplishment is
a handful of determined men, ready to jeopardize their
lives for the welfare of the opprest population. And it
matters little that the daring revolutionists may not have
the support or sympathy of the majority of the population:
the great majority of the population never knows its
own interests, and appreciates a brave and noble
deed only after it has been successfully accomplished.
All great revolutions, argue the anarchists, have been accomplished by small minorities, and all great public benefits have been forced upon mankind.

Consistently with these views anarchists reject political
action as a useless farce, and deprecate all efforts of trade-
unions and socialists to ameliorate the present condition of
the working class as tending to retard the revolution by
smothering the dissatisfaction of the workers with their
present conditions. The efforts of the revolutionary an-

archists are directed toward sowing the seed of revolt among the poor, and carrying on a personal war with those whom they regard as responsible for all social injustice— the high and mighty of all nations. Their weapons are the "propaganda of the word" and the "propaganda of the deed."

Anarchism is thus the extreme but logical deduction of the individualist philosophy of the French and English schools. The theories of Herbert Spencer and those of John Most differ in degree, but not in quality.

The first man to formulate the theory of modern anarchism was the French reformer and economist, P. J. Proudhon, whose work, "Qu'est-ce que la Propriété," published in 1840, contained the first allusions to the new social theory, and who developed his system of anarchism more minutely in his principal work, "Système des Contradictions Economiques." [2]

The system was somewhat modified and popularized by Michael Bakounin, whose name we have had occasion to mention in connection with the history of the International. In recent days its chief apostles have been Prince Kropotkin and John Most. Each of these men has added something to the theory, and has in turn been called "the father of anarchism." Altho the fundamental premises of all these authors are identical, the conclusions drawn by them vary indefinitely. It has frequently been said that there are as many anarchistic systems as there are anarchistic authors. The latest contribution to these systems is the theory of "anarchistic communism," a rather awkward attempt to combine the principle of extreme individualism with that of collectivism.

Under the influence of Bakounin's agitation, anarchism at one time gained considerable ground in France, Spain, Italy, Austria, and Switzerland. In Germany it was little known. It is generally a noteworthy fact that anarchism thrives least where the socialist movement is strongest.

In the United States the first manifestation of anarchism

[2] See George Plechanoff, "Anarchism and Socialism," Chicago, 1908.

appeared about the same time that the Socialist Labor Party showed signs of decline. Already at the Allegheny convention of 1879 a division between the moderate and more radical elements of the party was noticed. Somewhat earlier, the socialists of Chicago and Cincinnati had organized military organizations of working men under the name of "Educational and Defensive Societies" (Lehr und Wehr Vereine). The National Executive Committee of the party was opposed to these organizations, on the ground that they tended to create a false impression of the aims and character of the socialist movement. "As they carried the red flag and acknowledged their socialistic tendencies, the public were informed that the socialists were determined to accomplish by force what they could not obtain by the ballot," Van Patten reported to the convention. The National Executive Committee publicly disavowed any connection with the military organizations, and requested all party members to withdraw from them.

The sponsors for the military labor organizations resented this interference of the Executive Committee, and when the convention assembled, moved for a vote of censure against the latter. The motion was adopted by a small majority after a heated debate.

On the whole, however, the convention was dominated by the moderate elements, and the radical wing soon developed an open dissatisfaction with the party administration. In November, 1880, a number of members of the New York sections [3] left the organization and formed a Revolutionary Club, which adopted a platform modeled in the main after the Gotha program of the German Social Democracy, but interspersed with some anarchistic phrases. The leading spirit of the movement was Wilhelm Hasselmann, an old Lassallean, and former deputy to the Imperial German Diet, who had once played a prominent part in the socialist movement of his fatherland, and who had then shortly arrived in New York. Other prominent men in the new movement were Justus Schwab and M. Bach-

[3] The local branches or subdivisions of the Socialist Labor Party were styled "sections."

mann. Similar revolutionary clubs soon sprang up in Boston, Philadelphia, and Milwaukee. But of the greatest significance were the Chicago clubs, of which Paul Grottkau, August Spies, and Albert R. Parsons were the leading members.

In October, 1881, a national convention of the revolutionary clubs was held in Chicago, and the "Revolutionary Socialist Labor Party" was organized.

The character of the new movement was as yet rather indefinite. It vacillated between socialism of a more radical type and outspoken anarchism. It lacked a leader of sufficient strength and influence to direct it into definite channels. The leader was soon found in the person of John Most.

John Most was born at Augsburg, Germany, in 1846, the son of a poor subaltern officer. A sickness of five years' duration, an operation which left his face deformed forever, a cruel stepmother, and later on a still more cruel employer to whom he was apprenticed, are the cheerless events which filled out the childhood of the future apostle of anarchism. He received a very scanty school education, but he read extensively, and as a young man traveled in Germany, Austria, Italy, and Switzerland. In the latter country he came in contact with the International, whose theories he eagerly adopted. He was ever since active in the International revolutionary movement.

In the summer of 1869 he was sentenced to one month's imprisonment for an inciting speech delivered in Vienna. The next year he participated in the organization of a large popular demonstration for the freedom of speech, press, and assembly, was arrested on the charge of high treason, found guilty and sentenced to state prison for a term of five years. After a few months he was pardoned, and after a few months more was expelled from Austria. During the seven years following, he took a leading part in the socialist movement of Germany, and in 1874, and again in 1877, he was elected to the Diet to represent the District of Chemnitz. During that time he served two terms of imprisonment, both times for riotous speeches, and in 1878, immediately after the enactment of the anti-socialist laws, he was expelled from Berlin. Most now settled in London, where he established a weekly magazine under the title *Freiheit* (Freedom). It was in that period that he gradually began to depart from the principles of social democracy, inclining more and more toward revolutionary anarchism.

On the occasion of the assassination of Alexander II. by the Russian Nihilists in 1881, Most published an article in his *Freiheit* gloryifying the deed and calling for its emulation by others. For this article he was tried by the English courts and sentenced to imprisonment at hard labor for sixteen months. Shortly after he had served out this sentence Most landed in New York.

For the members of the revolutionary clubs, or the "Social Revolutionists," as they styled themselves, Most was no mean acquisition. A forceful and popular speaker, a brilliant journalist, and a "martyr" to the cause, he was the ideal man to gather the disheartened and demoralized elements in the socialist movement of America under the banner of revolt and destruction.

The great mass-meeting arranged for his reception in the large hall of Cooper Union Institute in December, 1882, turned into a veritable ovation for the "victim of bourgeois justice," and his tour through the principal cities of the country in the early part of 1883 resembled a triumphal procession His meetings were large and enthusiastic, they were extensively reported by the press, and a number of anarchistic "groups" were organized as a result of his agitation.

In October, 1883, a joint convention of the social revolutionists and anarchists was held in Pittsburg. The convention was attended by representatives from twenty-six cities, Most, Spies, and Parsons being among the delegates. Letters of congratulation and encouragement were received from many parts of the United States, and from anarchistic groups in France, England, Mexico, Italy, Spain, and Holland. The convention created a national organization of all social-revolutionary and anarchistic groups under the uame "International Working-People's Association." The administration of the groups remained autonomous, and a general "Information Bureau" for the purpose of communication between the groups, but without executive powers, was established, with headquarters in Chicago.

The principal work of the convention was the adoption of a declaration of principles, which has since become famous as the "Pittsburg Proclamation," and is still regarded as the classic exposition of "communistic anarchism." This declaration of principles, like the theory of communistic anarchism itself, is a rather peculiar mixture of many not always very consistent elements.

The Declaration of Independence is curiously interspersed with the conflicting theories of Marx and Proudhon, and the philosophy of the French encyclopedists of the eighteenth century. The object of the movement is stated to be "the destruction of the existing class government by all means, i. e., by energetic, implacable, revolutionary, and international action," and the establishment of a system of industry based on "the free exchange of equivalent products between the producing organizations themselves and without the intervention of middlemen and profit-making."

The Pittsburg convention and the repeated lecture tours of Most and other prominent anarchists had their effect. Anarchism became a power in the radical circles of the labor movement of the United States, especially in the German-speaking part of it. The "groups" multiplied from year to year, and their membership increased steadily. The *Freiheit* gained in circulation; some of the former socialist papers, such as the Chicago *Arbeiter-Zeitung* and *Vorbote*, deserted the socialist camp and joined the anarchist movement, and several new anarchist organs were established.

The growth of the movement served to deplete the weakened ranks of the Socialist Labor Party still more. Disheartened by their recent failures in politics, and despairing of the final success of the slow methods of socialist propaganda, many members lent a willing ear to the convenient anarchist theories of general negation, and section after section seceded from the party to join fortunes with the Internationalists. In 1883 the membership of the Socialist Labor Party had shrunk to about 1,500, and its leaders were forced to concentrate their energies on an effort to prevent further inroads.

A spirited controversy ensued between the *Freiheit* and the *Bulletin,* the official organ of the Socialist Labor Party. The controversy was conducted with a great deal of earnestness by the latter, and with considerable wit and skill by the former. On the whole, it may be said that if the *Freiheit* did not always have the best of the argument, it mostly had the laugh on its side, and was generally the more successful combatant.

Defeated in this struggle and disheartened by the general condition of things in the party, Philip Van Patten, who had been its national secretary over six years, in despair, abandoned the fight. On the 22d day of April, 1883, he suddenly disappeared, announcing in a letter left behind him his intention to commit suicide. It subsequently appeared, however, that the letter was only a stratagem calculated to divert the attention of his former comrades from his trail. In reality Van Patten had sought and found a more peaceful and remunerative existence in the employ of the Government. The loss of Van Patten at that juncture was a hard blow to the organized socialist movement. He was an American of good family, with an excellent education, and had been active and prominent in the socialist movement, without interruption, for ten years. He was a man of much enthusiasm and devotion, but by no means a strong and popular leader. It was not so much the loss of his personality as the moral effect of his retreat that reflected deep discouragement on the socialist movement. Van Patten was succeeded in the office of national secretary by one Schneider, and when the latter resigned in October, 1883, Hugo Vogt was elected to fill the vacancy until the next convention of the party, which was to be held in December.

When the Pittsburg convention of the social revolutionists was held earlier in the year, the Socialist Labor Party had been invited to send delegates to it, but the National Executive Committee declined the invitation, declaring that there could be no common ground between social democrats and anarchists.

The "proclamation" adopted at Pittsburg, however, was much more moderate than was expected, and seemed to afford some ground for united action. The International Working-People's Association created by the Pittsburg convention was not as yet a purely anarchistic body, but rather a confederation of radical socialist and revolutionary organizations of all shades. As soon as the results of the convention were published, voices for union with the new body were raised in the Socialist Labor Party. Now that the party was thoroughly disorganized, the clamor for union became general. In December, 1883, some prominent members of the Socialist Labor Party took it upon themselves to propose formally a consolidation of the party with the Internationalists. This was done by means of a written communication addrest to the Chicago "groups," and signed by Alexander Jonas, Henry Emrich, George Lehr, and H. Molkenbuhr. The brunt of the writers' argument was the wisdom of united action and the similarity of views in the two organizations. "Reading the Proclamation of the Internationalists as adopted at the Pittsburg convention," they declared, "we can hardly find anything in it with which the Socialist Labor Party has not always agreed, except perhaps some obscure clauses of a reactionary coloring."

The answer came from A. Spies, writing in behalf of the Chicago "groups." It exprest anything but enthusiasm over the proposed union, and in substance advised the Socialist Labor Party to dissolve into autonomous groups to be affiliated with the International Working-People's Association in the same manner as the other groups of that body. It was in these circumstances that the fourth national convention of the Socialist Labor Party met at Baltimore from December 26 to 28, 1883.

It was the most dismal convention ever held by the party.

Only sixteen delegates attended, and of these, four came from Baltimore and ten from New York and vicinity. The convention made some changes in the platform and constitution of the party, with an apparent view to placating the more radical elements. The office of national secretary was abolished, the powers of the National Executive Committee were curtailed, and the sections were accorded greater autonomy in the administration of their own affairs. In addition to the party platform, the convention, following the Pittsburg precedent, issued a "proclamation." The document was more radical in tone than any previous pronunciamentos: politics were recommended as a means of propaganda only, and the conviction was exprest that the privileged classes would never surrender their privileges without being compelled to do so *by force*. Having made these concessions to the "social revolutionists," the convention proceeded to define its attitude toward outspoken anarchism in very unambiguous language.

"We do not share the folly of the men who consider dynamite bombs as the best means of agitation," the delegates declared; "we know full well that a revolution must take place in the heads and in the industrial life of men before the working class can achieve lasting success."

The principal significance of the convention lay in the fact that it drew a sharp line of demarcation between socialism and anarchism. The somewhat vague species of "social revolutionism" rapidly disappeared; the more moderate leaders of the movement, such as Paul Grottkau, rejoined the ranks of the Socialist Labor Party, and the extremists cast their lot definitely with the anarchists. Henceforward all attempts at conciliation were abandoned as useless, and there was nothing but war between the two camps.

The socialist as well as the anarchist papers of that period are filled with controversial articles on the merits and demerits of the theories and practices of the two contending movements, and public discussions on the subject were frequent and heated. The most notable of these was the debate between Paul Grottkau and John Most held at Chicago, on the 24th day of May, 1884. It was a well-matched contest, the opponents being equally well versed in the subject, and both fluent speakers and ready debaters. The discussion was very thoroughgoing and dealt with almost every phase of the subject. It was reported stenographically, published in book form,[4] and widely circulated.

Of considerable benefit to the party were the lecture tours of Alexander Jonas, F. Seubert, H. Walther, and O. Reimer, undertaken at about the same time. The tours were arranged by the party's Executive Committee. The special mission of the lecturers was to combat anarchism. The speakers visited the most important centers of the anarchist movement, addrest public meetings as well as some meetings of social revolutionary clubs, exposing the weak points of anarchism, and urging the party members to new activity. Simultaneously with this oral work the agitation against anarchism was vigorously conducted by means of leaflets published under the supervision of the National Executive Committee, and distributed in many thousand copies.

But the activity of the party at that period was by no means limited to the struggle with anarchism. A systematic campaign of education was conducted, principally through the medium of socialist tracts and pamphlets, of which no less than 160,000 were disposed of during the years 1884 and 1885.

The result of this renewed activity was a steady growth of the Socialist Labor Party. In March, 1884, the party consisted of about thirty sections; during the two years following the number was doubled. Three party papers in the English language—*The Voice of the People* in New York, the *Evening Telegram* in New Haven, and the *San Francisco Truth* in San Francisco—had been established at different times, but all were compelled to suspend publication after a brief trial. Of the German party papers, the *New Yorker Volkszeitung* and the *Philadelphia Tageblatt* were the only ones to survive. The *Sozialist*, a weekly magazine in the German language, was created as the official organ of the party under the editorial manage-

[4] "Discussion über das Thema 'Anarchismus oder Communismus,' gefürt von Paul Grottkau und Joh. Most," Chicago, 1884.

ment of Joseph Dietzgen. On the 5th day of October, 1885, the fifth national convention of the Socialist Labor Party met at Cincinnati. Forty-two sections were represented by thirty-three delegates. The principal work of the convention was to regulate the party's methods of work and to strengthen its organization.

The Socialist Labor Party had now somewhat recuperated from the onslaughts of anarchism, but it had by no means vanquished the foe. On the contrary, the International Working-People's Association, during the last two years, had gained more in proportion than the Socialist Labor Party. In the year 1885 the International embraced about eighty organized groups, with a total of 7,000 enrolled members, and its press was represented by seven German, two English, and two Bohemian papers.

3. The Chicago Drama

The main strength of the anarchist movement lay in Chicago, in which the "Information Bureau" was located, and the *Arbeiter-Zeitung,* the *Vorbote,* and the *Fackel,* as well as the English *Alarm,* edited by Parsons, were published. Toward the end of 1885 the city contained no less than twenty groups, with a membership of about 3,000.

What made the ground especially favorable for the propaganda of anarchism at that time was the new industrial crisis which set in about 1884 and lasted until 1886. As in 1877, the large industrial cities of the country were again filled with throngs of destitute and embittered working men out of employment, and these supplied eager and appreciative audiences for the apostles of anarchism.

Here again Chicago was in the lead. The Internationalists of that city held numerous mass-meetings, a great street demonstration was arranged by them for Thanksgiving Day in 1884, and the *Freiheit,* the *Alarm,* and other anarchist papers counseled their adherents to arm themselves, and even published minute instructions for the preparation and use of dynamite. Similar instructions were contained in a pamphlet written by Most, under the title "Revolutionary Science of War," which was reprinted by several anarchist papers and had an extensive circulation. The climax of the agitation, however, was reached in 1886.

In 1884 the annual convention of the Federation of Trades and Labor Unions of the United States of America had decided to revive the movement for an eight-hour work-day, and the first day of May, 1886, was afterwards fixt upon as the day on which the new system should be in-augurated. As the ominous day approached, the movement gained in extent and determination. The trade-unions of the country doubled and trebled their membership, eight-hour leagues were formed, and the subject was warmly agitated in public meetings and in the labor press.

In Chicago excitement ran highest. In 1885 the "Eight-Hour Association" was organized on the initiative of George A. Schilling and others. The Trade and Labor Assembly, the principal central body of organized labor in Chicago, immediately fell in line. The Central Labor Union, a smaller body dominated by anarchist influence, followed, and the movement soon became general.

The Internationalists of Chicago were at first quite in-different to the movement, and even deprecated it as a com-promise with capital and as a hopeless and useless battle. But when the eight-hour movement assumed larger propor-tions and became the all-absorbing topic in labor circles, the anarchists gradually changed their position, and ulti-mately supported it. Parsons, Spies, Fielden, Schwab, and other anarchist orators became the most popular speak-ers at eight-hour meetings, and at such meetings, as well as in their press, the anarchists frequently took occasion to advise the working men to provide themselves with arms on the first day of May.

The first serious trouble occurred among the striking em-ployees of the McCormick Reaper Works. These had been "locked out" from the works in February. The battle between employers and employees was fought with unusual bitterness, still more intensified by the fact that the Mc-Cormicks had hired no less than 300 armed Pinkerton detectives to protect the strike breakers whom they had

employed. On the third day of May the Lumber Shovers'
Union, of which the majority of the locked-out McCormick
employees were members, held a mass-meeting in the vicinity of the works to discuss the terms of a peace proposal
to be submitted to the employers. Spies was addressing
the meeting with "unusual calmness and moderation," as
he relates in his autobiography, when the bell of the Mc-
Cormick factory rang and the "scabs" were seen leaving.
An excited crowd of about 150, separating themselves from
the meeting, made an advance toward them. A street battle ensued, stones being liberally thrown on both sides.
The police were telephoned for, and a patrol-wagon filled
with officers immediately rattled up the street. A few
minutes later about seventy-five policemen followed the patrol-wagon on foot, and these were again followed by three
or four more patrol-wagons. The officers were assaulted
with stones, and in turn they opened fire on the crowd,
shooting indiscriminately men, women, and children, killing
six and wounding many more. Frantic and infuriated beyond measure, Spies hurried back to the office of the
Arbeiter-Zeitung, and there composed the proclamation
to the working men of Chicago which has since become famous as the "Revenge Circular."

It was headed "REVENGE!" and called upon the working
men to arm themselves and avenge the "brutal murder"
of their brethren. Five thousand copies of the circular,
printed in English and German, were distributed in the
streets. The next evening a mass-meeting was called at
Haymarket for the purpose of "branding the murder
of our fellow workers." About 2,000 working men responded to the call, and Spies, Parsons, and Fielden spoke.
Mayor Carter H. Harrison of Chicago, apprehending
trouble, was present at the meeting, and what occurred was
subsequently described by him in the following language:

"With the exception of a portion in the earlier part of
Mr. Spies' address, which for probably a minute was such
that I feared it was leading up to a point where I should
disperse the meeting, it was such that I remarked to Captain Bonfield that it was tame. The portion of Mr. Par-

sons' speech attracting most attention was the statistics as to the amount of returns given to labor from capital, and showing, if I remember rightly now, that capital got eighty-five per cent. and labor fifteen per cent. It was what I should call a violent political harangue against capital. I went back to the station and said to Bonfield that I thought the speeches were about over; that nothing had occurred yet or was likely to occur to require interference, and I thought he had better issue orders to his reserves at the other stations to go home.''

Mayor Harrison left at about ten o'clock, and the meeting was then practically ended. At least two-thirds of the audience had dispersed, in view of the heavy clouds which had gathered foreshadowing a storm. Fielden addrest the remaining crowd, a very few hundred in number. He had spoken about ten minutes, when 176 policemen suddenly marched upon the little crowd in double-quick step. Captain Ward, in charge of the squad, commanded the meeting to disperse. Fielden retorted that the meeting was a peaceable one. At this juncture a dynamite bomb was thrown from an adjoining alley; it alighted between the first and second companies of the policemen and exploded with a terrible detonation, killing one policeman and wounding many more. Instantly an indiscriminate firing was opened on both sides, which lasted about two minutes without interruption. When it was all over it appeared that seven policemen had been killed and about sixty wounded, while on the side of the working men four were killed and about fifty wounded.

Who threw the bomb which precipitated the riot? The question has never been satisfactorily answered. One Rudolph Schnaubelt, a brother-in-law of Michael Schwab, is commonly credited with the fatal deed, but Schnaubelt fled immediately after the Haymarket tragedy, and through the anarchistic press of Europe he has repeatedly denied any connection with the act. The opinion was also frequently exprest that the bomb was thrown as an act of personal vengeance by some relative or friend of a victim of the police brutalities perpetrated on the preceding day, and there were not wanting those who believed that the dastardly act had been committed by an "agent provocateur" at the behest of the powers interested in breaking up the eight-hour agitation, which had just then assumed very powerful proportions.

But be this as it may, the Haymarket incident was laid at the door of the anarchists, and popular indignation against them and their agitation knew no bounds. The daily press loudly clamored for the heads of the leading anarchists. All labor meetings were broken up, and the *Arbeiter-Zeitung* was placed under censorship of the chief of police. The speakers at the Haymarket meeting and the entire editorial staff and the force of compositors of the *Arbeiter-Zeitung* were immediately placed under arrest. Parsons, who could not be found by the police, surrendered himself voluntarily at the trial. On the 17th day of May the grand jury convened and found an indictment against August Spies, Michael Schwab, Samuel Fielden, Albert R. Parsons, Adolph Fischer, George Engel, Louis Lingg, Oscar W. Neebe, Rudolph Schnaubelt, and William Seliger, charging them with the murder of M. J. Degan, the policeman who was killed by the fatal bomb. Of these, Schnaubelt made his escape, Seliger turned State's evidence and was granted immunity. The eight others were placed on trial.

The men thus singled out were not only the backbone of the local anarchistic movement, but were among the most prominent and influential leaders in the eight-hour agitation, and generally popular in the labor movement of Chicago.

August Spies was at that time thirty-one years of age. He was born in Germany and emigrated to the United States in 1872. In 1877 he became a member of the Socialist Labor Party. He was business manager and then editor-in-chief of the Chicago *Arbeiter-Zeitung*. He retained the latter position until his arrest. Upon the advent of the "social revolutionary" clubs, he joined the movement and later became an avowed anarchist. His anarchism, however, was of a rather mild and philosophic type. He was a Marxian student, spoke and wrote English and German with equal fluency, and was by all odds the most cultured and intellectual of the defendants.

Albert R. Parsons was born at Montgomery, Ala., in 1844. At the age of fifteen he learned the trade of type-setting. He fought in the civil war on the Confederate side, but in 1868 he published a newspaper for the defense of the rights of the colored race, and thereby incurred the enmity of his relatives. In 1875 he joined the Social Democratic Labor Party, and one year later organized the Chicago Trade Assembly of the Knights of Labor. He was one of the first to affiliate himself with the "social revolutionary" movement of 1880, and after 1884 he edited the ultra-anarchistic *Alarm*. He was an eloquent and magnetic speaker and talented organizer, and between 1875 and 1886 is said to have addrest no less than 1,000 mass-meetings and to have traveled over sixteen States as organizer for the Socialist Labor Party, and later for the International Working-People's Association.

Michael Schwab was a man of smaller caliber than either Spies or Parsons. He was a German of good education, thirty-three years old, and at the time of his arrest had been eight years in the United States. He was associated with Spies on the editorial staff of the *Arbeiter-Zeitung*, and was a lucid tho not original writer and a fluent speaker. His influence in the labor movement was due principally to his great earnestness and unbounded devotion to the cause of the working class.

George Engel was the oldest of the defendants. He was born in 1836 in Kassel, Germany. A life of hardship and privation had early matured in him a spirit of bitterness. His hatred of existing society was a personal sentiment rather than the result of his social philosophy. He joined the anarchistic movement upon the first signs of its appearance in the United States, and was one of its extremest and most earnest devotees ever since.

Louis Lingg was only twenty-two years old. He was a passionate and enthusiastic fanatic and an untiring worker for the cause of anarchy.

Samuel Fielden was born in England in 1847. He was successively a weaver, a lay Methodist preacher, and a driver. His knowledge of socialism and anarchism had been gathered mostly from newspaper articles and public discussions. His speeches were direct, somewhat abrupt, passionate, and eloquent, and he was a great favorite with the masses.

Adolph Fischer was only two years older than Lingg. He was born in Germany, but emigrated to the United States at the age of fifteen. His education in socialism was received from his parents. He turned anarchist a few years before his arrest, and was one of the most indefatigable workers in the movement.

Oscar Neebe was born in New York in 1849. He settled in Chicago in 1866, and since that time was identified with almost every phase of the labor movement. He had been a delegate to the National Labor-Union, and later joined first the Socialist Labor Party and then the International Working-People's Association. He was never very prominent in the anarchist propaganda, but was always active in the trade-union movement, and took a leading part in the eight-hour agitation of 1886.

The trial of the eight men began on the 21st day of June, 1886. It was presided over by Judge Joseph E. Gary, and lasted forty-nine days. The defendants were not charged with personal participation in the killing of Degan. The theory of the prosecution was that they had by speech and print advised large classes of the people to commit murder, and that in consequence of that advice somebody not known had thrown the bomb that caused Degan's death.

The trial of the anarchists has been called a farce by many impartial observers who were in no way connected with the anarchist movement, and it is hard to read the records of the case without coming to the conclusion that it was the grossest travesty on justice ever perpetrated in an American court. The jury was not drawn in the customary way. Judge Gary appointed one Henry L. Ryse as a special bailiff to go out and summon such jurors as he might select. Out of a panel of about 1,000 only five were working men, and these were promptly excused by the State. Most of the talesmen declared that they had a prejudice against anarchists and a preconceived opinion of the guilt of the defendants, but upon their statement that they believed their prejudice could be overcome by strong proof of innocence, the judge ruled that they were qualified to serve as jurors. The most important witnesses for the State were Seliger, who had betrayed his comrades for a promise of immunity, and a number of detectives and newspaper reporters, many of whom contradicted themselves in the trial to such an extent as to render their testimony of no value. With all that, the prosecution did not succeed in establishing the most vital point of its theory—*i. e.*, that the person who threw the bomb did so upon the advice, directly or indirectly, of any of the defendants, or that he was in any way influenced by their teachings. Since the identity of the actual culprit was unknown, his acts could, of course, not be brought into any connection with the defendants.

The most revolting feature of the trial was the partial manner in which it was conducted by the judge: not only did he rule all contested points in favor of the prosecution, but his repeated insinuating remarks made within the hearing of the jury were of such a nature that they could not fail to influence the latter against the defendants. In vain did Spies and Fielden disclaim any connection with the tragedy; in vain did Parsons show that he did not anticipate any violence at the meeting, since he had permitted his wife and children to accompany him to it; in vain did Fischer and Engel show that they were quietly at home playing cards while the Haymarket meeting took place; in vain did Schwab, Lingg, and Neebe prove that they had not been at the Haymarket meeting, and that they did not know of the preparations for it; and in vain did their attorney, Captain Black, demonstrate that the State's case was built on perjured testimony. The Haymarket affair was only a pretext. What the defendants were really tried for was not the murder of Degan, but their anarchist views. They were bound to be convicted, and convicted they were.

On the 20th day of August the jury brought in the following verdict:

"We, the jury, find the defendants, August Spies, Samuel Fielden, Michael Schwab, Albert R. Parsons, Adolph Fischer, George Engel, and Louis Lingg guilty of murder in the manner and form charged in the indictment, and fix the penalty at death. We find the defendant, Oscar W. Neebe, guilty of murder in the manner and form as charged in the indictment, and fix the penalty at imprisonment in the penitentiary for fifteen years."

An appeal was taken to the Supreme Court of the State, and the judgment was affirmed. A further appeal to the Supreme Court of the United States was dismissed on the ground that the court had no jurisdiction in the matter. The only other recourse left was a petition to the governor for executive clemency. Some of the condemned men adopted this course, with the result that the sentences of Schwab and Fielden were commuted to life imprisonment. Lingg committed suicide in his cell by exploding a cartridge in his mouth. Spies, Parsons, Fischer, and Engel were hanged on the 11th day of November, 1887. They died bravely. "The time will come when our silence in the grave will be more eloquent than our speeches," declared Spies as the noose was placed about his neck. Parsons' last words were: "Let the voice of the people be heard," and Fischer's dying statement as he ascended the scaffold with elastic step and radiant face was: "This is the happiest moment of my life." Six years later John P. Altgeld, then recently elected governor of Illinois, granted an absolute pardon to Samuel Fielden, Oscar Neebe, and Michael Schwab, accompanying it by a thoroughgoing analysis of the trial before Judge Gary, and a scathing arraignment of the unfair and partial methods of the judge.

4. PERIOD OF RECONSTRUCTION

The Chicago incident was practically the closing chapter in the history of anarchism as an active element in the labor movement of this country. While the anarchists disclaimed responsibility for the particular act of throwing the fatal bomb, it could not be denied that the act was in accord with the methods of violence countenanced by them. The Haymarket tragedy and its direful consequences were a concrete illustration of anarchism reduced to practice, and had a sobering effect on its adherents and sympathizers.

Whatever support organized labor had heretofore given to the movement was now rapidly withdrawn. The organized anarchist movement was henceforward confined to a few insignificant "groups" in the East with little power or influence.

The field was now once more clear for the propaganda of socialism, and the socialists were not slow to take advantage of the favorable situation. The work of reviving the movement was begun in earnest, and was greatly facilitated by the industrial and political struggles of labor at that period.

The Socialist Labor Party gained in membership and strength. New party papers were established, new "sections" organized, and extensive lecture tours arranged. Of the latter the most noteworthy were those undertaken by Wilhelm Liebknecht, the veteran leader of the German Social Democracy, in conjunction with Eleanor Marx Aveling, the eloquent and brilliant daughter of Karl Marx, and her husband, Dr. Edward Aveling. This tour was arranged by the Socialist Labor Party in the fall of 1886. The lecturers addrest about fifty meetings in all the principal cities of the Union, Liebknecht speaking in German and the Avelings in English. Their work had a marked effect on the socialist movement.

In the month of September, 1887, the sixth national convention of the Socialist Labor Party was held in Buffalo. The convention was attended by thirty-seven delegates, representing thirty-two sections. The full number of party sections was reported to be about seventy. The most interesting feature of the convention was the discussion on the question of the proposed unity between the Socialist Labor Party and the International Working-Men's Association.

The International Working-Men's Association (not to be confounded with the "International Working-People's Association," created in Pittsburg in 1883) had been organized in the latter part of 1881. It was composed principally of American working men and farmers, and had its main strength on the Pacific coast. The social views and principles of the organization were a somewhat curious mixture of anarchism and socialism.

With the anarchists these Internationalists disdained the use of the ballot. "We believe," [5] they declared, "that if universal suffrage had been capable of emancipating the working people from the rule of the loafing class, it would have been taken away from them before now, and we have no faith in the ballot as a means of righting the wrongs under which the masses groan."

But they differed from the revolutionary anarchists inasmuch as they discountenanced methods of violence and laid greater stress on education and propaganda.

Their aims and objects were stated by them to be: "To print, publish, and circulate labor literature; to hold mass-meetings; to systematize agitation; to establish labor libraries, labor halls, and lyceums for discussing social science; to maintain the labor press; to protect members and all producers from wrong; to aid all labor organizations, etc." The Association was organized on the "group" system. Its principal organ was *Truth,* published in San Francisco under the editorial management of Burnette G. Haskell. It was established as a weekly in 1882, but in the beginning of 1884 was converted into a monthly magazine. Toward the end of the same year it suspended publication for lack of subscribers. *Truth* was succeeded by the *Labor Enquirer,* published in Denver.

In 1887 the International Working-Men's Association claimed an enrolled membership of about 6,000, distributed in the following manner: In Washington Territory and Oregon, about 2,000; in California, 1,800; in Colorado, Utah, Montana, Dakota, and Wyoming, about 2,000. About 200 members were scattered in the South and East.

Mr. Haskell, who conducted the negotiations in behalf of the Association, made several demands upon the Socialist

[5] R. T. Ely, "The Labor Movement in America."

Labor Party as conditions precedent to the unification of the two organizations, the most important of these being that the party change its name to "Socialist League" or "Socialist Association;" that it declare against political action; that it devote less means to the support of the socialist movement in Germany and more to propaganda at home; that it admit the Chicago anarchists to membership, and continue the publication of the *Labor Enquirer*. After a somewhat lengthy discussion, the following resolution was adopted by the convention:

"*Whereas*, A friendly offer of union with our party has been received from the Denver Socialist League;

"*Resolved*, That we, in the spirit of fraternity, reciprocate the offer and welcome the outstretched hand; and

"*Whereas*, The platform and principles of the Socialist Labor Party are acknowledged to be complete, comprehensive, and satisfactory to our brothers of the International Working-Men's Association and the Socialist Leagues connected therewith;

"*Resolved*, That said platform be the basis of the union.

"*Whereas*, Many other socialist organizations in Chicago and other places in the Middle and Western States are believers in our platform and principles, tho still isolated;

"*Resolved*, That we welcome them, with our comrades of the Socialist League, to our party upon a formal acceptance of our platform under the provisions of our constitution, to the end that the socialist agitation and propaganda may be made the more effective, and our common cause may finally triumph."

As no formal union was thus accomplished, the International Working-Men's Association soon disbanded. Next to the matter of unity the larger portion of the convention's deliberations was occupied with the subject of political action. The views of the delegates were divided on the question of continuing to cooperate with the various political labor parties then in the field, entering the political arena independently, or abstaining from politics altogether. A temporary compromise was finally effected by the adoption of a resolution recommending the members, "where-ever one or more labor parties are in the field, to support that party which is the most progressive."

The adoption of the resolution by no means disposed of the controversy. The disappointing experience of the socialists with the several "Progressive" or "Radical" labor parties in the ensuing elections accentuated the difference of views. The New York *Volkszeitung* and its adherents held that socialist politics were as yet premature, and advised the party to concentrate attention on the trade-union movement, while the official party organs, *The Workmen's Advocate* and *Der Sozialist,* were enthusiastic advocates of independent socialist politics, and rather inclined to underrate the importance of socialist activity in the trade-unions.

The antagonism between the two camps grew more pronounced within the next two years, and finally developed into open hostilities. The *Volkszeitung* was charged by the party officers with disloyalty, and retorted by styling the National Executive Committee an incompetent clique. In this controversy the bulk of the membership of "Section New York," which had elected the members of the national committee and had the right to recall them, sided with the *Volkszeitung.* In the month of September, 1889, the section preferred charges of incompetency against the national officers of the party, and called a meeting for the purpose of investigating the charges. The meeting deposed the national secretary, W. L. Rosenberg, and the members of the national committee—Hinze, Sauter, and Gericke—and elected in their places S. E. Schewitsch, Otto Reimer, C. Ibsen, and R. Praast. This summary action precipitated a crisis within the party organization. The deposed officers refused to recognize the validity of the procedure by which they had been removed. They continued to assert their rights as the national committee of the party, and called a convention, to be held at the end of the same month in the city of Chicago. In the meanwhile the new national committee entered on the discharge of its duties.

The "sections" were pretty evenly divided in their allegiance between the two committees, and in the ensuing chaos the "control committee" of the party, with head-quarters at Philadelphia, stepped in, suspending both contesting committees from office and taking temporary charge of the administration of the party affairs.

The control committee postponed the date of the convention to October 12th. This date was accepted by the *Volkszeitung* wing of the party, but the Rosenburg faction adhered to the date originally fixed by the deposed committee. Thus two separate conventions were held by the party sections, each claiming to represent the regular organization and denouncing the other as irregular.

The convention of the Rosenberg faction was poorly attended. The majority of the delegates were "proxies." The organization led a rather precarious existence for several years more. Efforts were repeatedly made to reunite the two factions, but no union was accomplished, and the remnants of the Rosenberg faction, or "Social Democratic Federation," as it styled itself in later years, ultimately was merged into the Social Democratic Party.

In the meantime the *Volkszeitung* faction held its convention in Chicago in October, 1889. Thirty-three sections were represented by twenty-seven delegates. Notwithstanding the recent split, the proceedings were marked by a spirit of confidence and hopefulness. The most important work was the adoption of a new platform drafted by Lucien Sanial. While all previous platforms of the party had consisted of concise and unimpassioned expositions of the abstract principles of modern socialism, the platform of 1889 was more of a campaign document, and acquired a national coloring by basing its arguments on the Declaration of Independence. This document was readopted with insignificant modifications at every succeeding convention of the Socialist Labor Party.

The next convention was held in Chicago in July, 1893, and was attended by forty-two delegates. At that convention the demand for the abolition of the office of President of the United States was struck from the platform.

The progress of the party continued undisturbed and steady for a number of years. In 1889 the number of "sections" was reported to be seventy. During the four years following 113 new sections were organized; of these, forty-three were German, thirty-nine American, fourteen Jewish, and the remainder made up of Poles, Bohemians, Frenchmen, Italians, and other nationalities. The sections were distributed over twenty-one States. Many of the newly organized sections disbanded, but others were organized in their stead, and on the whole the number increased. In 1896 the national secretary reported over 200 sections in twenty-five States. In that year the ninth national convention of the Socialist Labor Party was held in the city of New York. It was opened on the 4th day of July, and remained in session seven full days. Ninety-four delegates attended, representing seventy-five sections in twelve States.

The proceedings of the convention were unusually animated and covered a wide range of subjects. Most significant and fateful was the attitude assumed by the delegates toward the trade-union movement. The subject was brought up by the introduction of a resolution to indorse the Socialist Trade and Labor Alliance, which had then recently been called into existence by several prominent party leaders in opposition to the American Federation of Labor and the Order of the Knights of Labor. The debate occupied several consecutive sessions of the convention, and at times grew exceedingly intense. A resolution condemning the existing trade unions as hopelessly corrupt and commending the organization of the Alliance was finally adopted by a vote of seventy-one to six.

Thus the Socialist Labor Party for the first time in the history of its existence declared war on the national bodies of organized labor. This was a radical departure from the established policy of the party toward the trade-union movement. How fateful the policy was to become to the organization the following chapters will show.

During the three succeeding years the number of sections increased to over 350, the operations of the party extended over thirty States, and the party press received several notable additions and gained in circulation. In 1899 the Socialist Labor Party had reached the zenith of its power.

III.—THE SOCIALIST LABOR PARTY IN POLITICS

I. INDEPENDENT POLITICS

THE Socialist Labor Party, or the Working-Men's Party of the United States, as the organization was named during the first years of its existence, was originally organized mainly for propaganda purposes. On the question of the party's attitude toward participation in politics, the Philadelphia Unity Convention adopted the following resolution:

"*Whereas*, The economic emancipation of the working class is the great end to which every political movement must be subordinated;

"*Whereas*, The Working-Men's Party conducts its struggles primarily on the economic field;

"*Whereas*, It is only the economic struggle in which the soldiers for the Working-Men's Party can be trained;

"*Whereas*, The ballot-box has in this country long ceased to be the expression of the popular will, but has rather become an instrument for its subversion in the hands of the professional politicians;

"*Whereas*, The organized working men are as yet by no means strong enough to root out this corruption:

"*Whereas*, This bourgeois republic has produced a multitude of middle-class reformers and quacks, and the penetration of these elements into the party will be largely facilitated by a political movement;

"*Whereas*, The corruption of the ballot-box and the reform humbug reach their highest bloom in the years of presidential elections, and the dangers for the Working-Men's Party are accordingly greatest in these years;

"For these reasons the Unity Convention of the Work-ing-Men's Party, in session at Philadelphia on the 22d day of July, 1876, *resolves*:

"The sections of this party and all working men gen-erally are earnestly requested for the time being to abstain from all political movements, and to turn their backs upon the ballot-box.

"The working men will thereby spare themselves many disappointments, and they can devote their time and en-ergies with much more profit to the organization of the working men, which are frequently injured and destroyed by premature action.

"Let us bide our time! It will come!"

It will be readily seen from the wording of the resolu-tion that the party's abstention from active participation in politics was a measure of necessity rather than a matter of choice. The reasons for that attitude may be easily traced in the condition of the party and the political sit-uation of the time. In 1876 the Working-Men's Party consisted of about 2,500 to 3,000 enrolled members. The overwhelming majority of these were Germans. The party had just been created by the union of several not quite homogeneous elements. Its organization was loose, its means were scanty, and its influence insignificant. In these circumstances an independent national campaign was not to be thought of. The prospects of fusion with any ex-isting reform party were by no means seductive. The only party which could lay claim to that title in the elections of 1876 was the Greenback Party, and this was very in-significant, and the issues presented by it were not of a nature to appeal to the labor interests. Abstention from politics was, therefore, the only course left open.

But the following year wrought many significant changes in the condition of the party. The industrial depression and the great railway strikes described in a preceding chapter had advanced social problems to the front. The ranks of the party had been swelled, and many of the new converts were American working men. Popular sen-timent was favorable to radical and reform politics, and the

Socialist Labor Party was not slow in following up its advantage.

From 1877 till 1879, during which time the labor excitements continued, the party conducted many spirited campaigns in the State and local elections, and in some of its strongholds met with considerable success. In Chicago in the fall of 1877 about 7,000 votes were cast for the Socialist Labor Party, and in the spring of the following year one of its members, F. Straubert, was elected to the Common Council. In the fall of 1878 the Chicago socialists elected three State Representatives—C. Ehrhardt, C. Meier, and Leo Meilbeck, and one State Senator, Sylvester Artley. These introduced in the legislature bills providing for the cash payment of wages, for the limitation of the hours of labor for women and children, for an employers' liability act, and several similar bills, all of which were promptly defeated. They did, however, succeed in inducing the legislature to establish a bureau of labor statistics. In the spring of 1878 four socialists—Altpeter, Lorenz, Meier, and Straubert—were elected aldermen. In these elections the Socialist Labor Party ticket was headed by Dr. Ernst Schmidt, as candidate for the office of Mayor. Dr. Schmidt was a popular and influential German physician, a noted Marxian scholar, and a steadfast friend of labor. He received over 12,000 votes.

In Cincinnati the party polled 9,000 votes in the fall elections of the same year, and in Cleveland it received 3,000 votes. In St. Louis the party received 7,000 votes at the same time, and elected five members of the school board and two aldermen.

In New York a State ticket was nominated in the fall of 1879, with Caleb Pink as the candidate for Governor and Osborne Ward as candidate for Lieutenant-Governor. The ticket was supported by the sections of the party in New York, Brooklyn, Albany, Troy, Utica, Syracuse, and Buffalo, but the State organization was extremely weak on the whole. The total vote did not reach 10,000.

Candidates were nominated in Detroit, Boston, New Orleans, and Denver. The party organizations in New

Jersey, Pennsylvania, Wisconsin, Iowa, Indiana, Kansas, and Kentucky took no part in the political campaigns of that period. In Louisville a "Workingmen's Party," composed principally of trade-unionists, but largely influenced by members of the Socialist Labor Party, polled over 9,000 votes out of the total of about 14,000 cast in the local election of 1877. In a few other places the socialists occasionally cooperated with the Greenbackers.

In California the organized working men, under the leadership of the eloquent agitator, Dennis Kearney, had organized for political action as the "Working-Men's Party of California." The Socialist Labor Party refrained from nominating candidates of its own, "deeming it unwise and imprudent to divide the forces of the labor movement." [6]

[6] The Kearney agitation forms one of the most picturesque pages in the history of the American labor movement. In 1877 California presented a most critical economic and political situation. The waves of the great industrial depression which had struck the East in 1873 reached the Pacific coast much later, and its effects were still felt very keenly in 1877. The crisis was rendered more acute by the wild stock speculations in which almost all persons in California had engaged during the preceding years. Business was practically suspended. Mines, factories, and shops were closed, and whatever work there was, was done principally by Chinese, who were at all times ready to work for half the customary wages.

The sufferings of the population became intense, and the notoriously corrupt and incompetent State officials showed themselves unable or unwilling to devise any efficient measures of relief. The army of unemployed working men in California, and particularly in San Francisco, swelled to tremendous proportions. Their discontent with the existing state of affairs grew louder and louder, and finally found expression in the formation of the "Working-Men's Party of California." The leading spirit of the party was Dennis Kearney, a man of little education and powers of reasoning, but endowed with the gift of popular oratory and possest of indefatigable energy. Under the leadership of Kearney the party soon became a power in local politics. Its open-air meetings on the "Sand Lots" of San Francisco were attended by thousands of enthusiastic listeners; its agitation became the all-absorbing topic of discussion in the press; its adherents grew daily, and when the city elections in San Francisco arrived the party elected the majority of officers. It was also the vote of the Working-Men's Party of California which brought about a revision of the State constitution, and when the Constitutional Convention assembled in 1879, the

The party as a whole did not participate in any national election, and its total voting strength at the period under consideration is, therefore, largely a matter of conjecture. It has been variously estimated as between 50,000 and 100,000.

This was certainly a promising beginning, considering the extraordinary difficulties with which the young organization had to cope. Enthusiasm ran high in the ranks of organized socialists in the United States.

But the subsequent developments by no means justified the enthusiastic expectations. Returning prosperity cut the ground from the socialist agitation, which had just begun to gain a foothold among American working men. The Socialist Labor Party lost rapidly in membership and strength, and when the presidential election of 1880 drew nearer, the party was in not much better condition to meet it than it had been in the election of 1876. "It is to be regretted," said Van Patten in his official report to the Allegheny convention (December 26, 1879, to January 1, 1880), "that our party has lost valuable opportunities offered during the past two years, but which could not be properly grasped, as our own organization had not the experience and confidence necessary to control the vast

party exercised a controlling influence in framing the document.

The new State constitution of California introduced a number of radical reforms intended for the purification of the State administration, legislature, and judiciary; the curbing of the powers of corporate capital, and the prohibition of Chinese labor. This instrument for a time occasioned a good deal of fear among the possessing classes, but subsequent events proved the apprehension quite unfounded.

The Kearney movement was only the expression of a vague and unenlightened discontent. It was not based on any definite social theory. It offered no constructive measures. Its battle-cry was: "Down with the rich!" and its platform was: "The Chinese must go!" The movement lasted as long as the industrial crisis continued. As soon as the first signs of returning prosperity appeared, it collapsed, leaving little, if any, traces behind it. The Working-Men's Party of California disbanded, and the new State constitution, which was its principal achievement, was so circumvented by succeeding legislatures and so "construed" and "trimmed" by the courts as to render it quite ineffective.

numbers of discontented workmen who were ready to be organized. It is especially to be regretted that we had not secured the election of at least a dozen representatives in the legislature of every Northern State, since a party which has elected a number of representatives is considered tolerably permanent, while one who has not, is regarded by the public as transient and uncertain.''

The same report recommended participation in the approaching presidential election. This recommendation was the subject of the most heated discussions in the convention.

With very few exceptions the delegates were agreed upon the advisability of taking part in the election, but the controversy turned on the question of entering the campaign independently, or in conjunction with other reform parties.

The National Executive Committee suggested that the party unite on a ticket with the Working-Men's Party of California, the Greenback Party, and the Liberal Party, which last organization had recently been called into existence by the Liberal League and had held a convention in Cincinnati in September, 1879, at which a semi-socialist platform was adopted. The suggestion was received with favor by a number of delegates—Parsons and McGuire among them—but was strenuously opposed by others. Upon a vote the motion to fuse with other reform parties was defeated by a narrow margin, and the convention decided to make independent nominations for the offices of President and Vice-President.

Caleb Pink, of New York, O. A. Bishop, of Illinois, and Osborne Ward, of New York, were placed in nomination. Of the twenty-four delegates present, nine abstained from voting, ten voted for Pink, four for Bishop, and one for Ward. Caleb Pink was thereupon declared the choice of the convention.

At a later stage of the proceedings, the vote whereby Pink was nominated was reconsidered, and a resolution adopted to the effect that the names of all three candidates be submitted to a general vote of the party members, the person receiving the highest vote to be the party's candidate for President, and the one receiving the next highest to be its candidate for Vice-President. This resolution changed the entire situation. The proposition to nominate independent candidates for the offices of President and Vice-President was rejected *in toto* by the party, and in the elections of 1880 the Socialist Labor Party supported the candidates of the Greenback Party.

2. THE GREENBACK PARTY

THE Greenback movement was the immediate result of the financial crisis of 1873. It was the first expression of popular protest against the aggressions of capital, and took the shape of a currency-reform movement. It was claimed that bankers and bondholders had conspired to depreciate the war greenbacks by depriving them of their character as legal-tender for customs and for the payment of the national debt; to buy United States bonds with such depreciated greenbacks; and to induce the Government to redeem the same bonds in gold. A popular agitation against this alleged conspiracy sprang up, and the movement finally crystallized in the Greenback Party. Its first convention was held in Indianapolis in 1874, when a platform was adopted demanding several currency reforms, chief among which were:

1. The withdrawal of national bank-notes.

2. That the only currency should be paper, and that such currency be exchangeable for United States interest-bearing bonds.

3. That coin be used only for the payment of such bonds as called expressly for payment in coin.

These demands appealed principally to farmers and small business men who had mortgages and other debts to pay. The movement was for a long time confined to those classes. Industrial laborers manifested little interest in it.

In 1876 the party nominated the well-known New York philanthropist, Peter Cooper, for President of the United States, and Samuel F. Cary, of Ohio, for Vice-President. The ticket received over 80,000 votes.

The movement had almost run its course when the great strikes and labor agitation of 1877 brought new life into it and gave it an entirely new turn. The currency issues were relegated to the background, and the demands of labor took their place. In 1878 the national convention of the party, held at Toledo, Ohio, was attended by a number of labor leaders, and the party name was changed to "Greenback Labor Party." The movement gained popularity among industrial workers of the East, and in the ensuing congressional elections the party polled about 1,000,000 votes and elected fourteen representatives to Congress. In the presidential election of 1880 the Greenback Labor Party nominated James B. Weaver, of Iowa, and B. J. Chambers, of Texas, as its candidates for President and Vice-President. But the popular excitement had already subsided, and the Greenback vote sank to 300,000. Henceforward the party declined steadily. The last national ticket nominated by it was that of 1884, when Gen. B. F. Butler, ex-congressman and ex-governor of Massachusetts, who had in turn been Democratic, Republican, and labor politician, was its candidate for President. Butler received the indorsement of the anti-monopolists, and polled a vote of about 175,000. After that election the Greenbackers drifted gradually into the ranks of the old parties and ceased to exist as an independent political factor.

As long as the Greenback Party had limited its agitation to currency reform, the Socialist Labor Party strenuously discountenanced all political alliances with it, but since 1878, when it came into closer touch with the labor movement, the party's attitude toward it became more friendly. As shown in the preceding chapter, some sections of the party had supported the Greenbackers in the elections of 1878 and 1879, but this support was unofficial; tolerated, but not encouraged, by the party administration. It was only in 1880 that the Socialist Labor Party, as such, officially decided to support the Greenback Party. As soon as the decision was reached, the National Executive Committee of the party issued a call to all sections and all trade-

unions in sympathy with it to send delegates to a conference in Chicago on August 8, 1880. The national
nominating convention of the Greenback Labor Party was
to be held in the same city on the 9th day of August, and
it was understood that the conference of August 8th would
practically be a caucus meeting of the socialist elements
expected to attend the Greenback convention. About
ninety prospective delegates responded to the call. Of these,
more than half were Chicago residents who had received
credentials as proxies from various minor sections, and
thirty-eight were direct representatives of their respective
sections. Among the latter were Philip Van Patten, the
party's secretary; Dr. Douai, P. J. McGuire, Albert R.
Parsons, Mrs. L. Parsons, T. J. Morgan, and other prominent members of the Socialist Labor Party.

In the socialist caucus it was decided to apply for admission to the Greenback convention as a body, and to vote as a
unit on all questions. It was further resolved that the
party insist upon the admission of twenty to fifty of its
delegates, and upon the appointment of seven socialists on
the platform committee.

Dr. Douai, as spokesman of the caucus, presented these
demands to the convention "in behalf of 100,000 voters
represented by the Socialist Labor Party."

The demands were substantially granted. The socialists
received the required representation on the platform committee and were allowed forty-four votes on the floor of
the convention. At a later stage of the proceedings, however, a ruling was made that all votes be taken by States,
to which ruling the socialists refused to submit, and during
the remainder of the convention they abstained from
voting.

The main work of the socialists in the convention was in
connection with the drafting of the platform. They strove
to bring the views exprest in that document as close to
their conceptions as possible. But they had an extremely
difficult task. The convention was composed of many heterogeneous reform elements with many incongruous social

views. The currency reformer, the land reformer, the anti-monopolist, the Chinese-exclusion advocate, and the pure and simple trade-unionist were all represented. Each demanded recognition in the platform for his special nostrum. In most instances the demands were acceded to with little regard for the unity and consistency of the document as a whole. The influence of the socialist thought was unmistakable in the opening planks of the platform, which were as follows:

"Civil government should guarantee the divine right of every laborer to the results of his toil, thus enabling the producers of wealth to provide themselves with the means for physical comfort and the facilities for mental, social, and moral culture; and we condemn as unworthy of our civilization the barbarism which imposes upon the wealth producers a state of perpetual drudgery as the price of bare animal existence.

"Notwithstanding the enormous increase of productive power, the universal introduction of labor-saving machinery, and the discovery of new agents for the increase of wealth, the task of the laborer is scarcely lightened, and the hours of toil are but little shortened, and few producers are lifted from poverty into comfort and pecuniary independence."

It was also on motion of the socialist Morgan that the convention, after much discussion, adopted a plank calling for the collective ownership of land.

On the whole, however, the socialists were not well satisfied with the platform and management of the Greenback Party, and participated in its presidential campaign in a half-hearted way. Immediately after the campaign the alliance with the Greenbackers was dissolved, never to be renewed again, except in a few isolated instances.

In the elections of 1881 the socialists took no part. "A socialist campaign in this country is useless," argued the New York *Volkszeitung*, "unless the American vote can be reached by it. But as the party is constituted at present, it can only reach the German working men." The *Volks-*

zeitung, therefore, advised members to concentrate their efforts on the establishment of an English socialist daily newspaper.

The disorganized state of the socialist movement during the following years, and the all-absorbing struggles with anarchism, made it impossible to conduct a systematic political campaign. Only local candidates were occasionally nominated by way of exception. Thus the party invariably nominated a candidate for Assembly in the Tenth Assembly District of New York, which during these years uniformly cast from 700 to 1,000 socialist votes.

In the presidential elections of 1884 the Socialist Labor Party nominated no candidates, and supported none of those nominated by other parties. The continued abstention from voting and the seemingly hopeless condition of American politics made the party skeptical as to the efficacy of the ballot-box, and the following statement, published in the Zurich *Social Democrat* on November 14, 1884,[7] is probably a correct expression of the contemporaneous attitude of socialists on the subject:

"Our comrades in America have taken no part in the elections, but have proclaimed abstention from voting. Both great political parties, the Republican and the Democratic, are capitalistic. The struggle against corruption was a war cry in which the socialists would surely have joined, but the men who first sounded it were of such quality that the incorrigible skeptics doubted their ability and even their desire to clean out the Augean stables. The third party, composed of former Greenbackers and others, with General Butler at the head, our party could also not support, because the society was a rather promiscuous one, and General Butler, a skilful demagog but by no means a reliable customer. To enter into the campaign independently, our party was too weak, and, what is still more important, it was of the opinion that the presidential elections are nowadays but a humbug and cannot be anything else."

[7] Reprinted in Waltershausen's "Der Moderne Sozialismus," p. 268.

It was only in 1886 that the Socialist Labor Party was roused from its political lethargy. The intense labor excitements of that year, engendered by a long period of industrial depression and the struggles for an eight-hour work-day, assumed the form of a political movement in many important places.

In few American cities was the eight-hour-day agitation as intense as in Milwaukee, where the Knights of Labor had succeeded in organizing the workers of almost all important industries. Many of the labor organizations, especially those largely composed of Germans, were strongly influenced by the socialists under the leadership of Paul Grottkau, who at that period edited the Milwaukee *"Arbeiter Zeitung."* Towards the first day of May the movement of the workers grew so strong, and the opposition to it on the part of the employers so determined, that an open battle became unavoidable.

Strikes and lockouts followed each other in rapid succession, and by the 5th of May it was estimated that about 15,000 workingmen, over one-half of the voters of the city, were idle. The excitement was general and intense. Several socialist and labor leaders, including Paul Grottkau, were arrested. The State militia was called out by Governor Rusk, and collisions of a serious nature occurred between the soldiers and the strikers. During one of such collisions, the militia fired on an unarmed crowd, killing two men and three boys and wounding several others.

The strike movement was eventually subdued, but the resentment of the workers survived and exprest itself in unmistakable language at the polls in the fall elections of 1886. In that year a "Union Labor Party" was organized in the State of Wisconsin by the Knights of Labor in conjunction with the remnants of the Greenback Party, and the movement was strongly supported by the socialists. Its principal strength was in the city of Milwaukee, where the party polled over 12,000 votes, electing its candidates for Congress and State legislature as well as for all county offices.

In Chicago a "United Labor Party" was organized on

the initiative of the Central Labor Union. The party was composed of members of the American Federation of Labor, Knights of Labor, radical elements of all kinds, socialists, and even anarchists. It cast over 20,000 votes in the fall of 1886 for its county ticket, and in the following spring mustered no less than 28,000 votes for its candidate for Mayor.

In Maine, New Hampshire, Connecticut, New Jersey, New York, Maryland, Ohio, Minnesota, Michigan, Iowa, Missouri, and Colorado similar parties were organized. They were composed principally of trade-unionists, Knights of Labor, and Greenbackers; and in New York, New Jersey, Missouri, and Ohio the socialists also supported the movement. The parties were known in different places as "United Labor Party," "Union Labor Party," "Industrial Labor Party," "Labor Reform Party," or simply "Labor Party." They reached their highest state in the fall elections of 1886, when several of their local tickets were elected. The next year witnessed a rapid decline of the movement, and in 1888 very few of them survived.

By far the most important political campaign of that period conducted by organized labor was that in the city of New York. Here the Central Labor Union initiated a movement for independent political action of working men in the early part of the summer of 1886. On the 5th day of July of that year a conference of representatives of labor organizations was held in Clarendon Hall for the purpose of launching the movement. Over 300 delegates were present, and on a vote being taken, 286 of these declared themselves emphatically in favor of nominating an independent labor ticket in the ensuing mayoralty campaign, and only forty opposed the plan. Several more conferences were held, and the movement grew in strength and enthusiasm from week to week. A municipal platform was adopted, and a permanent party organization was created under the name of "United Labor Party" of New York. On the 2d day of September, 1886, a city convention of the party was held in Clarendon Hall, and amid deafening cheers and shouts of enthusiasm the convention nominated as its candidate for Mayor and the standard bearer of the young movement—Henry George.

3. THE HENRY GEORGE MOVEMENT

Henry George was born in Philadelphia in 1839. He finished his school education at the age of thirteen, worked a short time as office boy, then went to sea, visiting many parts of the world. At the age of sixteen he returned to Philadelphia and learned the trade of typesetting, but following his irrepressible love for travel, soon enlisted again on shipboard, went to Calcutta, and thence to San Francisco, where he finally settled.

In San Francisco he worked successively as compositor and reporter, and in 1871 he was one of the founders and part owners of the San Francisco *Evening Post*. It was at this time that George became interested in the study of social problems. In 1871 he published his first work, "Our Land and Land Policy," which attracted scant attention. But an altogether different reception was accorded to his second work, published eight years later under the title "Progress and Poverty."

As intimated by the rather striking title, the work is devoted to an inquiry into the causes of the persistence of general poverty alongside of increasing wealth. Our present era, argued George, has been marked by a prodigious development of wealth-producing power. It should have been expected that the increase of general wealth and material comfort would benefit mankind as a whole; that poverty would vanish; that all vices and crimes engendered by it would disappear, and that a state of general social happiness and contentment would ensue. But instead of this we see the increased blessings of civilization enjoyed by a comparatively small number of men, while the greater part of the population still succumbs to poverty, and destitution is most appalling where luxury is greatest. There is evidently some factor in our system of wealth production and distribution, concluded the author, which associates poverty with the progress of our civilization. What is that factor? Henry George found it to be the private ownership of land, *i. e.*, all "natural opportunities," such as soil, mines, rights of way, etc., exclusive of the improvements on them. There can be no right to property in land, he declared. Man has a right to the possession of the products of his labor. A man who makes a coat, builds a house, or constructs a machine, has an exclusive right of ownership in it. But who made the earth, and what man can claim the right to give or sell it? The value of land has no reference to the cost of production or the labor expended on it. The value of the labor expended on it is the value of the improvement, but the value of land as land depends on natural causes, such as fertility; or social causes, such as the agglomeration of a vast number of people in a certain area. Justice, therefore, requires that the land and the increase of its value be the common heritage of the whole nation. But, instead, it is being monopolized by a small class of landowners, who appropriate all the benefits of it, and exact a high rent for its use and occupation. This system makes it possible for a number of men to hold large areas of land for speculative purposes, thus withdrawing it from actual use. And as land is in the last analysis the source of all wealth, the withholding of any part of it results in the curtailment of wealth production for the nation.

Furthermore, so long as land is free to all, everybody can gain his subsistence by agriculture or by industrial pursuits on a small scale, but as soon as land becomes private property, it is only the man who can afford to pay a high rent—the capitalist—that can engage in any industry, while the poor man is compelled to sell his labor for the best price obtainable.

And, lastly, rent being an arbitrary tax on production, draws from the profits of capital and the wages of labor alike, impoverishes both, gives rise to industrial crises, and produces an unjust distribution of wealth which is building up immense fortunes in the hands of a few while the masses grow relatively poorer and poorer. "Nothing short of making land common property can permanently relieve poverty," concluded George.

This object, however, the author desired to attain gradually by means of an increasing tax on land values, so that the tax should ultimately equal the full rental value of the land, with the result that, tho the title to it might still be nominally in the individual owner, all income from it would go to the State.

George proposed to abolish all taxes save this tax on land values, and his plan hence is known as the "Single Tax."

To understand the great influence of his book it must be borne in mind that it appeared at a time when social problems and land-reform theories were warmly agitated. The fascinating style in which the book was written and the tone of self-assurance and sincerity of conviction with which the novel and bold conclusions of the author were announced, contributed largely to its success. It was one of the popular books which, like popular leaders, appear occasionally as the embodiment of a vague public sentiment, and give color and direction to that sentiment.

The book aroused spontaneous enthusiasm. It was printed in many editions, translated into many languages, and became a universal topic of discussion in labor circles and scientific publications. The obscure Western journalist all of a sudden found himself one of the most famous men of his day. His name was a household word in all parts of the United States. He gained thousands of ardent disciples in this country as well as in Europe, and numerous "land and labor clubs " were organized for the purpose of propagating his theories. George was an eloquent and convincing speaker, and the extensive lecture tours arranged for him in the principal cities of the United States, as well as in Ireland and England, served to enhance his popularity still more.

Such was the man whom the working people of New York chose for their leader in the municipal campaign of 1886.

George did not accept the nomination without attaching a rather unusual condition to it. He demanded that his constituents obtain the signatures of at least 30,000 citizens and residents of the city of New York to a statement that they desired his nomination and would vote for him. This, he explained, would accomplish two purposes: It would demonstrate that there was a popular demand for his candidacy, and would show to the indifferent that he had good chances of being elected, so that they could vote for him without fear of "throwing away" their votes. This extraordinary condition did not impair the enthusiasm of the movement by any means. On the contrary, it instigated the working men to greater activity. Within a very short time more than the required number of signatures were obtained, and the campaign was in full swing. Meetings were held by the score, campaign literature was distributed broadcast, and when, toward the end of September, a street demonstration was arranged, no less than 35,000 people marched in line enthusiastically shouting the name of Henry George under the loud applause of the sympathetic crowds of bystanders. In October the United Labor Party established *The Leader,* a daily newspaper published in the interest of the Henry George campaign. It was a four-page paper, sold at one cent, and soon reached a circulation of 100,000.

The movement assumed such proportions that the old parties took alarm and sought to offset the popularity of George by nominating the strongest available candidates at the head of their tickets. The Democrats nominated the noted philanthropist and son-in-law of Peter Cooper, Abram S. Hewitt, while the Republicans nominated Theodore Roosevelt, then a young and promising politician.

The day of election was one of great excitement for the city of New York. When the vote was finally counted it was announced that George had received over 68,000 votes to about 90,000 cast for Hewitt and 60,000 for Roosevelt.[8]

[8] The supporters of Henry George contended that the latter had actually been elected Mayor and that he had been "counted out." This belief caused George and his followers to agitate for the introduction of the Australian secret-ballot system in the State of New York, a reform which has since been realized, not only in that State, but throughout the Union.

Thus closed the most memorable political campaign ever conducted by the working men of New York.

The socialists were at no time in sympathy with Henry George as the apostle of a new social creed. While they agreed with his criticism of the present system of wealth production and distribution, they differed widely from him in the analysis of the causes of the evil and the remedy proposed.

The single-taxer regards land-ownership as probably the most fundamental factor in our industrial life; the socialist considers modern factory production the dominant feature of present civilization. The single-taxer recognizes but one form of economic exploitation—rent, *i. e.*, the return made for the use of land; the socialist asserts that "surplus value," *i. e.*, the unpaid part of the working man's labor, is the source of all exploitation, and that it is from this "surplus value" that rent as well as interest and profit are drawn. The single-taxer thus consistently sees the root of all social and economic evils of our civilization in the private ownership of land—in which term he includes all franchises and special privileges for the use of land—while the socialist opposes the private ownership of *all* socially necessary means of production, machinery, etc., as well as land as above defined.

The single-taxer would abolish the landlord and monopolist of "land values," but continue the existence of the capitalist and wage-worker; the socialist strives to wipe out all class distinction and to introduce complete economic freedom. The single-tax theory professes to be an absolute and scientific truth applicable to all ages and conditions alike, while socialism claims to be a theory growing out of modern economic conditions, and relying for its realization largely upon the steadily growing concentration and socialization of industry. The single-taxer, lastly, is an earnest supporter of the competitive system of industry, while the socialist is an ardent collectivist.

Thus the two social theories differ very materially in their views, aims, and methods.

The socialists of New York never attempted to conciliate or minimize this difference. They supported the Henry George movement solely for the reason that they saw in it a movement of labor against capital, and they indorsed the candidacy of Henry George "not on account of his single-tax theory, but in spite of it," as the *Volkszeitung* put it.

Nor did Henry George and his most prominent supporters feel any friendlier toward the socialists. The platform of the United Labor Party as originally drafted consisted substantially of the so-called "immediate demands" of the Socialist Labor Party, and wound up with the classic declaration of the Communist Manifesto that "the emancipation of the working class can only be accomplished by the working class itself." As soon as George accepted the nomination, the platform was replaced by a document of an entirely different tenor, based in the main on the land theory of Henry George, and demanding various land, currency, and tax reforms, along with some factory and labor legislation.

During the campaign the antagonism between the two camps was carefully represt by both sides, but as soon as the election was over, it broke out into open hostility.

The war was first conducted on purely theoretical grounds: the socialist press combated the single-tax theory as such, while George retorted in kind by criticizing the theories of socialism in his *Standard*.

But when the campaign of 1887 drew nearer, the controversy assumed a more practical aspect, and finally led to an open rupture. The immediate pretext was the interpretation of Article 1, Section 2, of the constitution of the United Labor Party, which required members of the organization to sever their connections with other political parties. On a previous occasion the New York County Executive Committee had decided that the section had no application to the Socialist Labor Party, since the latter was not a political party in the accepted sense of the term; but when the County general committee met on August 4, 1887, the point was raised again, and the previous decision was reversed, thus virtually expelling the

members of the Socialist Labor Party. The decision precipitated a general commotion in the organization. Several
Assembly districts protested against the ruling, and demanded its rescission, others approved of it, and in a few
instances the question produced schisms in the district organizations.

It was in these circumstances that the State convention of
the United Labor Party assembled in Syracuse on the
17th of August. It was expected that it would deal
with the status of the socialists in the party, and both sides
were represented in full numbers. Out of the 169 delegates who presented credentials, twenty-six were avowed
socialists, while many more were in sympathy with them.
The Eighth, Tenth, and Fourteenth Assembly Districts of
New York were each represented by two rival delegations,
one elected by the socialist elements within the organization,
the other by the anti-socialists, and the debate arose on the
question of the regularity of the contesting delegations. In
the ensuing discussion great latitude was allowed, and all
phases of socialism were drawn into the debate.

Socialism was warmly defended by S. E. Schewitsch,
Walter Vrooman, Lawrence Gronlund, Hugo Vogt, Col. R.
J. Hinton, and others, while the campaign against it was
led by Henry George himself, who was ably seconded by
McGlynn, McMackin, and others. The discussion lasted
about eighteen hours, and when a vote was finally taken,
it was found that the socialists were barred from the convention by a large majority.

The convention thereupon nominated a State ticket,
headed by Henry George as candidate for the office of Secretary of State, adopted a platform, and adjourned.

The breach between the Socialists and the United Labor
Party had the effect of weakening the organization to a
great extent. The socialists had been energetic and devoted workers in the movement, and much of the success of
the campaign of 1886 had been due to their activity. Besides, the labor excitement of 1886 had been greatly allayed,
the eight-hour-day agitation relaxed its intensity, and the
working men gradually lost interest in their political or-

ganization. The United Labor Party was on the decline, and its dissolution was accelerated by the strife among the leaders. In the contest between George and McGlynn for supremacy within the organization the latter prevailed. George withdrew from the United Labor Party and cast his fortunes with the Democratic Party.

Under the leadership of McGlynn the United Labor Party conducted one more political campaign, that of 1888, but the results were so insignificant that the movement was abandoned as hopeless, and no attempt was made to revive it in the following election.

4. INDEPENDENT POLITICS AGAIN

The fate of the socialist delegates in the Syracuse convention of the United Labor Party had only served to enhance the popularity of their cause. The expulsion of the socialists from the organization on technical grounds was resented by many adherents of Henry George and caused a revulsion of feeling in favor of the socialists.

When the defeated delegates returned to New York, they were received with a veritable ovation. Their report and comments were heard by several thousand working men at a mass-meeting held in the large hall of the Cooper Union Institute, and it was then and there decided to call a conference of all radical labor organizations to consider the advisability of organizing a political party in opposition to the United Labor Party.

The first meeting of the conference was held on the 4th of September, 1887, at Webster Hall, in the city of New York. Eighty-seven organizations were represented, fifty-six of these being trade-unions and thirty-one political organizations, mostly subdivisions of the Socialist Labor Party.

The conference constituted itself a political party under the name of Progressive Labor Party, adopted a platform which was practically identical with the one the United Labor Party originally had adopted and subsequently discarded, and called a State convention for the purpose of nominating candidates.

The convention was held in New York on the 28th of September. John Swinton was nominated for Secretary of State against Henry George, but he declined on account of failing health, and J. Edward Hall [9] was substituted in his stead.

The campaign of the Progressive Labor Party, practically confined to the city of New York, was brief and rather weak. The total number of votes cast barely exceeded 5,000. This was the last political campaign conducted by the Socialist Labor Party in conjunction with any other political organization.

The enthusiasm of the movement of 1886 had aroused the socialists from their political lethargy, while the disappointments of 1887 had demonstrated to them the futility of fusion politics. Henceforward the socialists adhered unswervingly to the policy of independent political action. The socialists of New York initiated the movement by placing a full ticket in the field in 1888. In the city of New York the gubernatorial, mayoralty, congressional, and presidential elections that year coincided. J. Edward Hall was nominated for Governor, Alexander Jonas for Mayor, and a full list of State, local, and congressional candidates was put in the field. But a rather embarrassing question arose on the nomination of a presidential ticket. A presidential ticket presupposes a national campaign, but the political activity of the party was practically confined to the city of New York. Besides, the platform of the Socialist Labor Party at that time contained a plank demanding the abolition of the Presidency of the United States, and it seemed inconsistent to nominate a candidate for an office to the existence of which the party was opposed. The difficulty was finally overcome by a rather ingenious device: the party nominated a full ticket of presidential electors with instructions to cast their votes in the electoral college for "No President."

In that campaign less than 3,000 votes were cast for the

[9] Born at Glen Cove, L. I., in 1851. He was a machinist by trade. and very prominent in the local socialist and trade-union movements alike. He died of consumption in 1889.

socialist ticket in the entire State of New York. Of this
number about 2,500 fell to the credit of the city of New
York, 232 were cast in Albany, 49 in Syracuse, and 32 in
Utica. Outside of the State of New York the socialists
had nominated candidates in only two places, Milwaukee
and New Haven. They received 586 votes in the former
and 82 in the latter.

The results were so disheartening that the New York
Volkszeitung, and with it some of the foremost party leaders, again counseled abstention from politics.

But the advocates of independent politics within the
ranks of the party were by no means discouraged by the
first failure, and urged the policy of continued participation in all elections regardless of results.

The next national convention met in Chicago in 1889 and
upheld the latter policy. In 1890 we find the socialists of
New York again actively engaged in politics. Some radical
reform elements led by the "nationalists," constituted
themselves as a "Commonwealth Party," and at first sought
to bring about a political agreement between themselves
and the socialists. But at the very first conference it became manifest that they differed materially in aims and
views, and the thought of political cooperation was abandoned. The Commonwealth Party did not succeed in obtaining the requisite number of signatures for its candidates
on the State ticket, and limited itself to local nominations in
the city of New York, where it polled less than 700 votes.
The Socialist Labor Party nominated a full State ticket
headed by Franz Gerau, a popular Brooklyn physician, as
candidate for the office of Judge of the Court of Appeals,
and polled 13,704 votes in the State.

What greatly contributed to the comparative success
of the ticket was the introduction of the Australian secret-
ballot system in the State of New York. Owing to this
system, the names of the party's candidates appeared on the
ballot in every one of the sixty-one counties of the State,
and, to the great surprise of the socialists themselves, every
county but one (Delaware) cast some votes for the ticket.

In the following year the socialist vote in the State of

New York rose to 14,651 for Daniel De Leon, the party's candidate for Governor. At the same time the socialists of Massachusetts and New Jersey made their début in politics, the former polling a vote of 1,429, and the latter, 472.

In 1892 the socialists for the first time nominated a presidential ticket in the United States. This step was decided upon in a "national" party conference held in the month of September at the party headquarters in the city of New York. The conference was attended by eight representatives coming from the States of New York, New Jersey, Massachusetts, Connecticut, and Pennsylvania. Simon Wing, of Boston, Mass., a manufacturer of photographic instruments, was nominated for President, and Charles H. Matchett of Brooklyn, N. Y., an electrician, for Vice-President. The party had tickets in six States and polled a total vote of 21,512. From that time on new States were drawn into the circle of socialist politics every year, and the socialist vote rose slowly but steadily, as the following figures will indicate:

1893—25,666;
1894—30,120;
1895—34,869.

In the presidential elections of 1896 the socialists nominated Charles H. Matchett for President and Matthew Maguire for Vice-President, and polled a total vote of 36,275 in twenty States of the Union.

In the following year, however, the Socialist Labor Party vote rose to 55,550, and in 1898 it reached 82,204.[10] This was the highest vote ever polled by the Socialist Labor Party.

[10] The figures are taken from Lucien Sanial's "Socialist Almanac."

IV.—THE SOCIALIST LABOR PARTY AND THE TRADE-UNIONS

1. Local Organizations

The efforts of the Socialist Labor Party to gain the good will of the trade-unions have been described in a previous chapter. These efforts, while not very successful on the whole, were not entirely barren of results.

A number of local trade-unions were in outspoken sympathy with the Socialist Labor Party, and the influence of the party was especially pronounced in some of the central organizations formed by such local unions. Of the latter type of organizations, the most important was the Central Labor Union of New York, of which the following is a brief historical sketch:

In the beginning of 1882, when the Irish land question was warmly agitated in this country, several labor organizations arranged a joint mass-meeting in the large hall of Cooper Institute, to express their sympathy with the Irish tenants. The meeting was attended by a number of representative trade-union members, and the formation of a permanent central committee of all trade-unions in the city of New York was then and there suggested. This suggestion was promptly taken up and on the 30th of January, 1882, the first meeting was held. Fourteen organizations were represented, the German unions predominating. The Central Labor-Union adopted a platform containing the principal socialist demands.

Philip Van Patten, national secretary of the Socialist Labor Party, delivered an address, and Matthew Maguire, another socialist, was elected secretary. Within six months, the number of organizations represented rose to forty-five, and in a very short time it became the most important factor in the labor movement of New York. The friendly relations of the Central Labor-Union with the Socialist Labor Party continued for several years.

In 1882, and again in 1883, the Central Labor-Union engaged in the municipal campaigns of New York as an independent organization, polling a little over 10,000 votes each time, and in 1886 it initiated the famous Henry George campaign.

The strength developed by organized labor during the latter campaign attracted the attention of the professional politicians, who now vied with each other in an endeavor to gain the good graces of the delegates to the Central Labor Union. As long as the enthusiasm of the George movement lasted, these attempts were unsuccessful, but with the collapse of the movement, a period of political demoralization set in, and many labor leaders were found to lend a willing ear to the promises of the old party managers. Rumors of "boodle" and "corruption" became common, factions were formed, and finally it came to an open breach. In February, 1889, after a stormy meeting in which charges of bribery in connection with the brewers' pool boycott were freely exchanged, about sixty delegates left the meeting-hall in a body, and formed a new organization under the name of Central Labor Federation. After a separate existence of a few months the two organizations opened negotiations for a reunion. Several conferences were held, some objectionable delegates were withdrawn from the Central Labor Union as a concession to the Federation, and the two bodies in December, 1889, were formally reunited.

But the union was not lasting. The antagonism between the opposing elements broke out anew, the meetings of the body were consumed in acrimonious discussions and mutual recriminations, and in June, 1890, another division took place, and the Central Labor Federation was revived.

The Central Labor Federation consisted originally of thirty trade-unions, but the number soon grew to seventy-two. Among these were some of the strongest and most progressive organizations. The Socialist Labor Party was formally represented in the body, and for a long time exercised a controlling influence on all its deliberations. In 1900 the two organizations again consolidated, assuming the name of CENTRAL FEDERATED UNION.

The Central Labor Union and the Central Labor Federation were by no means the only organizations of that kind in the United States. Similar organizations under the same or different names sprang up in most industrial cities and some of them, notably the Central Labor Federations of Brooklyn and Hudson County, the Central Labor Unions of Rochester, Buffalo, Cincinnati, and Cleveland, the Trades Council of New Haven, and the Trade and Labor Assembly of Chicago, were in avowed sympathy with the socialist movement.

Its greatest support, however, the Socialist Labor Party received from the German trade-unions in the city of New York, which in 1885 had organized a separate central body under the name of the UNITED GERMAN TRADES OF THE CITY OF NEW YORK. This body was called into existence primarily for the purpose of supporting the labor press. During the four years of its existence it rendered valuable services to the New York *Volkszeitung* by extending its circulation, increasing its advertisements, and raising funds for its publication. It was also on the initiative of the United German Trades that the English organ of the Henry George campaign, the daily *Leader,* was established in 1886, and when that paper later on passed into the hands of the socialists, the German Trades assisted it financially and otherwise to the end of its brief career. The United German Trades were organized by the representatives of about twelve trade-unions, but the number was soon quadrupled.

The example of New York was followed by Brooklyn, Philadelphia, Cleveland, Baltimore, Buffalo, and some other places, in all of which central bodies of German trade-unions were formed, and in 1887 the New York organization initiated a plan to form a national confederation of German trade-unions. But the plan never materialized, and the United German Trades soon began to decline. As long as these bodies adhered to the original object of their creation, which was the support of the labor press, they performed a useful function and prospered, but when toward 1888 they began to occupy themselves with general trade matters, they came in conflict with existing older and stronger central labor bodies, and not infrequently caused considerable confusion in the local movement. Many trade-unions disapproved of the new policy, and withdrew their delegates, and the United German Trades gradually disintegrated.

An organization similar in scope and character to that of the United German Trades was the UNITED HEBREW TRADES, organized in New York toward 1888. In the beginning of the eighties the immigration of Russian Jews to this country had assumed enormous dimensions. Thousands of these immigrants landed at New York every week, and the majority of them settled on the lower East side. Their principal industry was tailoring, and within a few years they acquired a practical monopoly of the trade. Within the bounds of their settlement in New York, which became the most congested spot on the face of the globe, hundreds of tailoring shops sprang up. These shops, popularly known as "sweat-shops," were as a rule conducted by middlemen or "contractors," with whose living rooms they were frequently connected. They were always dingy, unclean, and ill-ventilated, and in them scores of men, women, and children were indiscriminately crowded together, working at times fifteen hours and more at a stretch for incredibly low wages.

Several attempts had been made from time to time to organize them, but they met with poor success until the spring of 1888. By that time the wages of the Jewish tailors had sunk so very low, and their conditions of work had become so very wretched, that even they, the men of few needs, rebelled.

A series of strikes was begun by them. The "knee-pants-makers" were the first to open fire. They were soon followed by the "pants-makers, cloak-makers, shirt-makers, and jacket-makers." Within a very few weeks an army of no less than 15,000 Jewish tailors laid down work, demanding better pay and shorter hours.

The strikers were unorganized and undisciplined, and it is very doubtful whether they would have accomplished anything substantial without the aid of the socialists. The latter practically assumed entire charge of the contest. They organized the strikers into trade-unions, collected funds for them, directed their battles, and led them to victory. It was shortly after that and likewise on the initiative of the Jewish socialists that the United Hebrew Trades were organized. It was, therefore, natural that there should have been at all times a strong bond of sympathy between the Jewish trade-union movement and the socialist movement: most of the organizers, leaders, and speakers of the Jewish trade-unions came from the ranks of the Socialist Labor Party, and in return the organized Jewish working men heartily cooperated with the party in all it undertook, and promptly responded to all of its appeals.

United Hebrew Trades after the pattern of the New York body were also organized in Newark and Philadelphia, and in one or two more places.

The Socialist Labor Party thus acquired considerable influence in several important local organizations, but its struggles for a footing in the great national bodies of trade-unions were much harder and less successful, as will be shown in the following pages.

2. THE KNIGHTS OF LABOR

The once powerful order of the Knights of Labor had a very humble beginning. In the sixties of the last century the garment-cutters of Philadelphia organized a union of their trade. It soon incurred the displeasure of employers, and its members were frequently compelled to choose between their organization and their jobs. In these circumstances it was deemed best to abandon the open organization, and in December, 1869, seven members, headed by Uriah S. Stephens and James L. Wright, organized a secret society under the name of the Noble Order of Knights of Labor.

The first election of permanent officers was held in January, 1870. The following officers were chosen: Venerable Sage, Past-Officer, James L. Wright; Master Workman, U. S. Stephens; Worthy Foreman, Robert W. Keen; Worthy Inspector, William Cook; Unknown Knight, Joseph S. Kennedy.

The society was originally composed exclusively of **gar-**

ment-cutters, and at the end of the first year of its existence numbered only sixty-nine members. In 1871, it was decided to extend the operations of the Order to other trades, and the period of growth of the Knights began. During the next year no less than nineteen new unions, denominated "Local Assemblies," were organized under its auspices in Philadelphia alone, and similar organizations soon followed in other cities and States.

In 1873 the "locals" of Philadelphia formed the first "District Assembly" of the Order. This plan of organization was adopted by other Local Assemblies, and in 1877 there were over fifteen District Assemblies in Pennsylvania, New Jersey, South Carolina, Connecticut, Ohio, and other States. District Assembly No. 1 of Philadelphia was by tacit consent regarded as the head of the organization.

Up to 1878 the Order remained a strictly secret organization. Even its name was not divulged to the uninitiated. On all official communications and calls it was designated as "N. and H. O. of the * * * * * of North America," the five asterisks standing for "Knights of Labor."

As the organization grew in membership and power, the veil of secrecy surrounding it gave rise to the most adventurous and absurd rumors. Inventive newspapers told gruesome stories of widespread communistic and incendiary plots hidden behind the cabalistic sign of the asterisks. The "criminal combination" was fiercely denounced from the pulpit. The unknown, ever present and dangerous organization seriously disturbed the peace of good citizens. In these circumstances, U. S. Stephens, the Grand Master Workman of the Order, issued a call for an emergency meeting "to consider the expediency of making the name of the Order public, for the purpose of defending it from the fierce assaults and defamations made upon it by press, clergy, and corporate capital." The meeting was held in Philadelphia in June, 1878, and the name, object and declaration of principles of the Order were made public.

During the same year the first national convention of the Knights of Labor was held in Reading, Pa., and a central executive body under the title of "General Assembly" was created.

After that the Order spread with unprecedented rapidity. At the third meeting of the General Assembly, in Chicago in September, 1879, it was reported that over 700 Local Assemblies had been organized, of which number, however, only 102 reported. In 1883 the membership numbered over 52,000; in 1884 it rose to 71,000, and in 1885 to 111,000. In the year 1886 the Order reached its high-water mark. The strike fever and labor struggles of that year caused a veritable rush of new members; hundreds of new Assemblies were organized; thousands of new members of all trades were admitted daily. The total number of members of the Order during that year was variously estimated at from 500,000 to 800,000.

The period of rapid growth was soon succeeded by one of reaction. The numerous defeats of the Knights in the strikes of 1886 created a spirit of dissatisfaction, and when the American Federation of Labor was organized at about that time, members deserted the Order in large numbers to join the new organization. In 1891 the total membership of the Knights of Labor was said to be less than 200,000, and it has been steadily decreasing until to-day a very few thousand men scattered in different parts of the country are all that is left of it.

U. S. Stephens, the founder of the Knights of Labor, was the Master Workman of the Order until 1879, when Terence V. Powderly was elected in his stead, and the latter remained in office continually until 1893, when he was in turn succeeded by J. R. Sovereign.

The first declaration of principles was adopted in 1878. It was in substance the platform prepared by George E. McNeil for the Rochester labor congress of 1874.[11] The

[11] A different and more romantic version of the origin of the docu, ment is given in the *Sozialist*, vol. iv, No. 10, by the author, writing under the *nom de plume* of "Loma." The writer, a socialist, and at one time a prominent "Knight," relates that on some occasions in 1881 he interrogated the old U. S. Stephens on the subject, and received the following reply: "In the course of my travels through Europe some thirty years ago, I made the acquaintance of a certain

preamble to the declaration opens with the following statement:

"The alarming development and aggressiveness of great capitalists and corporations, unless checked, will inevitably lead to the pauperization and hopeless degradation of the toiling masses.

"It is imperative, if we desire to enjoy the full blessings of life, that a check be placed upon unjust accumulation and the power for evil of aggregated wealth."

The Order further declares it to be one of its aims: "To secure for the workers the full enjoyment of the wealth they create," and among others, makes the following demands upon the State:

"IV. That the public lands, the heritage of the people, be reserved for actual settlers; not another acre for railroads or speculators; and that all lands now held for speculative purpose be taxed to their full value."

"XVIII. That the Government shall obtain possession, by purchase, under the rights of eminent domain, of all telegraphs, telephones, and railroads; and that hereafter no charter or license be issued to any corporation for construction or operation of any means of transporting intelligence, passengers, or freight."

One of the immediate tasks of the Order is stated to be the establishment of cooperative works, "such as will tend to supersede the wage system by the introduction of a cooperative industrial system."

This declaration of principles has never been changed or modified in any substantial feature. The radical tone of the document, and especially the passages quoted above,

London tailor by the name of Eccarius. Later on, when I organized the Clothing-Cutters' Union of Philadelphia, I received from time to time from the same tailor quantities of agitation pamphlets, among them this 'Manifesto.' I had never read the pamphlet before, but I found it contained pretty much everything I had thought out myself, and I used it largely in the preparation of the Declaration of Principles of the Order." The Eccarius referred to by Stephens was the well-known Internationalist and coworker of Marx and Engels, and the pamphlet sent by him was the famous "Communist Manifesto."

have frequently given rise to the belief that the order of
Knights of Labor was a socialist organization. But as a
matter of fact it was far from it. The founders of the
Order were undoubtedly men of radical views on social
problems, as appears from the public utterances of U. S.
Stephens and his early associates. The déclaration of
principles, apparently influenced by socialist thought,
probably exprest their actual views, but in later years,
and especially since the advent to power of T. V. Powderly,
it became a dead letter, and the efforts of the socialists to
gain a foothold in the Order were productive of poor
results.

As early as 1881 several leading members of the Socialist
Labor Party, among them Philip Van Patten, the National
Secretary, joined the Order, and the official organ of the
party repeatedly exprest its sympathy with the aims
and objects of the Knights of Labor. But the relations
of the two organizations remained purely platonic, and
only when the Order was already on the decline, toward
the beginning of the nineties, did socialists gain actual
influence in the organization. In the city of New York
one Local Assembly, known as the "Excelsior Club," was
composed almost exclusively of socialists, and many other
"locals" were in sympathy with socialism. In 1893 the
Socialist Labor Party obtained control of the New York
District Assembly, the erstwhile famous District Assembly
49 of the Knights of Labor, and succeeded in having some
of its members elected delegates to the General Assembly.
The socialist delegates were largely instrumental in the
defeat of Powderly for reelection that year, and their influence in the Order was so great that J. R. Sovereign, the
newly elected Master Workman, promised to appoint a
member of the Socialist Labor Party to the editorship of
the *Journal of the Knights of Labor,* the official organ of
the Order. The promise was not kept, and gave rise to a
heated controversy between Sovereign and Daniel De Leon,
the leader of the socialists in the Order and editor of
The People, the official organ of the Socialist Labor Party.

As a result of the controversy the annual convention held in Washington, in December, 1895, refused to seat De Leon as a delegate from District Assembly 49. The greater portion of the District withdrew, and all connections between the Socialist Labor Party and the Knights of Labor were severed.

3. THE AMERICAN FEDERATION OF LABOR

The ultimate aim of the Knights of Labor was to unite all working men of the United States into one body. The organization was effected not by trades, but by localities. It was strictly centralized, the General Assembly being the supreme authority for all organizations within the Order, and no national trade-union being allowed within it. This form of organization, as well as the complicated ritual and ceremonies which still survived after the veil of secrecy had been removed, and the autocratic demeanor of its officers largely impaired the usefulness of the organization for purposes of practical labor struggles. The feeling of discontent grew steadily, and in 1881 representatives of several national organizations called a convention of "international and national unions, trade councils, and local unions" for the purpose of forming a confederation of autonomous labor organizations for mutual support and for the furtherance of the general interests of labor.

The convention met in Pittsburg on the 15th of November, 1881. An organization was formed under the name "Federation of Organized Trades and Labor-Unions of the United States and Canada." The Federation was not at that period regarded as a rival of the Knights of Labor. No less than forty-eight of the 107 delegates who assisted in the formation of the new body represented "locals" of the Knights of Labor.

The second convention of the Federation was held in Cleveland in November, 1882. It was attended by only seventeen delegates. The Knights of Labor were not represented. The first note of hostility between the two bodies was sounded by the adoption of a resolution setting forth the objects of the Federation. The resolution contained the following passage aimed at the Knights of Labor:

"The Federation seeks to attain the industrial unity of the working men not by prescribing a stereotyped, uniform plan of organization for all, regardless of their experience or necessities, nor by antagonizing or aiming to destroy existing organizations, but by preserving all that is integral in them and widening their scope, so that each, without submerging its individuality, may act with the others in all that concerns them."

The third convention was held in the city of New York in August, 1883. Twenty-two organizations were represented by twenty-seven delegates, among them one woman, representing the National League of Working Women. Significant of the spirit prevailing was the passage of a resolution demanding of the Republican and Democratic Parties that they make public declarations at their next national conventions, of their attitude on the questions of the enforcement of the eight-hour law, the incorporation of national trade-unions, and the establishment of a national bureau of labor.

The fourth annual convention was held in Chicago in October, 1884, and was attended by twenty-five delegates. Resolutions condemning child labor were adopted, and the Supreme Court of New York was censured for having declared unconstitutional the law against manufacturing cigars in tenement-houses. But the most important and far-reaching act of the convention was the adoption of a resolution "that from May 1, 1886, eight hours shall constitute a legal work-day, and that all labor organizations should prepare for it."

The fifth convention met at Washington in December, 1885, attended by only eighteen delegates. Further preparations for the struggle for an eight-hour day were made, but in other respects the proceedings were of no significance. In the meantime the labor movement of the country had developed enormously. The eight-hour agitation initiated by the Federation, and the industrial prosperity had encouraged a general movement among the workers for improved conditions of labor. The ranks of existing trade-unions were rapidly swelled, and new organizations were formed.

At the same time the rivalry between the Order of Knights of Labor and the Federation of Organized Trade and Labor Unions developed into open hostility. Some attempts at conciliation and unification of forces were made by the Federation, but its advances were uniformly repelled by the Knights, who insisted on their narrow and oligarchic form of organization. The result was that a number of unaffiliated trade-unions, mistrusting the efficiency of both bodies, called an independent convention of labor organizations, to be held on December 8, 1886, in Columbus, Ohio. The Federation of Organized Trade and Labor Unions showed its diplomatic acumen by calling its convention for December 7th, at the same place. Here delegates from twenty-five national organizations, affiliated and unaffiliated, representing a membership of 316,469, met for a common purpose. The old Federation was dissolved, and the American Federation of Labor was founded in its stead.

The convention radically modified the declaration of principles and the constitution of the old Federation, appointed an executive committee of five officers, provided for larger revenues, and elected Samuel Gompers its first president.

After the reorganization the Federation progrest with large strides. Its annual convention of 1887 was attended by fifty-eight delegates, representing a membership of 618,000, according to official reports.

The convention of 1888, held at St. Louis, fixt the 1st day of May, 1890, as the date on which the general movement for an eight-hour work-day was to be inaugurated. A similar resolution was adopted one year later by the first international convention of socialists assembled in Paris, and the First of May has since become an international holiday of labor.

The resolution of the Federation was partly carried out.

In 1900 the United Brotherhood of Carpenters and Joiners, who were selected to lead the movement, struck for an eight-hour day; the brotherhood was successful in 137 cities and benefited over 46,000 working men of the trade. The cigar-makers and German typesetters had gained a similar reduction of hours of labor about two years earlier.

At the tenth annual convention of the Federation in Detroit in December, 1890, eighty-three organizations were represented by 103 delegates. The president reported having issued 282 charters during the preceding year, and the national organizations had established over 900 branches during the same period; since the convention of 1889, 1,163 strikes had taken place, of which 989 were successful, 98 terminated by compromise, and only 76 were lost.

The Federation grew in popular favor and routed the Knights of Labor completely. After 1887 the total number of its members had oscillated around the figure of 300,000, but since 1900 every year has marked a new increase.

The declaration of principles and objects of the American Federation of Labor is much more conservative in tone than that of the Knights of Labor, but the former organization was probably the more radical of the two. The Order of the Knights of Labor was an aristocratic body removed from the uninitiated world by a cover of secrecy and a complex system of rituals and ceremonies. The Federation, on the other hand, was at all times a democratic organization, freely and openly discussing all labor problems brought to its attention, in touch with the labor interests of the country, and ever engaged in open struggle with capital.

It is largely for these reasons that the Federation became a favorite field of operation for the socialists from the very start. Out of the 107 delegates who assisted at the formation of the body in 1881, six were outspoken socialists; and even Samuel Gompers, the president of the Federation, who in later days became a most decided opponent of socialism, was at that time very friendly to the movement. Some papers even went so far as to class him with the socialists.

Every convention of the Federation had a larger or smaller representation of socialists, who endeavored to utilize the occasion for the propaganda of their theories.

At the convention of 1885, the socialists for the first time introduced a resolution advocating independent political action by the working class. The resolution was defeated, but at its next annual convention the Federation by a large majority decided to urge upon its members "to give cordial support to the independent political movements of the working class."

At every one of the subsequent conventions the socialists managed to bring up their theories for general discussion in one form or another. At the convention of 1890 the subject received the most thorough treatment. In the summer preceding that convention the Central Labor Federation of New York applied to the American Federation of Labor for a charter. The charter was refused on the ground that the list of organizations affiliated with the body contained the name of the "American Section" of the Socialist Labor Party. This, Mr. Gompers declared, was in direct contravention of the provisions of Article IV., Section 5, of the constitution of the Federation, which prohibits affiliation with political parties.

The Central Labor Federation appealed from this decision to the convention, and sent Lucien Sanial, the representative of the "American Section," to argue the appeal.

The debate was long and heated. The socialists contended that their organization was not a political party in the ordinary sense of the term; that the Socialist Labor Party was an organization devoted to the interests of labor exclusively, and that its participation in politics was merely an incident in its struggle for the emancipation of the working class.

Gompers and his followers, on the other hand, argued that a political party is a political party, no matter what its ultimate objects may be. The issue was by no means drawn squarely as to the indorsement of socialism. Several delegates expressly declared that they were not hostile to socialism or to independent political action, but that they would vote against the seating of Sanial on the ground that they were opposed to the introduction of politics into the Federation. Still the ultimate vote on the admission of the Central Labor Federation—525 for to 1,699 [12] against—was probably a good test of the strength of socialism in the Federation at that time.

The subject of socialism was brought before the Federation in a more direct manner at its Chicago convention of 1893, when Thomas J. Morgan, a member of the Socialist Labor Party, introduced the following resolution:

"*Whereas,* The trade-unionists of Great Britain have, by the light of experience and logic of progress, adopted the principle of independent labor politics as an auxiliary to their economic action; and

"*Whereas,* Such action has resulted in the most gratifying success; and

"*Whereas,* Such independent labor politics are based upon the following program, to-wit:

"1.   Compulsory education;

"2.   Direct legislation;

"3.   A legal eight-hour work-day;

"4.   Sanitary inspection of workshop, mine and home;

"5.   Liability of employers for injury to health, body, or life;

"6.   The abolition of the contract system in all public works;

"7.   The abolition of the sweating system;

"8.   The municipal ownership of street-cars, and gas and electric plants for public distribution of light, heat, and power;

"9.   The nationalization of telegraphs, telephones, railroads, and mines;

"10.   The collective ownership by the people of all means of production and distribution;

[12] The vote in the conventions of the Federation is by representation, each delegate having one vote for every one hundred constituents.

"11. The principle of referendum in all legislation; therefore,

"*Resolved*, That this convention hereby indorses this political action of our British comrades; and

"*Resolved*, That this program and basis of a political labor movement be and is hereby submitted for the consideration of the labor organizations of America, with the request that their delegates to the next annual convention of the American Federation of Labor be instructed on this most important subject."

The resolution was discust with much earnestness and skill on both sides, but the socialists had decidedly the better end of the debate: the general destitution of the working men brought on by the industrial crisis of that year had made the minds of the delegates more receptive to radical social views, and the fact that the resolution called for a referendum vote on its final adoption, placed its opponents in the unpleasant position of withholding an important question from the consideration of their constituents. The resolution was carried by a comfortable majority, and during the next year the members of the numerous labor organizations affiliated with the Federation were discussing and voting on it. The socialists have always claimed that the resolution *in toto* had been overwhelmingly indorsed on this popular vote; their opponents in the trade-union movement deny it. Neither contention could be substantiated by proof, for, at the next convention of the Federation in December, 1894, when the resolution came again before the delegates for a vote in accordance with their instructions, the managing powers of the convention succeeded in side-tracking the issue by a clever trick. When the vote was to be taken on plank 10, which was the very substance of the resolution, calling as it did for the collective ownership of all means of production and distribution, a substitute was suddenly offered, calling for the grant of public lands to actual tillers of the soil only. The substitute was adopted after some debate, and the original motion was thus superseded by it.

The issues of socialism were introduced in the three succeeding annual conventions of the American Federation of Labor in the shape of one resolution or another, and on the average such resolutions received about one-fourth of the delegates' votes.

In 1898, the Kansas City convention of the Federation, after defeating a socialist resolution introduced by Max S. Hayes, of Cleveland, defined its attitude on the question in the following language:

"We hold that the trade-unions of America, as comprised in the American Federation of Labor, do not now, and never have, declared against discussion of economic and political questions in the meetings of the respective unions. We are committed against the indorsement or introduction of partizan politics, religious differences, or race prejudices. We hold it to be the duty of trade-unionists to study and discuss all questions that have any bearing upon their industrial or political liberty."

4. THE SOCIALIST TRADE AND LABOR ALLIANCE

The battles for socialism in the conventions of the Federation had since 1890 been waged by individual members of the Socialist Labor Party, without the direction or sanction of the official party administration. The recognized party leaders and the official party press had withdrawn their support and sympathy from the Federation ever since the Sanial incident at the Detroit convention, and, while many prominent party members, such as Thomas J. Morgan of Chicago, Max S. Hayes of Cleveland, and J. Mahlon Barnes of Philadelphia, continued their efforts to infuse the principles of socialism in the Federation, the party officials, headed by Daniel De Leon, engaged in a campaign to capture the Knights of Labor with the results shown above.

When the breach between the Socialist Labor Party and the Knights became final in November, 1895, the former, for the first time in the history of its career, found itself in open opposition to both existing national bodies of trade-union organizations.

The experience of the editor of *The People* and his associates during their brief but tempestuous careers in the American Federation of Labor and in the Order of the Knights of Labor had utterly discouraged them. They renounced all hope of ever winning over the "corrupt" bodies to socialism. The creation of a rival organization —THE SOCIALIST TRADE AND LABOR ALLIANCE—followed.

When the leaders of the Socialist Labor Party first laid their plans to obtain control of the Order of the Knights of Labor, they induced a number of friendly trade-unions in the city of New York, consisting principally of German and Jewish working men, to join the Order. These unions remained loyal to the Socialist Labor Party, even after the final breach between the party and the Knights; and when, in December, 1895, De Leon publicly repudiated the Order and called on them to withdraw from it, the great majority followed the call.

These seceders from the Knights of Labor formed the nucleus of the Socialist Trade and Labor Alliance, and other labor-unions in sympathy with the socialist movement followed their lead.

Within the first two or three years of its existence the Alliance issued over 200 charters to various labor organizations, the most important among them being the Central Labor Federation of New York with twenty-seven unions, the United Hebrew Trades of New York with twenty-five, the Socialist Labor Federation of Brooklyn with twelve, the Socialist Labor Federation of Newark with seven, and a Chicago central organization consisting of eight.

The Alliance had besides a number of local organizations in New York, New Jersey, Massachusetts, Rhode Island, Pennsylvania, Ohio, Illinois, and other States, and in the period of its bloom its membership was said to exceed 20,000.

The Socialist Trade and Labor Alliance, altho an organization of trade-unions, was to be a kind of auxiliary to the Socialist Labor Party.

In direct opposition to the views of the Federation and the Knights, it laid more stress on the political action of the working class than on their economic struggles; it invited the various "sections" of the Socialist Party to send representatives to its local councils; it requested the party as a whole to be represented in its conventions, and exacted a pledge from every local and national officer "that he would not affiliate with any capitalist party ·and not support any political action except that of the Socialist Labor Party."

In form of organization the Socialist Trade and Labor Alliance was an almost exact copy of the Order of Knights of Labor. The separate organizations were denominated Local Alliances, the "locals" of a city formed a District Alliance, and the supreme power of the organization was vested in a General Executive Board.

The Alliance was a failure from the start. Its inconsistent and rather vague aims and its highly centralized and antiquated system of organization rendered it inefficient for practical labor struggles, and the dictatorial policy of its leaders made the organization distasteful to many of the most important organizations affiliated with it. The first organizations to leave the Alliance were the Brewers' Unions of Brooklyn and Newark, of whom the General Executive Board had demanded that they sever their connections with their national organization. Other unions soon followed the lead of the brewers. Out of the 228 organizations chartered by the Alliance between December, 1895, and July 4, 1898, only 114 survived at the opening of its third annual convention, held at Buffalo in July, 1898, and of these only 54 were paying dues to the Alliance.[13] Shortly after the Buffalo convention the Central Federated Union of New York, by far the strongest organization of the Alliance, seceded, and the latter was left with a mere handful of men.

The Socialist Trade and Labor Alliance continued a practically nominal existence until the formation of the Industrial Workers of the World (which will be treated in a later chapter), into which its remnants were merged.

[13] "The Attitude of the Socialists toward the Trade-Unions," by N. I. Stone, New York, 1900.

Chapter IV

THE SOCIALIST PARTY

I.—RECENT FACTORS OF SOCIALIST GROWTH

MANY events in the industrial and political life of the nation during the closing decade of the last century contributed to the spread of socialist sentiment in this country. The tendency toward the concentration of industry had never before been so marked. "Not less than $500,000,000 is in the coal combination," reported Lloyd in 1894,[1] "that in oil has nearly, if not quite $200,000,000, and the other combinations in which its members are leaders foot up hundreds of millions more. Hundreds of millions of dollars are united in the railroads and elevators of the Northwest against the wheat-growers. In cattle and meat there are not less than $100,000,000; in whisky $35,000,000, and in beer a great deal more than that; in sugar, $75,000,000; in leather, over $100,000,000; in gas, hundreds of millions. . . . There are in round numbers $10,000,000,000 claiming dividends and interest in the railroads of the United States. Every year they are more closely pooled."

These immense combinations of capital had the effect of uniting vast armies of labor in each of the industries mentioned. The gigantic trusts called forth formidable trade-unions. The class lines were drawn more distinctly, and the class struggles grew more embittered and assumed larger proportions. Hardly a year passed without witnessing one or more powerful contests between capital and labor.

The earlier part of this remarkable decade was particularly replete with such struggles, and, without attempting to give anything like an adequate account of them, we

[1] Henry D. Lloyd: "Wealth against Commonwealth."

will mention a few of the most noteworthy strikes of that period.

The first of this series of strikes to attract universal attention was that which broke out in the iron and steel works of Carnegie & Company, at Homestead, Pennsylvania, in July, 1892.

Homestead was a town of about 12,000 inhabitants founded by Andrew Carnegie and his associates, and its population consisted chiefly of employees of the steel-works. These were organized by the Amalgamated Association of Iron and Steel Workers, and it had been their custom to fix their wages by periodical agreements with their employers. The last of these agreements expired on June 30, 1892. When that date approached, the owners of the works announced a reduction of wages and demanded that the new scale be made to terminate in January instead of June. The employees rejected the proposed terms principally on the ground that they could not afford a cessation of work in midwinter, and would not be in a position to resist further reductions of wages, if any were to be attempted upon the termination of the agreement. A lockout followed, and the battle began.

The employers were by no means unprepared for the struggle. Weeks in advance Mr. H. C. Frick, the active manager of the concern, had surrounded the works by a fence three miles long, fifteen feet in height and covered with barbed wire. The fortification was dubbed by the operatives "Fort Frick."

The next step of the employers was to import a force of 300 Pinkerton constables armed to the teeth, who arrived by water in the early morning hours of July 6th. The coming of these men precipitated a scene of excitement and bloodshed almost unprecedented in the annals of the labor struggles of this country. As soon as the boat carrying the Pinkertons was sighted by the pickets, the alarm was sounded. The strikers were aroused from their sleep, and within a few minutes the river front was covered with a crowd of coatless and hatless men armed with guns and rifles, and grimly determined to prevent the landing of the

Pinkertons. The latter, however did not seem to appreciate the gravity of the situation. They sought to intimidate the strikers by assuming a threatening attitude and aiming the muzzles of their shining revolvers at them. A moment of intense expectation followed. Then a shot was fired from the boat, and one of the strikers fell to the ground mortally wounded. A howl of fury and a volley of bullets came back from the line of the strikers, and a wild fusillade was opened on both sides. In vain did the strike leaders attempt to pacify the men and to stop the carnage—the strikers were beyond control. The struggle lasted several hours, after which the Pinkertons retreated from the river bank and withdrew to the cabin of the boat. There they remained in the sweltering heat of the July sun without air or ventilation, under the continuing fire of the enraged men on the shore, until they finally surrendered. They were imprisoned by the strikers in a rink, and in the evening they were sent out of town by rail. The number of dead on both sides was twelve, and over twenty were seriously wounded. After this incident Homestead was placed under martial law, and State troops were stationed in the town for several weeks, displaying great severity in their treatment of the strikers. The contest ended with the defeat of the strikers.

The strike at Homestead was still in progress when a struggle of almost equal intensity broke out in the far Northwest, in the Cœur d'Alene district of the State of Idaho. The rich silver and lead mines of the district had for a long time been operated by the miners themselves, individually or in small groups. But with the onward march of civilization the mines attracted the attention of enterprising capitalists. They were purchased and syndicated, and the former independent miners were reduced to wage-workers, whose wages steadily decreased. The miners organized, and their demand for higher wages having been refused, they struck. Their places were soon filled, and an armed battle ensued between the strikers and strike breakers, as a result of which several men were killed and wounded on both sides. The strikers remained in control of the situation, driving those who had taken their places from the mines. They were 1,200 strong and well-armed, while the entire State militia consisted nominally of 196 men. In this emergency the governor appealed for federal troops, and the latter were promptly and liberally furnished. The strike was suppressed, the leaders arrested and thrown into prison, and suit was instituted to dissolve the miners' union as an unlawful combination.

Within less than one month from the happenings described two new strikes of large dimensions occurred simultaneously in widely different parts of the country—Buffalo and Tennessee.

THE BUFFALO STRIKE.—In 1892 the legislature of the State of New York enacted a law limiting the work time of railway employees to ten hours a day. The passage of this law had been warmly agitated as a measure of relief to the overworked employees as well as a measure of safety for the traveling public. But when it had finally been enacted, it was found to contain a "rider" in the shape of a provision permitting the roads to exact from their employees overtime work for extra compensation. This provision had the effect of nullifying the entire law. The companies reduced the wages of their employees more than sufficiently to allow for extra compensation for overtime, and as a result the wages of the railroad workers somewhat decreased, while the hours of labor remained unchanged.

The employees to suffer most from this state of affairs were the switchmen, who not infrequently were kept at work thirty-six hours in succession without as much as an intermission for meals. In Buffalo the number of switchmen employed by the several roads was over 400, and on the 13th day of August, 1892, they struck for shorter hours and better pay. The attempts of the companies to fill the places of the strikers were unsuccessful, the strike gained ground, and railroad traffic around Buffalo was blocked. The switchmen had the sympathy of the population, and the local militia, which was called into requisition at an early stage of the contest, did not seem inclined to interfere with their "picketing." The prospects looked bright for

the strikers, when the railroad officials by threats and ca-
joling forced the somewhat reluctant sheriff to call on the
governor for troops. Within forty-eight hours almost the
entire militia of the State—about 8,000 in number, as
against the 400 strikers—appeared on the scene of battle,
and the situation was at once changed. Under the protection of the militia the companies procured men to take the
places of the strikers; picketing and other methods of warfare usually employed by strikers were not tolerated, the
backbone of the strike was broken, and the strike was declared off on the 24th of August.

An entirely different state of facts led to the labor
struggles in the coal regions of Tennessee about the same
time. There the trouble arose over the employment of convict labor in the mines. Under the prison system of the
State the authorities had for a number of years been in the
habit of hiring out convicts, principally of the colored race,
to the mine-owners on yearly contracts, and as a rule,
convict labor and free labor were employed in the same
mines. This competition and the humiliating associations
were a standing source of grievance for the miners, and
more than once the sturdy Tennesseeans had rebelled, and
with armed hand driven the convicts out of the mines.

The troubles of 1892 were a repetition of the same occurrences, except that the operations were conducted on a
larger scale. The first skirmish took place at Tracy City,
where the free miners captured about 300 prison workers,
set them at large and burned their barracks. Two days
later the same procedure was reenacted at the iron-mines
of Inman, on August 17th in the coal-mines of Oliver
Springs, and on the 18th in Coal Creek.

Several troops of militia despatched by the governor of
the State were captured on the way, disarmed and sent
back; telegraph wires were cut and railroad tracks demolished. The miners remained in absolute control of the
field, until finally the entire State militia was concentrated
in the mine regions. Then the strikers were defeated and
unmercifully punished. Warrants were out for all leaders
of the movement. No less than 500 arrests were made

within a few days, churches and schoolhouses were converted into prisons, and indictments for murder, riot, conspiracy, etc., were found by the score. The rebellion was quelled, and quiet restored in Tennessee.

But the most far-reaching and sensational of the strikes of that period was the Pullman or Chicago strike of 1894. Pullman had been founded in the vicinity of Chicago in 1880 by the famous palace-car builder, George M. Pullman. It is a factory town provided with "model" tenement-houses, schoolhouses, churches, stores, and a library, all owned by the Pullman Palace Car Company. It was not a philanthropic experiment like the famous New Lanark of Owen, but a pure business enterprise, and a very remunerative one at that. The company furnished not only the dwellings, but the gas, water, and all other necessaries and comforts of the tenants—at high prices. At the same time the wages of the operatives were very low, and the entire town was at all times deeply in the company's debt. In the spring of 1894 the employees owed the company the sum of $80,000 for rent alone, and not infrequently, after a deduction of the rent from their pay-roll, had nothing left for living expenses.

It was in these circumstances that the Pullman Palace Car Company announced another reduction of wages, amounting to about twenty-five per cent. on the average. The employees refused to submit to the reduction, and were locked out. Numerous efforts were made in behalf of the men to induce the Pullman Company to submit the controversy to arbitration, but all such overtures were met by the unbending and unvarying declaration, "We have nothing to arbitrate."

This situation had continued for many weeks, when the American Railway Union, which had recently organized the Pullman employees, took the matter in hand.

The American Railway Union was created in June, 1893, through the tireless efforts of Eugene V. Debs. It was a combination of different organizations of railway employees, and, in 1894, was said to number no less than 150,-

000 members. When the annual convention of the Union met in Chicago, in June, 1894, it appointed a committee to again request the Pullman Company to consent to a submission of the grievances of their employees to arbitration. No heed was paid to the committee, and the convention, amid cheers of enthusiasm, decided to boycott the Pullman cars, and to refuse to do work on any trains to which such cars might be attached.

The battle now grew general. On the part of the employees the strike was conducted by Eugene V. Debs with great ability and courage, while the campaign of the railroad companies was directed by the "General Managers' Association," an organization of the principal railroad companies, created largely for the purpose of reducing wages throughout the railway service of the country. The strike grew in dimensions and intensity from hour to hour. Within a few days all railway traffic in Chicago, Cincinnati, Cleveland, Omaha, San Francisco, and in many other important points of the Middle and Western States, was paralyzed. The transportation of meat and agricultural products was seriously impaired, and many industries all over the country were crippled. The American Railway Union seemed sure of victory when the United States courts stepped in and issued injunctions forbidding the strikers to prosecute the boycott of the Pullman cars. The first injunctions were issued by Judges Wood and Grosscup in Chicago, and their example was followed by judges in other States.

The situation was now very tense, but it assumed a still acuter aspect when the President of the United States, over the protest of Governor Altgeld, sent federal troops into Illinois, and issued proclamations to the good citizens of Chicago, North Dakota, Montana, Idaho, Wyoming, Washington, Colorado, and California, and the Territories of New Mexico and Utah, to preserve the peace and withdraw to their houses. The proclamations and the presence of federal troops and State militia placed a vast territory of the country practically under martial law. But notwithstanding these strenuous measures, or, perhaps on account of them, serious disorders and acts of violence occurred in many places.

In the meantime the United States district attorney for Chicago, under the directions of United States Attorney-General Olney, had impaneled an extraordinary grand jury, which found an indictment for conspiracy against Debs and other strike leaders. The accused men were arrested and released under heavy bail. Immediately upon their release they were rearrested on the charge of contempt of court. This time Debs and his comrades refused to furnish bail and were sent to the Cook County jail to await trial. The strike was broken. "It was not the railways, nor the mines that beat us, but the power of the United States courts," Debs subsequently testified before the United States Strike Commission, appointed to investigate the famous labor war.

The number of persons killed during the strike was 12. There were 515 persons arrested by the State police, and 190 by the United States courts. Bradstreet's estimated the loss occasioned by the strike to the country at large at about $80,000,000.

In September of the same year Debs was tried on a charge of contempt of court, found guilty and sentenced to six months' imprisonment in the Woodstock jail.

The strikes thus briefly described by no means exhaust the list of violent struggles between capital and labor which marked the closing years of the nineteenth century. Similar strikes occurred from time to time in various parts of the country, and most of them presented substantially the same features. They were conducted on a large scale, and not infrequently shook the industrial foundation of the country. For the greater part they were as brief in duration as they were intense in character, and in a majority of cases were quelled by the aid of the local police force, State militia, or federal troops. The injunction which had first shown its great effectiveness in the Chicago strike grew rapidly in favor as a method of settling labor disputes, and became a regular feature in every important strike. The phrase "government by injunction," which played so prominent a part in later political history, owes its origin to this period.

With few exceptions the strikes resulted in the defeat of the workmen.

These events created a certain dissatisfaction with the existing order of things in large sections of the working class and made them more accessible to the teachings of socialism. Nor was the social discontent wholly limited to the city workers. The rural population of the country had its own grievances. The number of agricultural workers, the hired farm hands, had grown very largely and their lot was in many instances worse than that of the industrial workers. And even the "independent" farmer had an ever harder struggle for existence. The closing decades of the last century had wrought great changes in the economic situation of the farmer. The development of the great railroad lines and the marvelous improvements in the transportation facilities had created a national market for farm products in this country, and the farmer was drawn into the mill of industrial competition as effectively as the manufacturer of the city.

"The farmer of to-day," said A. M. Simons, in 1902, "is creating some special kind of wealth, not because he expects himself to use it, but because he hopes to sell it in the general market, and then to take the money received on that market and buy back the things he really wishes to use from the same impersonal, unknown market. He is a specialist producing for sale instead of a creator of wealth for his own use. His customer is not some individual who particularly desires the article to be created but the great impersonal, competitive world market." [14]

This transformation signified a complete revolution on the farm. The greater specialization in agriculture necessitated more efficient, complete and expensive farm implements and machinery; it widened the distance between

[14] "The American Farmer," by A. M. Simons, Chicago.

the farmer and the consumer, and put the former into the power of the railroads, the "commission" merchants and bankers.

The farmers found it more difficult every year to make both ends meet, and the practice of mortgaging farms grew with alarming rapidity. In 1890 the total mortgage indebtedness of the farmers was no less than $1,085,995,960, and the indebtedness bore interest at a rate exceeding 7 per cent. Only 47 per cent. of the farmers owned their farms unencumbered. Of the remaining 53 per cent., 34 per cent. did not own the farms which they were cultivating, and 19 per cent. owned them subject to mortgages. Rent and interest reduced the meager income of the farmer to a minimum, and the statement was made on good authority that the average net income of the American farmer was $200 per year or less.[15]

Alongside these industrial conditions and movements, and no doubt partly in consequence of them, a new and radical spirit was rapidly developing in the social and political life of the country. This spirit manifested itself in a variety of ways, but found its most pronounced expression in the Nationalist and Populist movements.

The Nationalist movement was founded on Bellamy's famous utopian novel, "Looking Backward." Edward Bellamy was born in 1850 at Chicopee Falls, Massachusetts, and was the son of a clergyman. He studied law, but soon discarded that profession for the more congenial pursuit of literature, and wrote several novels, which met with moderate success. In 1887 he published his "Looking Backward." The original plan of the novel, it is related, did not include the treatment of social or industrial problems. The author merely intended to write a playful fairy tale of universal harmony and felicity. But as he progressed with his work his subject assumed a more definite tendency and more direct application. The novelist gradually yielded to the reformer, and the projected work of fiction was turned into a social and political treatise.

15 Ibid.

Bellamy was not familiar with the modern socialist philosophy when he wrote his book. His views and theories were the result of his own observation and reasoning, and, like all other utopians, he evolved a complete social scheme hinging mainly on one fixed idea. In his case it was the idea "of an industrial army for *maintaining* the community, precisely as the duty of *protecting* it is entrusted to a military army." "What inference could possibly be more obvious and more unquestioned," he asks, "than the advisability of trying to see if a plan which was found to work so well for purposes of destruction might not be profitably applied to the business of production, now in such shocking confusion?"

The historical development of society and the theory of the class struggle, which play so great a part in the philosophy of modern socialism, have no place in Bellamy's system. With him it is all a question of expediency; he is not an exponent of the laws of social development, but a social inventor.

But this feature, which would have been a source of weakness in a work of science, by no means detracted from the success of the novel. "Looking Backward" was written in an easy and pleasing style; it had the charm of originality, and touched a live cord in the heart of the people. The book at once became the literary sensation of the day. Within a few years it reached a sale of over half a million copies in this country alone, and it was translated into almost all modern languages.

A "Bellamy Club" was organized in Boston soon after the appearance of the book, and in 1888 the club was renamed the "Nationalist Club." This was the beginning of the Nationalist movement. Other clubs patterned after the Boston prototype were formed in all parts of the country. In 1891 no less than 162 Nationalist clubs were reported to be in existence. The origin of the term "Nationalist" is accounted for by Bellamy in the following manner:

" . . . This is called Nationalism because it proceeds by the nationalization of industries, including the

minor application of the same principle, the municipaliza-
tion and State control of localized business. Socialism implies the socializing of industry. This may or may not be
based upon the national organism, and may or may not
imply economic equality. As compared with socialism,
nationalism is a definition, not in the sense of opposition or
exclusion, but of a precision rendered necessary by a cloud
of vague and disputed implications historically attached
to the former word.''

The Nationalist clubs were principally propaganda
organizations. In politics they displayed but little activity, occasionally nominating independent candidates,
but more frequently cooperating with the Populists.

The Populist movement originated in the State of Kansas, where a call for a convention of all the radical element with the view of forming a new political party was
issued in April, 1890. The convention met in June of the
same year, and was attended by ninety delegates, representing the Farmers' Alliance, Knights of Labor, Single-
Tax clubs, and other reform organizations. The ''People's
Party of Kansas'' was organized, and in the ensuing State
election succeeded in electing a majority of the lower house
of the State legislature. The movement spread rapidly to
all Western, Middle, and some Southern States. In 1891
a national convention was held in Cincinnati. It was attended by no less than 1,418 delegates, who were, however,
chiefly recruited from the States of Kansas, Ohio, Indiana,
Illinois, Missouri, and Nebraska.

The next convention of the party, held in Omaha, Neb.,
in 1892, was of a more representative national character.
Delegates were present from all parts of the country. An
independent presidential ticket was nominated and a party
platform adopted.

The People's Party was chiefly an organization of and
for the small farmers, and thrived principally in the agricultural West and Middle West. But while the leaders
and promoters of the movement recognized this character
of their party, and in all their platforms and public decla-

rations laid particular stress on the interests of the farming population, they appreciated that the party could not expect to attain significance in national politics without the aid of the industrial workers of the East, and they endeavored at all times to gain the support of the latter.

"Wealth belongs to him who creates it," declares the Omaha platform, "and every dollar taken from industry without an equivalent is robbery. . . . The interests of rural and civic laborers are the same; their enemies are identical."

In the presidential elections of 1892 the People's Party united over 1,000,000 votes on its candidate for President, General Weaver, and in 1894 its vote rose to 1,564,318. But in 1896, when William J. Bryan was nominated by the Democratic Party on a platform favoring the free coinage of silver, the Populists refrained from nominating a rival candidate and indorsed Mr. Bryan's nomination. This was practically the death of the People's Party, and the further history of the movement is one of rapid disintegration. After the fusion of 1896 the larger division of the party practically remained an appendix to the Democratic Party, while the more radical elements, known as the Middle-of-the-Road Populists, seceded from the parent organization, forming a political party of their own. In the elections of 1900 their candidate for President of the United States, Mr. Barker, polled a little over 50,000 votes.

In connection with the reform movements above described the schools of Christian Socialism and Fabian Socialism must also be mentioned. Both schools appeared in the United States at the period under consideration, and, while they did not influence the social and political views of the people to the same extent as Nationalism or Populism, they still contributed in some degree to the formation of modern socialism in this country.

In the countries of Europe the school of Christian Socialism had been in existence for more than half a century, and assumed a variety of forms and attitudes. In the United States the movement made its first definite appearance in 1889, when the Society of Christian Socialists was organized in Boston; it soon branched out to several other cities, principally in the East.

The doctrines of the Christian Socialists of that period may be summed up in the following statement, taken from the declaration of principles of their society:

"I. We hold that God is the source and guide of all human progress, and we believe that all social, political, and industrial relations should be based on the fatherhood of God and the brotherhood of man, in the spirit and according to the teachings of Jesus Christ.

"II. We hold that the present industrial and commercial system is not thus based, but rests rather on economic individualism," etc.

And the objects of the society were stated to be:

"(1) To show that the aim of socialism is embraced in the aim of Christianity.

"(2) To awaken members of Christian churches to the fact that the teachings of Jesus Christ lead directly to some specific form or forms of socialism; that, therefore, the Church has a definite duty upon this matter, and must, in simple obedience to Christ, apply itself to the realization of the social principles of Christianity."

The society never gained much influence, and after a struggling existence of a few years disbanded. The most prominent figures in the movement in this country were Rev. William D. P. Bliss, Prof. George D. Herron, and Prof. R. T. Ely. Mr. Bliss was one of the organizers and most active workers of the Society of Christian Socialists. For several years he published *The Dawn,* a monthly magazine, in which he advocated the usual political measures of the socialist program along with the general principles of Christian Socialism. Professor Herron occupied the chair of Applied Christianity at Iowa College, and expounded his views in numerous books and pamphlets, in public lectures and from the chair. He was outspoken in his denunciations of the existing order of things, but refrained from offering a positive program of action. His socialism was rather of an ethical than political nature.

In later years Professor Herron declared himself unreservedly for political socialism, and he is now a member of the Socialist Party.

In the summer of 1894 Professors Ely and Herron organized at Chautauqua, N. Y., the American Institute of Christian Sociology, which was designed to furnish literature for the Christian Socialist movement in churches and colleges. Professor Ely was president, Professor Herron was principal of instruction, and Prof. J. R. Commons was secretary. The Institute exerted some influence, but finally failed through the protests of the clergy and college instructors against the radicalism of Professor Herron's teachings. The Christian Socialist League, of Chicago, organized by Edwin D. Wheelock, also exerted a measure of local influence for some time. But the movement as a whole never reached considerable proportions, and disappeared within a few years.

The Fabian Socialist movement in the United States can hardly be considered more than an unsuccessful attempt to emulate the activity of the Fabian Society in England. The latter was organized in London in 1883 by a number of well-known socialists for the special purpose of promoting the educational side of the socialist movement. Its members delivered many lectures before clubs and societies, and published and circulated numerous tracts and pamphlets, among them the famous series of "Fabian Essays on Socialism," and brought about several important measures of municipal reform in London and in other cities of the United Kingdom.

The American Fabian Society was organized in 1895. It had branches in New York, Boston, Philadelphia, San Francisco, and in several other places. The society issued a few tracts, and for some time published a monthly magazine under the title, *The American Fabian*. The leading spirits of the movement were W. D. P. Bliss and Laurence Gronlund.

All these and other reform movements of that time, were short-lived and fleeting, but they left their mark on the political life of the nation.

They drew the attention of thousands of American citizens in all parts of the Union to the social problems of the day. Many of them discarded their traditional views and severed their old party affiliations, and when the reform movements collapsed one after the other, their former votaries in many cases turned to socialism.

II.—THE DISINTEGRATION OF THE SOCIALIST LABOR PARTY

THE Socialist Labor Party was founded at a time when socialism in this country was an academic idea rather than a popular movement. The socialists were few in number, and consisted largely of persons who had formed their social views and philosophy in European countries, principally in Germany. They were little in touch with the American population, and moved almost exclusively within their own limited circle. This character of the movement reflected itself on their organization: the mode of administration and methods of procedure of the Socialist Labor Party were those of a religious sect rather than of a political party of the masses.

This organization was quite sufficient for a period of about twenty years. The movement during that time made little progress among the native population, the party grew slowly, and whatever new members it acquired were gradually assimilated.

But the events described in the preceding chapter worked a great change in the character of the socialist movement in America. The movement outgrew the narrow bounds within which it had been confined up to that time, and the Socialist Labor Party was fast becoming inadequate for its new requirements. Its highly centralized form of organization did not suit the political institutions and traditions of the country, and its rigid adherence to all canons of dogmatic socialism and strict enforcement of party discipline were not calculated to attract the masses of newly converted socialists. A radical change had become necessary if the party desired to maintain its hegemony in the socialist movement. But, unfortunately for the Socialist Labor Party, its leaders did not appreciate the situation. The prolonged activity within the vicious circle of their own had made them men of extremely narrow vision. They had become used to regard membership in their party as the privilege of the chosen few, and were rather reluctant to open it to the masses. They eyed all newcomers with ill-concealed suspicion, and refused to relax the rigidity of party requirements in any way.

Nor was their attitude toward the trade-union movement of the country any more conciliatory. When the Socialist Trade and Labor Alliance was first organized and sprung as a surprise on the convention of 1896, several delegates had considerable misgivings as to the innovation. Fear was exprest that the organization would only serve to antagonize existing trade-unions, while accomplishing little good, and that it would ultimately lead to an estrangement between the party and the rest of the labor movement in the country.

But these fears were allayed by the repeated assurances of the spokesmen of the Alliance, that the latter did not intend to interfere with existing organizations, and would confine its activity to the task of organizing the unorganized.

As soon, however, as the convention adjourned, these promises were forgotten. The Socialist Trade and Labor Alliance accomplished hardly anything by way of organizing unorganized working men, and whatever strength it ever attained was drawn from existing trade-unions. The Alliance was besides not always very scrupulous in its methods, and it has even been accused of organizing strike breakers in opposition to striking workmen on several occasions. This course naturally provoked the hostility of organized labor toward the Alliance, and the hostility was extended to the Socialist Labor Party, which was considered practically identical with it. Thus the administration of the Socialist Labor Party within a few years suc-

ceeded in placing the party in a position of antagonism to
organized labor, as well as to all socialistic and semisocialis-
tic elements outside the party organization.

This policy was by no means always approved by the
membership, and voices of protest were occasionally raised.
But the opposition only served to accentuate the unbending
attitude of the men at the head of the party. A relentless
war was opened on everything within and without the
party that did not strictly conform to their conception of
orthodox socialist principles and tactics. The columns of
the official party paper, *The People,* edited by Daniel De
Leon, and the *Vorwaerts,* edited by Hugo Vogt, were filled
from week to week with violent tirades against the "corrupt pure and simple labor-unions" and their "ignorant and dishonest leaders," and against the Populist, Nationalist, and other reform "fakirs."

Side by side with this crusade against the "fakirs" outside of the party a process of "purification" of the party
members was begun. Had the party officers heretofore
been strict disciplinarians, they now became intolerant fa-
natics. Every criticism of their policy was resented by
them as an act of treachery, every dissension from their
views was decried as an act of heresy, and the offenders
were dealt with unmercifully. Insubordinate members
were expelled by the scores, and recalcitrant "sections"
were suspended with little ceremony. This "burlesque
reign of terror," as Lucien Sanial subsequently characterized the *régime,* continued for several years, and in 1899
reached such an acute stage that the members finally rose
up in arms against it.

The crisis was precipitated by a controversy between
the *New Yorker Volkszeitung* and the official party organs.
The immediate occasion for the dispute was the *Volkszeitung's* adverse criticism of the party's attitude toward
trade-unions; but as the controversy continued, it extended
to the whole range of the policy and methods of the party
administration. The discussion waxed more heated with
every issue of the papers. Members took sides with one or
the other of the combatants. The socialists of New York,

where the headquarters of the party were located and *The
People* and *Volkszeitung* were published, were divided into
two hostile camps—the "administration faction" and the
"opposition faction."

In these circumstances the month of July, 1899, arrived,
and with it the time for the election of new delegates to the
general committee of "Section New York." This election
was of more than local importance. The convention of
1896 had delegated to the city of New York the power to
elect and recall the national secretary and the members of
the national executive committee, and the latter in turn
elected the editors of the party organs. Thus the New
York Socialists held the key to the entire situation. The
election was to demonstrate the relative strength of the
factions.

The contest was a spirited one all along the line, and its
results were awaited with intense interest. The new general committee met on July 8th, when it became at once apparent that the opposition was in the majority. The committee did not proceed far. The nomination of a temporary
chairman precipitated a violent clash between the hostile
camps, and the meeting broke up in disorder.

That very night the opposition delegates issued a call for
a special meeting of the committee. The meeting held on
the 10th day of July was attended by the opposition delegates only, and proceeded with the party administration
in a summary manner. The offices of the national secretary, of the members of the national executive committee,
and of the editor of *The People* were declared vacant, and
their successors were then and there elected. Henry L.
Slobodin, who had taken a very active part in the overthrow of the old administration, was elected national secretary, and guided the much troubled course of the party
during the succeeding period with great skill and circum-
spection.

The war within the Socialist Labor Party was now on in
earnest. The deposed party officers repudiated the acts
of the general committee as invalid and continued in office.
The party officers elected by the general committee insisted

on the legality of their election, and proceeded to the discharge of their duties. Each side styled itself the Socialist Labor Party, each had its own national committee, its own secretary and headquarters, and each published a paper called *The People*.

The situation was somewhat analogous to the one created just ten years earlier by the deposition of Rosenberg and his associates, except that in the present case the battle was more intense.

In the beginning the administration party had decidedly the better end of the contest. The insurgents were practically confined to the East and a very few cities in the West and the Middle West while the majority of the sections in the country knew little about the merits of the controversy, and many of them adhered to the old party officers on general principles. The latter, however, did not possess the tact or skill to follow up their advantage. Their dictatorial tone toward their own followers, and their policy of abuse toward their opponents, repelled the sections wavering in their allegiance between the two committees, and one by one they turned to the opposition.

This was the state of affairs when the general elections of 1899 approached. Each of the two factions had nominated a ticket, and each side claimed its ticket to represent the only regular nominations of the Socialist Labor Party. In the State of New York the contest was taken into the courts, which decided in favor of the faction headed by the old party officers.

The decision was a severe blow to the opposition. The latter had at that time undoubtedly the support of the large majority of the members, and some of the most prominent ones among them, and had almost the entire party press on its side. Its organization was growing steadily, and it soon regained in some quarters of the labor movement the sympathy which the party had forfeited through the perverse trade-union policy of its former officers. But with all that its legal existence and identity had always been enshrouded in much doubt, and now that the courts had decided adversely on its claims to the party name, the organization was thrown into a state of indescribable confusion. To put an end to the chaos, the national committee issued a call for a special convention of all sections supporting its administration. The convention was held in the city of Rochester, and the character of the gathering and the efficiency of the work accomplished by it exceeded the most sanguine expectations of its promoters. It was attended by fifty-nine delegates, and remained in session five consecutive days. All questions of principle, organization, and policy were subjected to a most searching scrutiny. The methods and tactics of the party were revised, and the party was reorganized on a basis more nearly in accord with the modern requirements of the movement.

Almost the first act of the Rochester convention was to repudiate the Socialist Trade and Labor Alliance and to proclaim its sympathy with the struggles of all trade-unions regardless of national affiliations. The convention also adopted a new platform, and enacted a new set of by-laws for the administration of the affairs of the party. The most momentous act of the Rochester convention was the adoption of the following resolution, paving the way for the unification of the party with the Social Democratic Party (see next chapter):

"The Socialist Labor Party of the United States, in national convention assembled, sends fraternal greetings to the Social Democratic Party of the United States.

"*Whereas*, The course of development of the socialist movement in the United States during the last few years has obliterated all differences of principle and views between the Socialist Labor Party and the Social Democratic Party, and both parties are now practically identical in their platform, tactics, and methods;

"*Whereas*, Harmonious and concerted action of all socialist elements of the United States is expedient for a successful campaign against the combined forces of capitalism;

"*Resolved*, That it is the sense of this convention that the interests of socialism will be best subserved by a speedy union of the Socialist Labor Party and the Social Demo-

cratic Party into one strong, harmonious, and united socialist party;

"*Resolved,* That we call upon the earnest and intelligent
socialists of the country in the ranks of both parties to discard all petty ambitions and personal prejudices in the face
of this great purpose, and to conduct the negotiations for
unity of both parties, not in the sense of two hostile camps,
each negotiating for peace with a view of securing the
greatest advantages to itself, but in the sense of equal
parties, hitherto working separately for a common cause,
and now sincerely seeking to provide a proper basis for
honorable and lasting union for the benefit of that cause;

"*Resolved,* That for the purpose of effecting union between the two parties on the basis outlined, this convention
appoint a committee of nine to act as a permanent committee on Socialist Union, until the question is definitely disposed of;

"*Resolved,* That the said committee be authorized to
delegate a representative or representatives to the next national convention of the Social Democratic Party in order
to convey this resolution to said party and to invite the said
party to appoint a similar committee; and

"*Resolved,* that any treaty of union evolved by the joint
committee on union, including the question of party name,
platform, and constitution, be submitted to a general vote
of both parties."

The resolution was adopted by a vote of fifty-five to one,
and the committee of nine, provided for by it, was elected.
Before adjournment the convention made nominations of
candidates for the ensuing presidential campaign. Job
Harriman, of California, a brilliant and magnetic speaker
and a successful organizer, who had become widely known
in Socialist circles through his work on the Pacific coast,
was nominated for the office of President of the United
States, and Max Hayes, of Ohio, equally popular in the
socialist and the trade-union movement, for Vice-President.

But in view of the pending negotiations for unity with
the Social Democratic Party, the nominations were not
considered final, and the committee on unity was author-

ized to make any changes in the ticket that might be required by the exigencies of the situation.

III.—THE SOCIALIST PARTY

THE policy of the Socialist Labor Party described in the preceding chapter had the double effect of repelling many old-time workers in the movement, who withdrew in large numbers, and of making the organization unpopular with the majority of newly converted socialists.

Thus about the middle of the nineties of the last century a new socialist movement gradually sprang up outside the ranks of the Socialist Labor Party. It was scattered all over the country and it manifested itself in many ways. It was grouped around such enterprises as the weekly papers of J. A. Wayland, *The Coming Nation*, and subsequently *The Appeal to Reason*, both of which reached a circulation unparalleled by that of any previous socialist publication in this country; it exprest itself in the foundation of socialist colonies, such as the Ruskin Cooperative Colony of Tennessee, and in the formation of a number of independent socialist and semi-socialist clubs and societies.

The movement, however, lacked clearness and cohesion, and stood sorely in need of an energetic and popular leader to collect the scattered elements and to weld them together into one organization. The man to accomplish that task finally appeared in the person of Eugene V. Debs.

Debs had always been a man of radical views on social problems, and his experience in the great Chicago strike had only served to intensify this radicalism. He utilized his enforced leisure in the Woodstock jail for the study of the philosophy of modern socialism, with the result that he left the jail with decided leanings towards it.

In the campaign of 1896 he still supported the candidacy of Mr. Bryan, but in January, 1897, he publicly announced his conversion to socialism.

The American Railway Union had by this time practically ceased to exist, with the exception of a small group of men who remained true to Debs. This remainder of the once powerful organization was reorganized on political lines and decided to unite with the Brotherhood of the Cooperative Commonwealth, a socialist organization of a utopian coloring, which had then recently been called into existence by *The Coming Nation.*

A joint convention of the two organizations was held in Chicago on June 18, 1897, with the result that a new party, the SOCIAL DEMOCRACY OF AMERICA, was created.

The aims and views of the party were originally somewhat crude and indefinite. Its declaration of principles was substantially socialistic, but its main feature of activity was the promotion of a fantastic plan of colonization. The scheme was to colonize in some Western State, to capture the State government, and introduce a socialist *régime* within the limits of the State. A colonization committee, consisting of Col. R. J. Hinton, of Washington, D. C., W. P. Borland, of Michigan, and C. F. Willard, of Massachusetts, was appointed. Funds for the purchase of territory were collected and in May, 1898, the committee announced that it had completed arrangements by which the party would acquire about 560 acres of land in the Cripple Creek region in Colorado for the sum of $200,000, of which a cash payment of only $5,000 was required.

The colonization scheme of the Social Democracy had opened the doors of the party to all varieties of social reformers, and even a number of prominent anarchists joined the organization in the hope of exploiting it for the propagation of their theories.

But gradually the practical socialist elements within the party grew in numbers and strength. Many former members and several entire sections of the Socialist Labor Party joined the new organization, and these together with several prominent leaders within the Social Democracy, headed by Victor L. Berger, of Milwaukee, Wisconsin, initiated a movement to substitute the ordinary socialist propaganda and politics for the colonization scheme of the party.

This was the condition of affairs when the first national

convention of the Social Democracy was held in Chicago, on June 7, 1898. The convention was attended by seventy delegates, representing ninety-four branches of the party, and it became at once evident that a pitched battle was to be expected over the question of politics as against colonization.

The debate was opened by the report of the platform committee. Two reports were submitted, a majority report favoring the abandonment of the colonization scheme and the adoption of the usual methods of socialist propaganda, and a minority report advocating colonization as the most prominent feature of the activity of the party. The debate lasted until 2:30 o'clock in the morning, when a vote was taken, showing fifty-three in favor of the minority report and thirty-seven for the majority report. No sooner was the vote taken, than the defeated minority withdrew from the convention hall in a body, in accordance with a prearranged plan, and the field was left clear to the colonization faction. The latter adopted its platform, elected its officers, and adjourned. The organization subsequently established two insignificant communistic colonies in the State of Washington, and quietly dropped out of existence.

In the meantime the thirty-seven bolting delegates met and called into life a new party under the name of "SOCIAL DEMOCRATIC PARTY OF AMERICA." Freed from the presence of the troublesome colonization advocates, the new party proceeded to eliminate all utopian planks from its platform. It organized on the lines of a socialist political party and elected a national executive board, consisting of Eugene V. Debs, Victor L. Berger, Jesse Cox, Seymour Stedman, and Frederic Heath.

The following two years witnessed rapid growth. The party nominated State or local tickets in Massachusetts, New Hampshire, New York, Connecticut, Maryland, Illinois, Wisconsin, Missouri, and California. In the fall elections of 1899 it elected the first socialist representatives in the Massachusetts State legislature—James F. Carey and Lewis M. Scates, and in December of the same year

the Social Democrats of Haverhill, Massachusetts, elected
John C. Chase to the office of mayor, while C. H. Coulter
was elected mayor of Brockton, Massachusetts, also on a
Social Democratic ticket. The party succeeded in electing to office a number of aldermen, councilmen, and school
commissioners in several towns of Massachusetts and Wisconsin. When the first national convention assembled in
Indianapolis, on the 6th day of March, 1900, it claimed an
enrolled membership of about 5,000.

The system of representation devised by the party was
a rather novel one for political conventions. Each member had the right to append his signature to the credential
of a delegate or proxy of his own choice, and each delegate
had as many votes in the convention as the number of signatures attached to his credentials.

The number of delegates who attended the convention
was sixty-seven, and the total number of individual signatures attached to their credentials was 2,136.

The all-absorbing topic at the convention was the question of amalgamation with the Rochester wing of the
Socialist Labor Party. On the second day of the session
a committee of the latter, consisting of Max Hayes, of
Ohio, Job Harriman, of California, and Morris Hillquit,
of New York, formally opened negotiations. Their
earnest plea for the unification of the socialist forces was
interrupted by round after round of applause. The great
majority of the delegates had come to the convention with
their minds firmly made up on the subject. They needed
no arguments or persuasion; they were enthusiastically for
union, and urged immediate measures for the accomplishment of the object.

The desire for union without reserve or qualification
was, however, confined to the mass of the delegates. The
party leaders were more cautious in the matter. The
name of Socialist Labor Party had an unpleasant ring
for them; they were somewhat apprehensive of the motives and sincerity of the new allies, and they proposed to
surround the negotiations for unity with all possible safeguards. They consented to the appointment of a commit-

tee of nine to meet with the similar committee of the
Socialist Labor Party and to evolve a plan of union as
called for by the Rochester resolution; but they recommended that the results of the deliberations of the joint
committee be submitted to a referendum vote of each party
separately, so that if either of the parties should not ap-
prove of the plan as a whole it might reject it and thus
frustrate the proposed union. They also insisted upon the
retention for the new organization of the name Social
Democratic Party.

These recommendations were the subject of a prolonged
and heated debate, at the conclusion of which they were
rejected by a vote of 1,366 against 770. A committee of
nine was thereupon elected with full power to arrange the
terms of union with the like committee of the Rochester
faction. To seal the treaty of peace, a presidential ticket
was nominated, with Eugene V. Debs, of the Social Democratic Party, for President, and Job Harriman, of the
Socialist Labor Party, for his running mate, with the understanding that the nominations would supersede those
made at Rochester.

The joint conference committee met in New York on the
25th of March, 1900, and the practical work of merging
the two organizations began in earnest.

The Social Democratic Party was represented by John
C. Chase, James F. Carey, Margaret Haile, Frederic Heath,
G. A. Hoehn, Seymour Stedman, William Butscher, and
W. P. Lonergan. Victor L. Berger, also a member of the
committee, did not attend.

The Socialist Labor Party was represented by Max
Hayes, Job Harriman, Morris Hillquit, F. J. Sieverman,
J. Mahlon Barnes, G. B. Benham, C. E. Fenner, W. E.
White, and N. I. Stone.

The conference lasted two full days. The questions of
party name, constitution, candidates, and platform were
discust in detail. The last two points were disposed of
with practically no debate. The Indianapolis nominations
were ratified and the Rochester platform was readopted as
the declaration of principles of the new party, while the

"demands" formulated by the Social Democratic Party were appended to the document.

But the questions of party name and headquarters gave rise to prolonged and, at times, heated controversies. The representatives of the Social Democratic Party insisted upon the retention of their party name for sentimental reasons and on the ground of expediency, while the others urged the name of United Socialist Party as more expressive of the character of the new organization. A compromise was finally effected by a decision to submit both names to the vote of the combined membership of both parties.

The party headquarters were located in Springfield Massachusetts, and a provisional national committee of ten was created to be selected from the membership of the two parties in equal numbers. The work of the committee was on the whole harmonious, and when the joint meeting adjourned, the union of the two parties was considered accomplished save for the formality of submitting the results of the deliberations to a general vote of the members for ratification. But the unexpected was to happen again. Hardly a week had past since the members of the joint committee finished their labors to the apparent satisfaction of all concerned, when the national executive board of the Social Democratic Party issued a manifesto, charging the Socialist Labor Party representatives with breach of faith, and calling upon the members of their party to repudiate the treaty of union.

The document caused a storm of protest within the ranks of both parties, and gave rise to a prolonged and acrimonious feud between the adherents of the national executive board and the supporters of union. When the vote on the manifesto was finally canvassed, the officers of the Social Democratic Party declared that union had been rejected by the members of their party by a vote of 1,213 against 939, and that the party would continue its separate existence.

But this declaration by no means disposed of the controversy. The adherents of union within the ranks of the

Social Democratic Party, the majority of its committee on unity among them, denied the legality of the procedure adopted by the board, and refused to recognize its authority longer to represent the party. They went on voting on the treaty recommended by the joint committee on union. The treaty having been ratified by the Rochester faction of the Socialist Labor Party and the pro-union faction of the Social Democratic Party, they proceeded to carry its provisions into effect.

Whether it was in the hope of disarming the anti-union elements or for any other reason, the name Social Democratic Party was adopted on the general vote, not only by the pro-union members of that party, but also by the overwhelming majority of the Socialist Labor Party members, and the new party consequently assumed that name. The climax of confusion in the socialist movement in this country was now reached. Both the Socialist Labor Party and the Social Democratic Party were torn in twain. The former maintained its headquarters in New York, the latter had one in Chicago and one in Springfield; each of these parties and factions had a separate set of national officers, and each was making war on the other. And, as if to emphasize the absurdity of the situation, the presidential elections drew near with the various socialist nominations in a state of indescribable chaos. The administration faction of the Socialist Labor Party had nominated a ticket of its own—Joseph F. Malloney, of Massachusetts, for President, and Val. Remmel, of Pennsylvania, for Vice-President.

The Rochester faction of the party had originally nominated Harriman and Hayes for its candidates, but, as related above, these nominations were abandoned for those of Debs and Harriman. The latter ticket, however, was nominated on the assumption that complete union between the Rochester faction and the Social Democratic Party was an assured fact. But now, when the negotiations for union had failed, the anti-union or Chicago faction found itself with Job Harriman, a member of a rival organization, on its own presidential ticket, while the pro-union or Springfield faction was in the same position with regard to its candidate for President, Eugene V. Debs. The warring factions of the Social Democratic Party decided upon the only course possible in the circumstances—the retention of the joint ticket and the maintenance of a tacit truce during the campaign. Notwithstanding this inauspicious situation, both wings of the Social Democratic Party conducted an energetic and enthusiastic campaign, and the vote polled for their joint ticket in this their first national campaign was 97,730, more than the Socialist Labor Party had ever succeeded in uniting on its candidates in its palmiest days.

The harmonious work of both factions of the Social Democratic Party for a joint ticket during the brief campaign had accomplished more toward effecting real union between them than all the prolonged negotiations of the past. The members had learned to know each other more closely, and their vague feeling of mutual distrust was dispelled. After the campaign there was no further reason or excuse for continuing the separate existence of the two factions. The Chicago board issued a call for a joint convention of all socialist organizations for the purpose of creating one united party. The Springfield faction, several independent local and State organizations, and, in fact, all socialist organizations, except the New York faction of the Socialist Labor Party, responded to the call. When the convention assembled in Indianapolis, on the 29th of July, 1901, it was found that the organizations participating in it represented an enrolled membership of no less than 10,000. The system of representation was the same that had prevailed at the preceding Indianapolis convention. One hundred and twenty-four delegates held 6,683 credentials from individual members. Of these, the Springfield faction was represented by ' 68 delegates, holding 4,798 credentials; the Chicago faction by 48 delegates, with 1,396 credentials; while three independent State organizations, with a total membership of 352. were represented by 8 delegates.

Mindful of the disappointing results of the labors of

the former joint committee on union, the convention decided not to take any chances again, but to complete all
arrangements for the final amalgamation of the organizations represented, then and there.

With this end in view, a new platform and constitution
were adopted. The headquarters were removed from the
seats of former troubles to St. Louis, and one Leon Green-
baum, who had not figured very prominently in the former
controversies, was elected national secretary.

The convention was the largest and most representative
national gathering of socialists ever held in this country
up to that time. Among the delegates there were men who
had been active in all phases of the socialist movement,
and alongside of them men of prominence who had
recently come into the movement. The socialist organizations of Porto Rico were represented by a delegate of their
own, while the presence of three negroes, by no means
the least intelligent and earnest of the delegates, attested
the fact that socialism had begun to take root among the
colored race.

The composition of the convention served to demonstrate
how much the character of the socialist movement had
changed during the preceding few years. Out of the 124
delegates no more than twenty-five, or about twenty per
cent., were foreign-born; all the others were native Americans. Socialism had ceased to be an exotic plant in this
country.

The convention assembled as a gathering of several independent and somewhat antagonistic bodies; it adjourned
as a solid and harmonious party.

The name assumed by the party thus created was the
SOCIALIST PARTY.

Within the first three years of its existence the enrolled membership of the Socialist Party more than doubled
in numbers. In the beginning of 1904, the party consisted of over 1,200 local organizations distributed all over
the United States. In that year it held its first
national convention, which lasted six days, from
May 1 to May 6, and was attended by 184 dele-

gates representing 36 States and Territories of the Union. The platform and constitution were thoroughly revised, and the solidarity of the party with the trade-union movement of the country was affirmed anew. The make-up of the convention, its methods and proceedings clearly indicated that the Party was rapidly developing into a full grown political force in this country.

But the formal organization represented only one aspect of its progress. The growth of the Socialist Party during the early period of its existence was demonstrated much more strongly by its political gains, its increasing influence in the labor movement of the country, and its press.

As already related, the party made its début in national politics with a vote of almost 100,000, cast for Debs and Harriman in 1900. This vote was materially increased in the spring and fall elections of the following year, but owing to the local character of these elections the vote was never fully reported.

In the congressional elections of 1902, however, the vote, to the surprise of all, reached very closely the quarter-million mark.

A part of this unexpected success must be ascribed to the effects of the popular excitement produced in the summer and fall of that year by the prolonged and far-reaching strike of the Pennsylvania coal-miners. But it would be a mistake to consider the large socialist vote as purely accidental on account of that fact. The gains were almost as much noticeable in places which, from their geographical location, were practically unaffected by the coal strike as they were within the immediate theater of the great labor contest.

Moreover, when the local spring elections of 1903 arrived and the strike sentiment had completely subsided, it was found that the socialist vote had not fallen off, but, on the contrary, had very substantially increased.

In the general elections of the year following, the presidential campaign of 1904, the political conditions of the country were exceedingly favorable for socialism. The two great political parties both nominated "safe" and conservative candidates (the Republicans Theodore Roosevelt and the Democrats Chief Judge of the New York Court of Appeals, Alton B. Parker), and the People's Party had been discredited by its former alliance with the Democrats and disorganized and divided in its ranks. The Socialist Party, therefore, was practically the only representative of true radicalism in politics, and in a position to muster its full legitimate force. The party was thoroughly alive to its opportunities, and began a campaign which for intensity, extension and effectiveness excelled all previous efforts of the socialist movement in this country. Large public meetings were addrest in all parts of the country by Eugene V. Debs, the party's candidate for president, and by Benjamin Hanford, an eloquent printer of New York, whom the party nominated for vice-president; thousands of other propagandists were busy proclaiming the gospel of socialism in numerous hall meetings and countless street meetings, and printed circulars and leaflets were distributed by the millions. The vote polled for Debs in that year was 402,321, while that of the People's Party was only 113,259.

Hardly less significant than its success at the polls were the gains made by the party in the trade-union movement. The growing sympathies of the trade-unions for the Socialist Party were manifested in a variety of ways, but on no occasion were they so clearly demonstrated as in the two national conventions of the largest bodies of organized labor, held in 1902.

In the month of June of that year, the Western Labor-Union, a confederation of most trade-unions of the Rocky Mountain States and Territories, with a total membership of about 150,000, met in annual convention in Denver. At the same time and in the same city, two of the strongest organizations affiliated with that body, the Western Federation of Miners and the United Association of Hotel and Restaurant Employees, also held their annual conventions. The principal topic of discussion at all three conventions was the relation of the organizations represented by them to the Socialist Party. The result of their deliberations was that all three declared themselves in favor of independent political action, recognized the Socialist Party as the representative of the working class in the field of politics, and indorsed the platform of the party.

The Western Labor-Union at the same time rejected the overtures of the American Federation of Labor for the amalgamation of the two bodies on account of the conservative views of the Federation and changed its own name to "American Labor-Union," thus indicating its intention to extend its operations beyond the limits of the West. The organization was almost as active in the socialist movement as in that of the trade-unions, and its official organ, *The American Labor-Union Journal,* was a spokesman of both movements.

In the month of November of the same year the annual convention of the American Federation of Labor was held in New Orleans. The socialist delegates introduced a resolution indorsing socialism, as they had been doing at all previous conventions of the Federation. The resolution this time read as follows:

"Resolved, That this twenty-second annual convention of the American Federation of Labor advise the working people to organize their economic and political power to secure for labor the full equivalent of its toil and the overthrow of the wage system."

The resolution provoked a lengthy and heated debate, and was finally rejected by a vote of 3,744 to 3,334. It had not aimed at any practical measures and whether it was accepted or rejected was of little practical importance to either side. But it was to some extent a test of the strength of the socialist sentiment in the ranks of the American Federation of Labor, and the fact that almost a full half of all the votes of the convention was cast in favor of it was some proof of the progress of socialism within the organization.

Another proof of the spread of the socialist sentiment within the period mentioned was the development of the party press. In former years the Socialist Labor Party had found it difficult, and at times almost impossible, to maintain a single weekly paper in the English language. In the year 1904 the Socialist Party was represented in the press by seven monthly magazines and by eighteen weeklies in the English language, published in the following States: New York, Pennsylvania, Illinois, Wisconsin, Minnesota, Wyoming, Iowa, Kansas, Montana, Utah, Colorado, Washington and California and in the Territory of Oklahoma. Of the German party papers three were dailies and seven were weeklies. The party was also represented by one paper in each of the following languages: French, Italian, Jewish, Bohemian, Norwegian, Polish and Slavonic.

The growth of the Socialist Party was accompanied by a corresponding decline of the Socialist Labor Party. The latter never recovered from the effects of the split of 1899. Altho the "administration faction" had gained a legal victory over the "faction of the opposition" in the litigation over the right to the use of the party name, its victory was of little practical benefit. The great majority of organized and unorganized socialists had lost their confidence in the leadership of the party and turned their sympathies and support to the Socialist Party. The further actions and policy of the Socialist Labor Party were by no means calculated to regain the lost confidence.

Its hostile attitude toward the trade-unions and its fanatic rigidity of discipline, which had provoked an open schism within its ranks, now became the sole excuse for its separate existence, and was intensified to ludicrousness. In June, 1900, the party held a national convention in the city of New York, which lasted a full week. The proceedings of the convention were characterized by almost childish abuse of the seceders, and of all "pure and simple" trade-unions, and the climax of hatred toward the latter was exprest in the following resolution adopted by a practically unanimous vote:

"If any member of the Socialist Labor Party accepts office in a pure and simple trade or labor organization he shall be considered antagonistically inclined toward the Socialist Labor Party and shall be expelled. If any officer of a pure and simple trade or labor organization applies for membership in the Socialist Labor Party, he shall be rejected.''

In the presidential elections of 1900 the party's vote fell from 82,204 polled by it in the general elections of 1898 to 34,191. In the Congressional election of 1902, in which the vote of the Socialist Party was almost trebled, the Socialist Labor Party increased its vote to about 50,000, which, however, declined to 33,536 in the Presidential elections of 1904.

At the same time the process of ''purification'' went on within the party at an ever-accelerating rate. State organizations, ''sections,'' and individual members alike were expelled from the party for various acts of heresy. As the influx of new members was slow, the ranks of the party thinned steadily. In 1904, the membership of the Socialist Labor Party was estimated at about 3,000.

The party published a daily newspaper in the English language (*The People*) in New York, and several weekly papers in foreign languages.

Chapter V

PRESENT DAY SOCIALISM

I.—UNREST AND REFORM

THE United States is steadily approaching the climax of capitalistic development—the trustification of industries. This process is measured not by generations but by years. Within the six years following the Census of 1900, capitalistic production probably made greater progress, absolutely and relatively, than within the ten-year period intervening between that year and the preceding census year.

From 1900 to 1905 the capital invested in large manufacturing increased from about $9,000,000,000 to $12,700,-000,000 in round figures, while the number of big manufacturing establishments remained practically stationary. The value of the annual product of the establishments comprised within that class rose within the same period from $11,500,000,000 to almost $15,000,000,000 and the number of wage workers employed by them from 4,715,000 to 5,470,000.

The Census of Manufactures, published by the Department of Commerce and Labor in 1906, reveals the astounding fact that, in 1904, 11.2 per cent. of the manufacturing establishments controlled 81.5 per cent. of all capital invested in manufacture in the United States, and supplied 79.3 per cent. of all products. Thirty-eight per cent. of the total values were produced by about 1900 establishments—less than one per cent. of the whole.

The development of the railroad industry easily kept pace with that of manufacturing, and both were overshadowed by activity and speculation in the world of finance. The last few years, more than ever, witnessed the growth of colossal fortunes and the formation of stupendous business combinations.

The march of capitalist progress degenerated into a mad, frenzied race for wealth, in which thousands participated, while millions were trampled under foot. Huge corporations, trusts and combinations became the order of the day. With them came the inevitable watering of stock and traffic in corporate securities. It is estimated that in 1907 the par value of such securities was no less than $40,000,000,000, almost one-third of the entire wealth of the country! Nor did the currency, banking and credit of the country lag behind the march of industrial expansion. Between 1898 and 1907, the United States produced $3,200,000,000 of gold, or about one-half as much as in the entire one hundred and fifty year period between 1700 and 1850. In 1907 there were no less than 14,000 banks in the country with a total of about $18,000,000,000 in deposits, and the greater part of it was loaned out or seeking investment in the industrial field. Mines, mills, factories and other works ran at full blast, workingmen of all trades were in large demand, and wages went up. When all the ordinary branches of industry were overstocked and overtaxed, our enterprising capitalists sought new fields frequently embarking in mad and adventurous schemes and involving flocks of trusting small investors with them. In all larger cities thousands of buildings were erected for purely speculative purposes, vacant land in the newer sections doubled and trebled in price, rents in the older sections were raised beyond all reason, and prices of commodities generally increased to an extent entirely unprecedented. In the ten-year period of 1896–1906, the cost of food alone increased over 20 per cent. in the average, and the cost of other necessaries rose about 30 per cent.

Money was abundant in the country, great fortunes were made over night; speculation and gambling took the place of industry and commerce. When the mad race had run its full course, the inevitable collapse came sudden and crushing. In the early part of 1907, it was found that much of the stock manufactured in anticipation of future sales could not be moved; retail dealers were oversupplied. The manufacturers, who had largely produced on credit, could not meet their obligations; an atmosphere of uncertainty and lack of confidence pervaded the markets; credit was suddenly contracted; the house of cards, called our "financial system," was blown asunder by the first gust of wind.

In the months of October and November, 1907, sudden "runs" were made by crowds of frightened depositors on many large financial institutions of the metropolis, including the Knickerbocker Trust Company. Several banks closed their doors and thereby caused the suspension of numerous banking institutions connected with them. The stock market, always responsive to the movements of the money market, experienced a violent drop in the values of all securities.

The first symptoms of an approaching industrial crisis were thus clearly and unmistakably revealed, and it soon asserted itself, in grim defiance of all official proclamations and declarations to the contrary. The end of the year 1907 showed 10,265 recorded business failures with total liabilities of $383,000,000 for that year, as against 9,385 failures with liabilities amounting to only $127,000,000 for 1906. Most railroad extensions and improvements begun or contemplated, were abandoned. The industrial effects of the abandonment of that work may be readily realized, if it is borne in mind that their estimated cost in New York and vicinity alone was about $500,000,000. At the same time, the freight and passenger traffic on all railroad lines was greatly diminished and thousands of railroad employees in all parts of the country were discharged or temporarily "laid off." The United States Steel Corporation cut down its work and employees to about one-half; the tobacco trust closed many of its factories entirely; the Chicago stock yards, the iron and glass works, and the other principal industries of America began to run part time or with diminished force, and in the building trades and building material factories employment became the exception, idleness the rule.

Towards the end of 1907 it was estimated that the army of unemployed in the United States had been augmented by about 1,500,000, and in 1908 the total number of unemployed workers was variously estimated at from 3,000,000 to 4,000,000. It was two years before the country began to experience some relief from the general depression.

During this period of rapid industrial rise and decline and intense competition, the political and business quarrels of the contending interests of finance occasionally assumed such dimensions that they were bound to reach the public at large. In the summer of 1904, Thomas Lawson, a Boston financier, who had fallen out with the powerful group of American money kings identified with the Standard Oil Company, began the publication of a series of graphic accounts of the methods of that combination, and the country stood aghast before the web of perfidy, baseness and corruption that characterized the dealings of eminent citizens with each other and with the public.

This revelation of the mechanism of high finance was supplemented, in 1905, by an official investigation of life insurance companies ordered by the legislature of New York State.

The business of life insurance in the United States is very extended. Hundreds of millions of dollars are invested in it by persons in all classes of society. These sums frequently constitute the sole provision for the widows and orphans of numerous policy holders. The legislative investigation revealed the most unscrupulous abuse of trust. The "high minded" financiers and prominent citizens, who, as a rule, managed the funds as trustees, did not scruple to dissipate them in extravagant salaries and fees to themselves, to manipulate them in their own financial transactions, and to draw on them freely for the support of the dominant political party and even for the purpose of wholesale bribery of State Legislatures.

The echo of the scandals in the financial world had barely died out when the Socialist novelist, Upton Sinclair, threw a bomb into the camp of industrial capitalism by the publication of his now famous novel, "The Jungle." This novel, containing a very realistic description of the revolting conditions in our principal stock yards, created such a profound impression on the public mind that President Roosevelt found himself impelled to make it the subject of an official investigation, which fully confirmed the charges of the novelist, and led to certain remedial legislation in Congress.

At the same time and through various causes, the bottomless corruption of the government of several of our largest cities was brought to light. New York, Chicago, Philadelphia, Minneapolis, Pittsburgh, Milwaukee and St. Louis were at one time or another shown to be in the clutches of rapacious political rings, whose unscrupulous trading in city franchises, property and offices threw a glaring light on the political methods and morals of our country. In short, the fruits of concentrated capitalism became painfully apparent to the large mass of the population.

The general popular discontent with existing conditions grew more wide-spread and deep-seated than ever, and found expression in all organs of our public life, and more particularly in our literature and politics.

If the literature of a country reflects the mental attitude of its people, then indeed Americans must be said to have manifested of late a very decided revolt against existing political and economic abuses and a decided leaning towards radicalism. Criticism of existing institutions and the discussion of proposed social remedies have been the keynote of our press and literature, ever since the beginning of the new century.

In the domain of fiction, the radical novel and even more so the socialist novel, took the first rank in order of importance and popularity. Not only were Jack London and Upton Sinclair, socialists and members of the Socialist Party, most widely read among novelists, but it almost became impossible for any new novel to attract large attention and popular favor unless it dealt with a social or socialistic motive. And generally socialism came to be the most frequent and vital topic of discussion in books, magazines and newspapers.

Another evidence of this spirit of the times was the "Literature of Exposure" which enlisted under its banner the most gifted of younger journalists and writers. This modern school of American literature did much to uncover the corruption of many political and industrial institutions, and gained an extension and influence paralleled only by the old Russian literature of exposure which accompanied the movement for the emancipation of the serfs.

And finally mention must be made of the pseudo-socialistic daily press which was trading upon the popular feeling of discontent and building up enormous circulations by feigning an ultra radical attitude on all questions agitating the public mind. The father of this modern brand of journalism is Mr. William Randolph Hearst, who has established a chain of newspapers of that type in the principal cities of the United States with a combined circulation sometimes estimated at two million copies per day.

If the general discontent and "social unrest" were the keynote of our recent literature, they were in an even greater degree the guiding star in our recent politics. Probably in no country of the world are the political parties so devoid of definite party principles and so alert to the changing spirit of the times as in the United States. Within the last few years our dominant political parties actually vied with each other in radicalism. The Republican Party, through its aggressive president, began a systematic warfare against the "abuses of trusts and monopolies;" Congress passed certain legislation for a stricter government supervision in the manufacture of food products, for the regulation of railroad rates, and restrictions of child labor, while the United States Courts for a time exhibited unwonted zeal in the enforcement of the anti-trust laws and the punishment of capitalist offenders. The Democratic Party, on the other hand, took occasion in numerous local and State platforms to denounce the villainous trusts and monopolies even more vehemently, and to demand the municipal and State ownership and operation of certain industries. At the same time, and as part of the same process, new reform parties and movements sprang up in various parts of the country.

The American Federation of Labor, the largest body of organized American working men, for the first time in its existence of a quarter of a century, violated its vow of political neutrality, when it interfered in the congressional elections of 1906.

In different parts of the country, notably in California, the local trade unions organized themselves into independent political parties under the name of the Union Labor Party. In San Francisco, the Western metropolis of America, that party succeeded three times in carrying the municipal elections.

But of far greater dimensions than these parties of labor were the numerous middle class reform movements of the most recent period of American politics.

The year 1905 was a banner year for these movements: it witnessed the election of Judge Edward F. Dunne as mayor of Chicago on a platform declaring for the municipal ownership of street railways and other municipal monopolies; the election into the gubernatorial chair of Missouri of Joseph W. Folk, who had made for himself a record in the prosecution of the criminal city officials and political bosses of St. Louis; the election as governor of Wisconsin, and subsequently as United States senator, of Robert M. LaFollette, a noted radical and reformer in politics, and finally the signal feat of William R. Hearst in the city of New York.

Mr. Hearst, who up to that time had played a somewhat inconspicuous part in Democratic politics, had through his papers raised the issue of municipal ownership in the New York city elections of 1905, and when the dominant political parties refused to endorse that issue, he renounced his former political affiliations, and initiated a movement of his own. The organization in which the movement crystallized was the Municipal Ownership League, and its candidate for the mayoralty of New York was Mr. Hearst himself.

The organization was formed in the haste of the electoral campaign, and never had much more than a nominal existence; it stood for municipal ownership, and a line of other rather confused demands radical in sound; but above all, it represented the spirit of revolt against existing conditions. The movement was at first not taken seriously by the old-time politicians of New York, but as the election approached, it gathered unexpected strength and extension. On the day of election the official count gave Mr. Hearst 222,929 votes as against 228,397 for his successful opponent on the Democratic ticket, George B. McClellan.

Encouraged by this unexpected success at the polls, the Hearst forces entered in the State elections of 1906 on a larger scale. In the State of New York Mr. Hearst reorganized his party under the name of "The Independence League" and accepted its nomination for governor of the State, on a somewhat indefinite, though on the whole, radical, platform. He also received the endorsement of the Democratic Party on a quite definite and decidedly reactionary platform, and polled 691,105 votes as against 749,002 votes cast for his successful Republican opponent. His running mates on the fusion State ticket were elected to office. The Hearst movement also played an important part in the election in Massachusetts where its candidate, Mr. Moran, received 192,295 votes out of a total of little more than 400,000, and in California, where the Hearst candidate for governor, Mr. Langdon, polled 45,008 out of a total of about 300,000.

The campaign of 1906 marks a turning point in the movement. The alternate alliance of Mr. Hearst with the Republican and Democratic Parties, both of whom he had previously denounced in his papers in immoderate terms, and his willingness to run for office on any platform, rapidly divested the movement of the character of a popular reform movement. It was never based on a definite and consistent platform of political or social reform; it was largely held together by the personal means of its founder and the influence of his chain of papers. The kaleidoscopic changes of Mr. Hearst's political programs and allegiance made it apparent that there was nothing definite or permanent in the "Hearst movement" except the personality of Mr. Hearst. In the presidential elections of 1908, the organization was re-christened the Independence Party, it held a national convention and nominated Mr. Thomas L. Hisgen, a wealthy Massachusetts business man, for President. But the campaign only served to emphasize the weakness of the movement as distinct from its founder. Mr. Hisgen polled only 83,628 votes in the entire country, less than one-third of the vote cast in 1905 for Mr. Hearst in the city of New York alone, and less than one-fifth of the vote of the Socialist Party.

In 1909, Mr. Hearst again accepted the nomination for the office of Mayor of the city of New York. This time his campaign was not even made on any definite reform issue. He received a vote of over 150,000.

II.—THE TRADE UNION MOVEMENT TO-DAY

THE period of the last few years has been very eventful in the trade union movement. For the American Federation of Labor, it has been a period of slow but steady growth and of intense struggle. During the five-year period of 1904–1908, the Federation issued about 1,650 new charters to different national, international and local unions. In the same period the paid-up membership of all organizations affiliated with it increased over 100,000. In his report to the annual convention of the Federation, held in November, 1908, President Samuel Gompers gives the following numbers of affiliated labor unions: International unions, 116; State Federations, 38; Central Labor Bodies, 606; Local Trade and Federal Labor Unions, 583; Industrial Departments, 2. The International Unions comprised no less than 28,700 local organizations of their respective trades. The paid-up membership of the Federation in the same year was 1,586,885, and the actual total number of members was estimated at about two millions.

The American Federation of Labor is by far the largest body of organized labor in the United States, but it does not comprise all of the trade unions in the country. It is estimated that 500,000 to 1,000,000 working men are organized in smaller trade federations and in unaffiliated national and local unions. These organizations likewise made substantial gains within the last few years. The most acute period of the industrial depression, the year 1908, witnessed a slight deterioration of the movement. But on the whole organized labor managed to maintain its numbers and even successfully to resist the contemplated wholesale reduction of wages during the crisis.

The growth and vitality of the trade union movement could not fail to spread alarm in the ranks of the employing classes, and to give rise to concerted efforts to check the progress of organized labor. The most noteworthy movement in that direction is the so-called "open shop" movement. The movement received special inspiration through an order of the President of the United States directing that the government printing office be operated as an "open shop, *i. e.*, that no discrimination be made in favor of union printers as against non-union printers. This was a blow aimed at the most vital principle of the trade union movement, the endeavor to bring all working men of the organized trades under the jurisdiction of their respective organizations. The employers of the country eagerly took up the shibboleth and inaugurated a movement for the destruction of trade unions in the name of the "open shop." The most important organ of the movement was the Citizens' Industrial Alliance, which was founded in Chicago in October, 1903. The organization adopted a declaration of principles in which it voiced its opposition to "joint agreements, government arbitration in labor disputes, and to all plans for the settlement of labor strife which eliminate the right of every man to work where, when and for what he pleases, and the right of an employer to hire whom he pleases and for what he pleases."

In November, 1904, the organization held a national convention in the city of New York, which was attended by 400 delegates representing all parts of the country. In the following year Mr. Edward H. Davis, the secretary of the association, claimed for it a membership of several hundred thousand "of the manufacturers and business men of the United States."

The Citizens' Industrial Alliance was closely connected with the National Association of Manufacturers formed in 1895. This association originally proclaimed its object to be that of "promoting trade, commerce and markets and the elimination of restrictions and barriers," but within late years, and especially under the administrations of its four last presidents, Messrs. Parry, Post, Van Cleave and Kirby, it centered its efforts principally on the task of combating the trade-union movement. It is said that between the years 1906 and 1907 the Association raised one million and a half dollars among its members as a war fund to be used in its crusade against organized labor. No less than twelve thousand men were employed by it to mingle with the organized workers, report their doings to employers and demoralize and disorganize their unions. The National Association of Manufacturers claims a membership of over 3,000 in the different parts of the country. It organized a large number of lockouts, caused many strikes, and instituted several court proceedings against labor organizations, but while it attained some notable victories in the courts, its efforts to weaken the labor movement have on the whole been a failure.

Another and more subtle attempt on the part of the employing classes to render the labor movement harmless is found in the organization of the National Civic Federation. This organization, devised by the cunning mind of the late Senator Hanna, consists of an incongruous mixture of millionaires, labor leaders and "prominent citizens." It has for its ostensible object "the voluntary conciliation between employers and employees as distinguished from arbitration," but in reality it serves to palliate the aggressive spirit of organized labor without offering any concessions on the part of organized capital. Of a certain conference held by that body in New York on May 7, 1904, it was said that it represented hundreds of millions of capital and more than 2,500,000 wage earners. The latter assertion referred no doubt to the presence of the president and some other officials of the American Federation of Labor, who unfortunately allowed themselves to be drawn into the movement, but the Civic Federation has at no time exerted any influence on the rank and file of the trade union movement.

An important event in the recent history of American trade unionism is the political activity of the Federation of Labor.

For a number of years the Federation had stood on the principle of abstinence from organized working class politics, and had followed the policy of seeking favors from the State legislatures and United States Congress by "lobbying" methods. The fruits of that activity were very meager indeed. Several States passed laws limiting the hours of labor of women and children and those of men in particularly dangerous or unhealthful callings; others adopted laws fixing a minimum wage for certain workmen employed in State or municipal work, and the National House of Representatives passed an eight-hour law for all employees of the federal government. But these laws proved of little real benefit to the working class.

Under the peculiar power of our courts to change laws by "interpretation" or to nullify them entirely on the ground of unconstitutionality, one labor law after another was eradicated from the statute books of the States. The years 1905–1908 marked a veritable epidemic in the slaughter of such laws.

At the same time the departments of the United States Government showed great reluctance in enforcing the Eight-Hour Law, and the various legislative measures fathered by the American Federation of Labor—a more effective eight-hour law, laws against cheap prison labor, against interference of courts in labor disputes by summary "injunction" orders, and all similar proposed labor measures— were systematically ignored or voted down by Congress.

The executive officers of the Federation finally grew weary, and after consultation with the presidents of 117 national unions, formulated what has become known as the "Labor's Bill of Grievances," a document reciting the persistent attempts of the American Federation of Labor to secure fair legislation from Congress, and honest enforcements of existing labor laws from government, and its uniform failure to secure either. It closed with a demand for the redress of these grievances.

The document, which was presented to the President of the United States, the president pro tempore of the United States Senate and the Speaker of the House of Representatives, concluded with this remarkable statement:

"We present these grievances to your attention because we have long, patiently, and in vain waited for redress. There is not any matter of which we have complained but for which we have in an honorable and lawful manner submitted remedies. The remedies for these grievances proposed by Labor are in line with fundamental law, and with the progress and development made necessary by changed industrial conditions.

"Labor brings these its grievances to your attention because you are the representatives responsible for legislation and for the failure of legislation. The toilers come to you as your fellow-citizens who, by reason of their position in life, have not only with all other citizens an equal interest in our country, but the further interest of being the burden-bearers, the wage-earners of America. As Labor's representatives we ask you to redress these grievances, for it is in your power so to do.

"Labor now appeals to you, and we trust that it may not be in vain. But if perchance you may not heed us, we shall appeal to the conscience and the support of our fellow-citizens."

The Bill of Grievances received scant attention from the President and the presiding officers of the Senate and House, and in the following campaign, in the fall of 1906, for the election of a new House of Representatives, the American Federation of Labor, true to its warning, took an active part in the campaign. Unfortunately the campaign was conducted by the officers of the Federation on the lines of the short-sighted, half-hearted policy, which always characterized their political views and actions. They

did not rise to the point of conscious working class politics;
they did not nominate candidates of their own; nor did
they support the candidates of the Socialist Party. In fact
the distinction between the Socialist Party as a party of
labor and the two old parties, as parties of the possessing
and employing classes, never dawned on them. The Federation limited its political activities to combating some Republican or Democratic candidates and supporting others
on the sole test of their supposed personal hostility or
friendship for organized labor.

The campaign thus conducted upon the platform of ''Re-
warding friends and punishing enemies'' made practically
no impression on the politics of the country, and it is possible that the Federation would never have undertaken a similar one, had it not been for the occurrence of an event of
particular importance at that time.

It was customary for the Federation to publish in the
columns of its official organ, the *American Federationist,*
the names of employers against whom organized labor had
special grievances. These names were published under the
heading: ''We don't patronize,'' and constituted the so-
called ''We Don't Patronize List'' of the Federation.

Sometime in 1907 the Buck's Stove and Range Company
of St. Louis made an attempt to increase the working hours
of its employees, members of the International Brotherhood
of Foundry Employees. The latter resisted the attempt.
A strike followed, and all efforts on the part of the Brotherhood and the Federation to adjust the dispute foundered on
the obstinacy of the president of the Company, Mr. J. W.
Van Cleave, who was also the president of the National
Association of Manufacturers and a notorious enemy of organized labor. The name of the Buck's Stove and Range
Company was thereupon published in the ''We Don't
Patronize List'' of the *American Federationist,* and the
company secured from Judge Clabough of the Supreme
Court of the District of Columbia an order to show cause
why the Federation and its officers should not be enjoined
from continuing to publish its name on that list. The action seemed so subversive of the principles of personal lib-

erty and freedom of the press and so opposed to established precedents, that the officers of the Federation did not take it very seriously.

But on December 18, 1907 Judge Gould not only granted an injunction in the suit, but made it one of the most sweeping documents of the kind ever issued by a court in the United States. The injunction order prohibited all officers and members of the American Federation of Labor and of all its affiliated organizations, their agents, friends, sympathizers and counsel, either as officials or as individuals, from making any reference whatsoever to the controversy between the Buck's Stove and Range Company and its employees, by printed, written or spoken word and particularly from referring to the boycott of organized labor against the Company. The Federation promptly discontinued the publication of the "We Don't Patronize List," but the proceedings in the suit and the effect of the injunction order were freely discust in the editorial columns of the *American Federationist,* and commented on in public addresses by the officers of the Federation. On the ground of these publications and utterances Messrs. Samuel Gompers, John Mitchell and Frank Morrison, President, Vice-President and Secretary respectively of the American Federation of Labor, were cited in July, 1908, to show cause why they should not be punished for contempt of court for having disobeyed Judge Gould's injunction order. The hearing on the application was very thorough. Every statement or act of the defendants in connection with Buck's Stove injunction was carefully and critically examined, and even the political speeches of Mr. Gompers, and the publication in the *American Federationist* of the injunction order itself, were made the basis of additional charges. The proceedings lasted several months, and terminated in a decision rendered by Judge Wright shortly after the general elections of 1908, by which the American Federation of Labor was denounced in scathing terms, and its principal officers, Gompers, Mitchell and Morrison, sentenced to jail terms ranging from one year to six months.

The Federation had always regarded the injunction as

one of the heaviest scourges of the labor movement, and had for years conducted an energetic campaign for the abolition of the use of that extraordinary mandate in labor disputes. But now, when its lash was applied to their own bodies in such a severe manner and with so little justification, the officers of the Federation threw the entire weight of their organization into the war against the injunction writ. A bill was introduced in the United States Congress aiming at the abolition of the use of injunctions in labor disputes, but notwithstanding all efforts and agitation of the American Federation of Labor, the bill was smothered in committee, and never even discust in the House.

The Executive Council of the Federation thereupon convened an extraordinary conference of the chief officers of all International Unions affiliated with it, in which representatives of the unaffiliated Railway Brotherhoods and of several farmers' organizations also participated. The conference was held at Washington, D. C., on March 18, 1908, and formulated a Protest to Congress and an Address to the Workers. In the former document the labor leaders urged Congress to speedily enact legislation tending to right the wrongs inflicted on organized labor by recent decisions and acts of the courts, notably the decision in the Danbury Hatters' case holding labor unions to be trusts and illegal combinations, and the indiscriminate use of injunctions in controversies between employers and workers. In the Address to the Workers they called upon all labor unions to hold public meetings throughout the country and to pass resolutions urging Congress to enact such laws. The meetings were held and resolutions adopted, but Congress, in the words of Gompers, "adjourned, the majority party in Congress boastfully declaring its indifference to Labor's appeal and demand for justice." At this juncture the Presidential elections of 1908 were approaching and all political parties were about to hold national nominating conventions. The Executive Council of the American Federation of Labor sent deputations to the conventions of each of the two leading parties, the Republican and Democratic, and presented to each of them a demand that it pledge its party to anti-injunction legislation along the lines advocated by the Federation. The Republican Party felt itself strong enough to carry the election without the somewhat doubtful aid of the American Federation, and flatly refused to accede to its demands. The Democratic Party, on the other hand, weaker than the Republican and making its appeal to the more radical portion of the community, eagerly availed itself of the opportunity to gain the support of organized labor, and accepted the demands of the Federation with great alacrity. This decided the political course of the officials of the American Federation of Labor in the electoral campaign of 1908. The "friends" to be rewarded in this election were all the Democratic candidates in the country, and the "enemies" to be punished, were all the Republicans. Mr. Gompers and other prominent officials of the Federation were openly and consistently active in behalf of the Democratic candidates; they issued millions of leaflets and proclamations in support of the Democratic campaign, and called upon the affiliated trade-unions to contribute money to the war chest of the Democratic Party. The American Federation of Labor almost suddenly found itself engrossed in a political campaign, but not as an independent political factor in accordance with the several resolutions from time to time passed by its conventions, but as a tail to the kite of one of the old capitalist parties.

The policy of Mr. Gompers in supporting the Democratic Party does not seem to have created much enthusiasm in the ranks of the American Federation of Labor. The labor vote promised, if it materialized at all, was not very strong; at any rate not strong enough to save Mr. Bryan, the Democratic candidate for President, from defeat, or to prevent the election of any of the most notorious foes of labor from among the Republican candidates for Congress. The American Federation of Labor had again missed a splendid opportunity for asserting its power as a working class party, and the greatest American organization of labor with its two million members and its tremendous influence in the world of labor, made a lamentably poor debut in politics.

III.—THE INDUSTRIAL WORKERS OF THE WORLD

THE last annual conventions of the American Federation of Labor were marked by two features in particular; the decline of discussions on independent working-class politics, and the growth of jurisdictional disputes between the affiliated unions.

In former years the socialist delegates to the annual conventions of the American Federation of Labor bent all their energies to a persistent effort to induce the Federation as a body to enter the political field on a radical working-class platform, and, as we have seen, in some instances they were not altogether unsuccessful.

These efforts on the part of the socialists were perfectly natural at a time when the political organization of socialism had not much more than a nominal existence in the United States, and practically the entire strength of organized labor was represented by the trade union movement. But when the Socialist Party had begun to demonstrate its ability to organize the working class of the country politically on the clear cut lines of international socialism, the wisdom of forcing the creation of another political party of labor, of a presumably less satisfactory character, began to be seriously questioned. The socialists in the American Federation of Labor have accordingly abandoned the efforts to "capture" the Federation bodily, and have transferred their energies to the task of educating the individual trade unionists, in local meetings and State and national conventions, in the proper understanding of the socialist philosophy.

In all discussions on socialism on the floor of the Federation conventions, Mr. Samuel Gompers and other officers and leaders of the organization, invariably took the somewhat antiquated position of "pure and simple" trade unionism and occasionally evinced a very decided hostility towards the socialist movement. This unprogressive stand of its leaders resulted in a sentiment of dissatisfaction with the Federation in certain sections of organized labor, and the sentiment spread to other sections on account of the frequent jurisdictional disputes between its different affiliated unions.

The American Federation of Labor is organized on the principle of strict trade autonomy, and with few exceptions each national union within the Federation has exclusive jurisdiction of its respective trade. Thus where working men of several trades are employed by one concern or in one enterprise, they are often divided into a number of separate organizations, who may happen to follow different and conflicting policies in their relations with the common employer. In such cases it may frequently happen that when occasion arises for concerted action against the employer, as for instance in strikes, the working men may fail for want of unanimity and mutual support. In some instances, notably in that of the building trades, the difficulty was early met by the formation of joint local boards, who are entrusted with the direction of all action against the common employer, but in other cases as f. i., those of the railway and brewery workers, the conflicting and sometimes antagonistic attitude occasionally taken by the separate trades in common employment, has often led to internecine feuds and acrimonious debates in the conventions of the American Federation of Labor.

The opposition to this feature of the Federation and the conservative attitude of its leaders, led to the formation of a rival body of organized labor—the INDUSTRIAL WORKERS OF THE WORLD. This is one of the most interesting of recent experiments in the field of organized labor.

It had its inception in a secret conference held in Chicago in the early part of January, 1905. The conference was attended by about twenty-five persons, most of them officials of trade unions not connected with the American Federation of Labor, and several prominent socialists without trade union affiliations.

The deliberations of the conferees resulted in the issuing of a Manifesto to the working class of America, which may be regarded as the declaration of principles of the new movement. The trend of argument of the noteworthy document is best shown by the following excerpts from it:

"Social relations and groupings only reflect mechanical and industrial conditions. The great facts of present industry are the displacement of human skill by machines and the increase of capitalist power through concentration in the possession of the tools with which wealth is produced and distributed.

"Because of these facts trade divisions among laborers and competition among capitalists are alike disappearing. Class divisions grow ever more fixed and class antagonism more sharp. Trade lines have been swallowed up in a common servitude of all workers to the machines which they tend. . . .

"The worker, wholly separated from the land and the tools, with his skill of craftsmanship rendered useless, is sunk in the uniform mass of wage slaves. He sees his power of resistance broken by craft divisions, perpetuated from outgrown industrial stages. . . .

"Laborers are no longer classified by differences in trade skill, but the employer assigns them according to the machines to which they are attached. These divisions, far from representing difference in skill or interests among the laborers, are imposed by the employers that workers may be pitted against one another and spurred to greater exertions in the shop, and that all resistance to capitalist tyranny may be weakened by artificial distinctions.

"While encouraging these outgrown divisions among the workers the capitalists carefully adjust themselves to the new conditions. They wipe out all differences among themselves, and present a united front in their war upon labor. . . .

"The employers' line of battle and methods of warfare correspond to the solidarity of the mechanical and industrial concentration, while laborers still form their fighting organization on lines of long-gone trade divisions. . . .

"Craft divisions hinder the growth of class consciousness of the workers, foster the idea of harmony of interests between employing exploiter and employed slave. They permit the association of the misleaders of the workers with the capitalists in the Civic Federations, where plans are made for the perpetuation of capitalism, and the permanent enslavement of the workers through the wage system. . . .

"Universal economic evils afflicting the working class can be eradicated only by a universal working-class movement. Such a movement of the working class is impossible while separate craft and wage agreements are made favoring the employer against other crafts in the same industry, and while energies are wasted in fruitless jurisdiction struggles which serve only to further the personal aggrandizement of union officials.

"A movement to fulfil these conditions must consist of one great industrial union embracing all industries—providing for craft autonomy locally, industrial autonomy internationally, and working class unity generally.

"It must be founded on the class struggle, and its general administration must be conducted in harmony with the recognition of the irrepressible conflict between the capitalist class and the working class. . . .

"Local, national and general administration, including union labels, buttons, badges, transfer cards, initiation fees, and per capita tax should be uniform throughout. . . .

"Transfers of membership between unions, local national or international, should be universal.

"Working men bringing union cards from industrial unions in foreign countries should be freely admitted into the organization. . . .

"A *central defense fund*, to which all members contribute equally, should be established and maintained."

The Manifesto concluded with a call for a convention for the purpose of forming a new organization based on these principles, and was signed by the members of the secret conference and several other persons well known in the radical labor movement of the country including the late presidential candidate of the Socialist Party, Eugene V. Debs.

The convention initiated by the Manifesto assembled in Chicago on June 27, 1905, and was rather disappointing to the originators of the movement. The expected secession of a number of national trade unions from the conservative American Federation of Labor did not materialize. Of the 212 delegates who participated in the convention, 5 represented the Western Federation of Miners with a membership of 27,000, 7 represented the American Labor Union, with a total membership of 16,780, and 2 delegates represented the United Metal Workers' International Union with 3,000 members. All these were organizations not affiliated with the American Federation of Labor. Most of all the remaining delegates represented small local organizations, while about sixty represented no organizations at all.

But what the convention lacked in numbers, it amply made up in enthusiasm. During the eleven days of its deliberations, the delegates submitted the methods of existing trade unions to a scathing criticism, ratified all points and planks of the Manifesto, assumed the grandiloquent name of "Industrial Workers of the World," elected officers and adopted a constitution.

The form of organization of the new body was devised in accordance with the views exprest in the Manifesto. In the language of the initiators of the movement, the organization was to be "builded as the structure of socialist society, embracing within itself the working class in approximately the same groups and departments of industries that the workers would assume in the working class administration of the Cooperative Commonwealth."

The organization is divided into thirteen Industrial Departments, such as the Departments of Mining, Transportation, Food Stuffs, etc., which together are supposed to cover the entire field of the modern industrial world. The departments are composed of separate unions of "closely kindred" industries. The affairs of each industrial department are administered by separate executive boards, subject, however, to the direction and control of a General Executive Board, which consists of one member from each of the thirteen departments. The executive head of the organization is the General President, who has general supervision of all its affairs. All members of the local union pay a uniform per capita tax of 25 cents per month, of which two-thirds go to the respective departments, and one-third to the general organization. A specified portion of the dues received by the general organization is applied for the accumulation of a central defense fund.

During the first year of its existence the Industrial Workers of the World made slow but steady progress, and at its second annual convention held in September, 1906, General President Charles O. Sherman was able to report a not inconsiderable increase of membership. But the progress of the new movement was suddenly checked by internal strife.

Among the organizations that assisted at the birth of the Industrial Workers of the World were also the remnants of the "Socialist Trade and Labor Alliance," the creature of the Socialist Labor Party, whose total membership had been reduced to 1,400 as claimed by its representatives, or to about 600 as asserted by its opponents. The Socialist Trade and Labor Alliance had a record of having caused more disputes and schisms within the socialist labor movements in America in recent years than any other single factor, and its affiliation with the new movement was fateful for the latter. Months before the second convention, the Alliance under the direction of the leader of the Socialist Labor Party, Daniel De Leon, laid plans to capture the administration of the Industrial Workers of the World, and through skilful manipulation of delegates, it succeeded in obtaining control of the convention. The delegates of the Socialist Trade and Labor Alliance and their supporters dominated the convention completely. They practically remodeled the constitution of the organization, abolished the office of General President, and chose a new Executive Board from among their own adherents. But the triumph of the Alliance was not lasting.

The adherents of the old *régime* claimed that the acts of the convention were not operative and that the newly elected officers could not assume the direction of the organization until such time as the membership of the Industrial Workers would ratify the proceedings of the convention upon a referendum vote. The supporters of the Alliance refused to accede to that contention, and the old officers promptly declared all acts of the convention illegal and void. The split within the ranks of the Industrial Workers was now complete. The two factions maintained rival sets of officers, and the dispute was taken into the courts. In the meanwhile, the Western Federation of Miners severed its connection with the organization. The withdrawal of the only important body of workingmen from the Industrial Workers and the split within the ranks of the remaining membership, left the organization in a state of weakness from which it never fully recovered. Of its two wings the one headed by Charles O. Sherman survived the split but a very short time, while the other, headed by Mr. Vincent St. John, formerly a prominent member of the Western Federation of Miners, now practically has the whole field to itself. This organization had a paid-up membership of but little over five thousand in the years 1907 and 1908, but these numbers were more than doubled within the last year. The Industrial Workers of the World consists of one hundred and six local unions, one National Industrial Union, that of the Textile Workers, and four "Propaganda Leagues." The membership is composed principally of textile, lumber, and railroad construction workers, coal miners and waiters.

The fate of the Industrial Workers of the World has thus, on the whole, not justified the sanguine expectations of its sponsors, at least not up to the date of this writing. But if the organization of the Industrial Workers has failed, the idea of industrial unionism has on the contrary made large progress in the American labor movement. The necessity of a more compact and harmonious organization of the working men of kindred trades is receiving ever greater recognition in the trade-union world, and within the last few years several important organizations within the American Federation of Labor have formed industrial alliances. The Railroad Department, the Allied Printing Trades Council, the Building Trades Department and the

Metal Trades Department, are among the most conspicuous of such organizations.

IV.—THE MOYER-HAYWOOD CASE

ONE of the most significant and interesting episodes in the recent history of organized labor and socialism in the United States is the dramatic labor struggle in Colorado, with its culminating point—the arrest and imprisonment of the leaders of the Western Federation of Miners—Moyer, Haywood and Pettibone, on the charge of murder.

The principal industry of Colorado is mining, and the greater part of the working population of the State consists of mine workers. These were a lot of sorely exploited, overworked, underpaid and abused men until the year 1893, when they and the mine workers of some neighboring States banded themselves together into an organization under the name "Western Federation of Miners." The Federation grew rapidly, and in 1899 it had gained sufficient strength and influence in Colorado to induce the Legislature to pass an eight-hour law for all workers in the mines.

The law was, as usual, declared unconstitutional by the Supreme Court on the first test, but nothing daunted, the laboring population of Colorado took up the fight anew, and in 1902, they succeeded in passing a constitutional amendment which made it mandatory on the incoming Legislature to enact an eight-hour law for the miners.

But the Legislature, bribed or cowed by the mine owners, ignored the constitutional command, and adjourned without passing such a law.

The organized working men of Colorado thus twice betrayed by the political representatives of their employers, and persistently persecuted on account of their allegiance to their union, resolved to take the battle into their own hands; they struck for an eight-hour day and for more humane treatment in the mines.

The strike was well organized and effective; the strikers were orderly and determined; they had the undivided sympathy of the population, and their victory seemed assured.

The mine owners of Colorado were now thoroughly alarmed. They decided to break the workingmen's strike and their organization by all means, fair or foul, and proceeded to the execution of their task with unscrupulous brutality. They evicted their employees from their homes and, where possible, cut off their food supply; they hired thugs to assault the strikers, and harassed, maltreated and persecuted their wives and children. But the strikers showed no signs of surrender. They camped out on the public highways, faced exposure, sickness and starvation, and still their ranks did not weaken; they remained grimly determined to fight out the battle forced on them by their employers.

It was then that the ruling classes of Colorado turned for aid to the Governor of the State, James A. Peabody. And the Governor promptly responded to their appeal. The peaceful mining districts were infested by a horde of unprincipled troops led by brutal commanders. Martial law was declared in the strike districts, and all safeguards of law and the constitution were swept away. The State of Colorado was with one fell blow reduced to the political level of Russia, with Governor Peabody and Lieutenant-General Sherman Bell as the undisputed autocrats.

The working men affiliated with the Western Federation of Miners, and the citizens suspected of sympathy with them, were dealt with as outlaws; they were arrested by the hundreds without warrant, crowded into monstrous "bull-pens," and without trial and conviction deported from the State. The reign of terror inaugurated by the Colorado mine owners stopped at nothing; public officials regularly elected by the people were ousted from office if found unwilling to join in the carousal of lawlessness; mines were forcibly closed if their owners permitted union men to work in them; the courts, the churches and the press were bribed or cowed to support this reign of infamy; the writ of habeas corpus was suspended; the civil powers of the State were ignored, and theft, arson, assault and murder were freely committed by the "better classes."

The strike was not broken, it was literally physically crushed. And when the devastation of the mining districts in Colorado was complete, the militia withdrew with military honors.

But the ruling classes of Colorado were not satisfied. Their triumph was not yet complete. For while the strike was crushed, the greater evil, the organization of the workingmen, the "lawless, criminal" Western Federation of Miners, was still alive. The experience of the Colorado laborers during the reign of the law and order vandals had only served to strengthen the tie that bound them together, the tie of common sufferings and common struggles. Their organization rapidly recovered from the severe blow, and was again thriving under the leadership of its efficient and trusted officials, Chas. H. Moyer, William D. Haywood and others. These leaders could not be bribed or bought, hence they must be removed in some other way, in some way which would bring them and their following into lasting disgrace and would stamp out organized labor for many years to come.

This was the persistent aim of the Western mine owners, and to this end they employed a large force of private detectives. They had the machinery of the government at their command; they had the wheels of justice greased, they only waited for the pretext.

And the pretext came. On December 30th, 1905, Frank Steunenberg, former Governor of Idaho, was killed by means of an infernal machine at the gate of his house. Steunenberg, during his administration, had been to Idaho what Peabody was to Colorado, and the inference naturally arose that his assassination was a deed of vengeance. But who committed the ruthless deed? For weeks this was a matter of speculation. Suddenly the world of organized labor was startled by the news that Moyer, Haywood and Pettibone, all leaders of the Western Federation of Miners, had been arrested, charged with complicity in the heinous crime.

The charge bore the mark of clumsy fabrication on its face. Moyer and the other prisoners were men of an advanced and enlightened type and members of the Socialist Party. They were well known in the labor world as foes of all acts of violence. During the bitterest persecutions in Colorado they had persistently counseled order in the ranks of the strikers and cautioned their followers not to allow themselves to be provoked by the lawless acts of the militia.

On the other hand, the mine owners in their former struggles with the mine workers had repeatedly attempted to fasten various crimes on the strike leaders, even going to the extent of organizing outrages such as derailing trains and blowing up railway stations, for the purpose of creating public sentiment against the strikers and removing influential strike leaders.

Furthermore, Steunenberg had for many years before his death retired from public life and ceased to be a factor in politics. There was, therefore, no motive for the Western Federation of Miners to commit the crime even if it possest the requisite moral depravity. And finally the entire charge rested practically on the alleged confession of one Harry Orchard, a criminal and degenerate of the lowest type, a confession procured by a private detective in the pay of the mine owners.

But what made the case still more significant was the manner of arrest of the accused. The prisoners were residents and citizens of the State of Colorado, the crime was committed in the State of Idaho. Under the provisions of the United States constitution each State has exclusive jurisdiction of crimes committed within its boundaries, but where a person charged with the commission of a crime "flees from justice and is found in another State," the Governor of such State may upon demand in proper form surrender the fugitive to the Governor of the State in which the crime was committed.

Moyer, Haywood and Pettibone had not been in Idaho at the time of the killing of Steunenberg, nor for a number of years before, and the Governor of Colorado was, therefore, without power to arrest the accused or to surrender them to the Idaho authorities. To overcome this difficulty, the Governors of Idaho and Colorado virtually entered into a conspiracy to kidnap the officers of the Miners' Federation and to hurry them over the State border without giving them a chance to appeal to the courts of their State or to assert their constitutional rights. And the conspiracy was carried out in all details. On Thursday, February 15, 1906, an agent of the State of Idaho arrived at Denver with a requisition for the arrest of Moyer, Haywood and Pettibone, but by agreement with the Colorado State authorities the arrest was deferred. On the following Saturday evening when the courts and law offices were closed, the accused were suddenly arrested and thrown into the county jail. They were not allowed to communicate with their friends or lawyers, and early on the following morning they were surrounded by a heavy armed guard and forcibly and hastily removed to Idaho on a special train.

The imprisoned union officials subsequently appealed to the United States Courts for release from their illegal imprisonment, but the courts refused to interfere in the case. In rendering its final decision on the case, the Supreme Court of the United States handed down a most remarkable opinion in which it held in effect that while the arrest of the prisoners was illegal and might have been brought about by fraud and by conspiracy between the Governors of the two States, the State of Idaho had possession of the accused, and that the latter were without remedy in law or under the Constitution of the United States. Justice McKenna, who dissented from the prevailing opinion of his colleagues on the Supreme Court Bench, denounced the action of the two Governors as a criminal conspiracy, and the arrest of Moyer, Haywood and Pettibone in the manner described as an act of kidnaping and a flagrant violation of the constitutional rights of the defendants.

The accused officials of the Miners' Union remained confined in prison without bail for about a year and a half awaiting trial. And in the meanwhile the powers of capital were busy preparing the way for their conviction.

The Governor of the State of Idaho loudly proclaimed his conviction of the guilt of the accused, and made no secret of his desire to see them hanged. The Legislature of the State voted special appropriations and retained prominent counsel for the prosecution of the miners; the reactionary press throughout the country periodically treated its readers to gruesome accounts of the alleged criminal career of the Western Federation of Miners, and assiduously poisoned the public mind against the prisoners, and finally the President of the United States capped the climax of incitement against the accused miners by publicly branding them as "undesirable citizens" in advance of their trial.

The trial finally began on the 9th day of May, 1907, and lasted with very few and brief interruptions for 84 days. In many respects the trial is without a parallel in the annals of criminal jurisprudence in the United States. By agreement of counsel the defendants were to be tried separately, and as the prosecution believed it had the strongest case against William D. Haywood, the secretary-treasurer of the Western Federation of Miners, it was the indictment against him that was taken up first. Formally the defendant Haywood was charged with the killing of the former Governor Steunenberg, but in point of fact the trial resolved itself into an inquiry into all incidents of the embittered war which had been waged for years between the mine owners of the West and their working men. Upon the theory that the assassination of Steunenberg was but one of the results of a general conspiracy on the part of the leaders of the miners' organization to remove and destroy their enemies, the prosecution was permitted to go into all crimes which had accompanied the long series of miners' strikes in Idaho and Colorado. Every assault, murder, outrage and act of violence which had occurred in the troubled district during the preceding ten years, was sought to be laid at the door of the Western Federation of Miners, and the leaders of the organization were represented as fiends professionally and systematically engaged in the business of assassination as part of the routine of their activity. The foundation for all the gruesome charges against the accused labor leaders was laid by Harry Orchard, and the testimony of this principal witness for the prosecution was as extraordinary as was the entire trial. On the witness stand he calmly confest to about twenty different murders committed by him at various times in his career besides every other species of crime enumerated in the penal code, from theft and gambling to bigamy and arson. Orchard proved himself to be a most abnormal and hideous criminal monster with a strong suspicion of insanity. But for the time being he could be used against the dangerous socialists and labor leaders of Colorado, and incredible as it may sound, the loathsome creature was made the pet of the capitalist moralists. In prison he was surrounded with all imaginable comforts, and the Governor of the State and other high officials fraternized with him. It was announced that he had become religious and repentant, prominent clergymen gave him a testimonial of character, an eminent Harvard professor proclaimed that he had ascertained his truthfulness and good faith by unerring scientific methods, the press throughout the length and breadth of the country sang his praise, a "reputable" magazine published his autobiography—in a word Orchard was the hero, almost the saint of our respectable classes.

As against this polluted testimony, almost entirely uncorroborated, the defense produced no less than eighty-seven witnesses, including Charles H. Moyer, the president of the Federation, and Haywood himself, who disproved the charges of the prosecution. The testimony of the witnesses, men and women of all classes and callings, rapidly unfolded the true facts of this most remarkable case, and although the most influential part of the daily press was careful to suppress or mutilate these damaging facts, enough leaked out to show that the true conspiracy in the case was not one of the miners' union against the mine owners, but vice versa: that the mine owners had for years maintained in the unions of the working men their hired spies charged with the mission of disrupting the organization and inciting its members to riots, and the indications were very strong that Orchard was just one of those hired spies. Many of the crimes charged up to the Federation were traced to such spies or to the mine owners direct, and the brutal dealings of the latter with their striking employees were fully and glaringly brought to light. The presiding judge subsequently struck from the records all testimony of the counter conspiracy against the mineworkers, but he could not efface its effect on the minds of the jury. The twelve jurors who tried the case were with one exception, farmers who had no understanding of or sympathy with the struggles of labor. They had all, and some of them intimately, known the assassinated former Governor of their State; they had all read the hostile newspaper accounts of the case, and they frankly stated that they entered the jury box with a prejudice against the accused. But the case of the prosecution was so weak, and the testimony for the defense so compelling, that they took but a very short time for their deliberations and decision.

The case was submitted to them by noon on the 27th day of July, and on the 28th in the morning they announced their verdict—"Not Guilty."

Pettibone, who was tried a few months later, was likewise acquitted, and Moyer was discharged without trial.

Thus ended one of the boldest and most determined attacks of capital on organized labor in the United States within recent years.

The attempt to crush a growing labor movement by means of judicial murder is not without a parallel in the history of this country. To those who were familiar with the details of the Chicago drama of 1886–7, its inception, development and methods employed, the events in Colorado and Idaho looked like a suspiciously close imitation of it.

But between the execution of the Chicago anarchists and the trial of Haywood, just twenty years elapsed, and conditions had greatly changed during that period. Within those twenty years the labor movement became a social factor of prime importance in the United States, and the socialist movement became strong and alert to all dangers threatening the working class.

Immediately upon the arrest of Moyer, Haywood and Pettibone, a powerful wave of protest and indignation against the attempted social crime swept the laboring population of the country from one end to the other. The annual convention of the American Federation of Labor held in Minneapolis in November, 1906, publicly branded the proceedings in the case as an outrage and travesty upon justice. Numerous national and local organizations contributed large sums of money for the defense of the accused mine workers, and passed resolutions in condemnation of the lawless conduct of the executives of Idaho and Colorado; the labor press devoted much space to the discussion of the case; millions of leaflets were distributed and thousands of public meetings were held before the trial in all parts of the country in order to arouse the people to a consciousness of the full enormity of the contemplated crime against organized labor, and an agitation was unfolded which eventually forced some influential daily papers to depart from the general policy of the press, and to join their voice to that of organized labor in criticism of the unlawful methods employed in the arrest and trial of the Colorado miners.

And finally when President Roosevelt in an unguarded moment so frankly aligned himself against the accused miners, the indignation of the organized workers of the United States was roused to the highest pitch; resolutions of protest were adopted and published by hundreds of labor unions, and labor delegates were sent to Washington to remonstrate with the chief executive of the nation for his unjustifiable and tactless utterance.

In all phases of the agitation in behalf of Moyer, Haywood and Pettibone, the socialists assumed the initiative and intellectual leadership. In every State and city they were the most tireless and influential workers in the movement, which has largely served to knit more closely the bonds of solidarity between them and the trade unions.

V.—RECENT PROGRESS OF SOCIALISM

THE events described in the preceding chapters served to increase the general sentiment of unrest and dissatisfaction and to create a favorable field for radical political and industrial movements. But on the direct political fortunes of the Socialist Party they had a rather deterring effect.

The numerous reform movements, holding out to the impatient masses the phantom hope of slight but instantaneous relief, often diverted their attention from the more thorough-going but slower remedies offered by the Socialist Party.

The subsequent industrial depression created a feeling of general political timidity and conservatism, as unfavorable to socialist politics.

In the elections of 1906, the banner year of political reform parties, the vote of the Socialist Party was reduced to 330,158 (the figures are based on the highest vote in every state), while the Socialist Labor Party polled only 24,880 votes. The local elections of 1907 showed no material change in the socialist vote.

This slight set-back, however, did not discourage the organized socialists of America. The presidential elections of 1908 found them prepared to enter into the campaign with greater vigor than ever. In that year the Socialist Party held its third national convention, which met in Chicago on May 10th. The representation was based on the enrolled dues-paying membership, each 200 members being represented by one delegate. On this basis the number of delegates in attendance was 219. The convention, which lasted eight days, again nominated Eugene V. Debs for the office of President and Benjamin Hanford for that of Vice-President of the United States, and made elaborate preparations for the conduct of the ensuing electoral contest.

The political situation was most inauspicious for the Socialist Party. The presidential election of 1904 had been conducted along general lines of conservatism and the Socialist Party was practically the only exponent of radicalism. As a consequence, it not only brought out its entire legitimate strength, but also received many votes from disgruntled radicals in the camps of the old parties. In the election of 1908, on the contrary, all political parties vied with each other in professions of radicalism. The Republicans were pledged to continue the "radical policies" of President Roosevelt which included the program of "punishing rich malefactors," regulating the trusts and large corporations, extending the liability of employers within the jurisdiction of the federal government and several other popular reform measures. The Democratic Party, still smarting under the effects of the heavy defeat of its conservative ticket and platform in the preceding election, revived all the slogans of its old time middle-class radicalism and re-instated the prophet of that brand of radicalism, William J. Bryan, in the leadership of the party. The "radicalism" of the Democratic Party was far exceeded by that of Mr. Hearst's Independence Party, and the latter was eclipsed by that of the People's Party. Under these conditions the vote of the Socialist Party was from the outset limited to thorough-going socialists.

But the radicalism of the other political parties was not the only circumstance militating against the success of socialism at the polls. The bulk of the socialist vote always comes from the working class. The industrial depression which was then at its height had caused large numbers of workers to migrate in search of work, thus depriving them of a fixed residence and disqualifying them as voters. And, last but not least, the direct and public endorsement of the Democratic Party by the officials of the American Federation of Labor and their appeal to organized labor for active support of the candidates of that party, could not but be detrimental to the socialist campaign.

The socialists realized the difficulties confronting them at this juncture, and endeavored to overcome them by redoubled zeal. From May 17, the date of the adjournment of the convention, until the day of election, November 8, the socialist campaign was in full blast. From thousands of meeting halls and street corners in almost all cities and towns of the Union, the voters were addrest by indefatigable socialist propagandists, and socialist literature was circulated in enormous quantities. The National office of the Socialist Party alone printed over 3,000,000 campaign leaflets, and the different State and local organizations of the party distributed at least three or four times that number.

A special feature of the campaign was the extraordinary speaking tour of Eugene V. Debs. In order to enable the eloquent candidate of the Socialist Party to speak in every part of the country, Mr. J. Mahlon Barnes, the party's resourceful secretary, conceived the idea of chartering a special "campaign train." This train was to consist of three cars, one to accommodate Mr. Debs and his companions, speakers, reporters, and managers of the enterprise; one to carry campaign literature, and one for the use of persons desiring to accompany the party over parts of the route. In this train Mr. Debs and his party were to cross the country from one end to the other, making several stops each day at minor points in order to address meetings from the tail end of the train and to distribute socialist literature among the audiences. The train was to stop every evening at some important place on the route, where a large meeting could be arranged in advance, and to continue the journey in the night, so as to reach the next point of destination early on the following morning. The plan seemed very promising, but it required a large sum of money for its realization, and the treasury of the Socialist Party was depleted.

This obstacle, however, did not deter the indomitable socialists. The officers of the party, relying on the never failing socialist enthusiasm and devotion, chartered a train, naming it the "Red Special," and called upon members for voluntary contributions to defray the expense. The call was issued on July 18, and during the three months following the National office was busy receipting contributions. A little less than $35,000 was required for the enterprise, but more than $40,000 was collected. This money was contributed by individual socialists and by socialist and radical labor organizations. It came in amounts ranging from a few cents to a few dollars. The number of individual contributions was probably no less than 15,000. From the point of view of socialist propaganda, the "Red Special" was a signal success. Between August 30, the date of its starting, and November 2, when the tour was ended, Eugene V. Debs and his companions spoke in more than 300 towns and cities in thirty-three States. They were received by eager and cheering crowds all along the line. "The Red Special," reported Debs in the early part of his tour, "has demonstrated beyond peradventure its great power as a propaganda machine. From the hour that it started it has made good a hundred-fold every inch of the way, and I am sure that not a comrade who has seen the train in action regrets having contributed to make it possible. The enthusiasm it inspires everywhere is a marvel to me. If nothing else it would be worth ten times its cost to the movement." Mr. Stephen M. Reynolds, who accompanied Debs all through the tour, estimates that the number of persons addrest by the socialist candidate and other speakers on the train exceeded 800,-000.

The vigor and enthusiasm of the campaign were such that the socialists confidently expected a large increase of their vote, and even the non-socialist press of the country freely predicted about a million votes for Eugene V. Debs. But the vote actually cast for him in that election was only 421,520, a slight increase over that of 1904, the party's former high record.

The Socialist Party has no representation in the United States Congress, but it has elected a number of its members to State and local offices in some parts of the country. Its political stronghold is the State of Wisconsin, and more particularly, the principal city of that State, Milwaukee, in which it has been growing steadily and rapidly until it has reached a strength equal, and sometimes superior to that of the two old parties. In the city election of 1909, the Milwaukee socialists carried the city by electing the head of the municipal ticket, an alderman at-large. The number of elected socialist officials in the State of Wisconsin is more than 100, among them one State Senator and three members of the Assembly. The town of Manitowoc has a socialist mayor, while in Milwaukee the party has elected ten out of the thirty-five members of the municipal council. The Socialist Party has also at various times within the last few years elected candidates to State or local offices in the States of Massachusetts, Montana, Ohio, Illinois, Colorado and Pennsylvania.

But, as already indicated, the progress of the socialist movement in the United States can by no means be measured by its political strength and achievements alone. Towards the end of 1904, the Socialist Party consisted of about 1500 local subdivisions with a total number of about 25,000 enrolled and dues-paying members. Within the period of the following five years the number of local organizations rose to over 3200, with a combined membership of about 50,000.

Another indication of the increasing strength of the movement in the United States is the growth of the socialist press. In 1904 the Socialist Party was supported by about forty publications in different languages. Within the last years the number of strictly socialist publications has increased to almost sixty. Of these about one-half are periodicals in the English language, four are daily newspapers, eight are monthly magazines and the rest are weeklies. Thirty socialist periodicals are printed in foreign languages as follows: Six in German (of this number two are daily newspapers), three each in Finnish, Slavonic and Jewish; two each in Polish, Bohemian and Lettish, and one each in the following languages: French, Italian, Danish, Hungarian, Lithuanian, Russian, Swedish, Norwegian and Croatian. The first important daily newspaper of the Socialist Party was launched in Chicago in the fall of 1906, under the name of *Chicago Daily Socialist,* and it was followed by the establishment of the *New York Daily Call* in New York, in May, 1908. In both cases the big enterprises were undertaken with ludicrously inadequate means, and the papers during the first period of their existence were engaged in a pathetic and seemingly hopeless struggle for life from day to day. The pluck and devotion of the men entrusted with the publication of the papers and the customary socialist enthusiasm exprest in liberal gifts of money and gratuitous work have so far managed to overcome the almost insuperable difficulties. To-day the Chicago paper is practically self-sustaining, and the New York *Call* bids fair to reach that condition within a short time. Of the English periodicals, the *Appeal to Reason,* a weekly paper, and *Wilshire's Magazine,* a monthly publication, have each a circulation of about a quarter of a million copies, while the *Jewish Daily Forward* is said to sell almost 100,000 copies per day. Among the monthly socialist magazines one, *The Progressive Woman,* is devoted primarily to the task of carrying the gospel of socialism to women, and two others, *The Progressive Journal of Education* and *The Little Socialist,* aim at educating the youth in the philosophy of socialism.

The socialist movement in the United States has also of late made substantial progress among the organized workers of the country. While discussions on socialism in the annual convention of the American Federation of Labor have largely been abandoned by the socialist delegates as inexpedient and fruitless, the individual organizations within the Federation have developed a livelier interest in the subject than ever, and have on numerous occasions declared themselves unreservedly as favoring the socialist program, or at least its most substantial points and planks. In 1907, sixteen national organizations of workingmen, representing a total membership of 330,800, had thus endorsed the socialist program,[1] and in 1909 the United Mine Workers of America, one of the strongest organizations within the American Federation of Labor, at its national convention declared itself in favor of the cardinal aim of socialism, the socialization of all material instruments of production. But more progress even than in the national organizations of labor, has been made in the various local trade-unions, and there are to-day but few important labor organizations in the country which do not include a larger or smaller contingent of socialists among their members.

In the beginning of 1908, the Socialist Party attempted to take a census of its enrolled members with the view of ascertaining their social positions, nationalities, trade-union affiliations, etc. The returns were unfortunately very incomplete, only 6,310 members, or less than one sixth of the total, having reported. But as the members reporting represent no less than 37 different States, it is fair to assume that their conditions are quite typical of the members of the Socialist Party as a whole. From the returns thus obtained it appears that 66 per cent. of the party membership, or about 33,000, were workingmen, skilled and unskilled. Of these 62 per cent. or about 21,000, were members of different trade-unions. The ratio of enrolled Socialist Party members to socialist voters in this country is about one to ten, and we may thus conclude that over 200,000 trade-union members vote the socialist ticket. Deducting from the number of organized workers all women, minors, aliens, and other non-voters, we may estimate that the total voting strength of organized labor in this country is less than one million, and that over twenty per cent. of it is socialistic. This is by no means a very good showing, but it represents a considerable advance over former years.

And the industrial workers are not the only class among whom socialism has made gains of late. The movement has made deep inroads among American farmers. In the

[1] John Curtis Kennedy in " International Socialist Review," December, 1907.

national socialist convention of 1904, the farmers made their first appearance with five delegates, and in the convention of 1908, a very substantial proportion of the delegates consisted of active and typical farmers. In the Socialist Party census, mentioned above, seventeen per cent. of all members gave their occupation as "farming," and in the last presidential election several purely agricultural states polled heavier socialist votes than some of the States noted for factory industries.

And even the so-called intellectual classes of American society, the professionals and middle-class business men were gradually drawn into the expanding circle of the socialist movement. Our schools and colleges, our press and churches are honeycombed with socialists or socialist sympathizers. In the fall of 1905, several well-known radicals, among them Oscar Lovell Triggs, Thomas Wentworth Higginson, Clarence S. Darrow and Jack London, issued a call for the organization of a society "for the purpose of promoting an intelligent interest in socialism among college men and women, graduate and undergraduate, through the formation of study clubs in the colleges and universities, and the encouraging of all legitimate endeavors to awaken an interest in socialism among the educated men and women of the country." On September 12, 1905, a number of people met in the city of New York in response to the call and organized the "Intercollegiate Socialist Society." During the short period of its existence, the society has distributed a large quantity of socialist literature among college students and teachers, and its members have delivered a number of lectures on socialism before college students. At the present writing socialist "study chapters" connected with the Intercollegiate Socialist Society have been organized in fifteen universities and colleges, among them Harvard, Princeton, Columbia, Cornell and the University of Pennsylvania.

In the summer of 1905, Mrs. Carrie Rand, mother-in-law of the well known socialist writer and propagandist, George D. Herron, bequeathed the income of a fund of about $200,-

000 for the establishment of an institution for the teaching of Socialism and social sciences. The bequest resulted in the foundation of the Rand School of Social Science in the city of New York, in which a number of eager students are receiving systematic instruction from a teaching staff composed of several well known college professors and equally well known socialist writers and lecturers.

Another noteworthy manifestation of the spread of socialism among the educated classes was the organization of the Christian Socialist Fellowship in June, 1906. The movement represented by the Fellowship differs from the earlier American movement of Christian Socialism in its substantial aims and character. While the Christian Socialism of the nineties of the last century was based upon a program of its own, distinct from that of the organized political parties of socialism, and built almost exclusively on ethical concepts, the later-day Christian Socialist Fellowship endorsed the program and methods of the Socialist Party in their entirety, and was organized for the purpose of active cooperation with the party. The main mission of the Fellowship was to carry the socialism of the Socialist Party to the churches and the church goers. In 1909, the Fellowship was reorganized, and adopted the name of the ''Christian Socialist League of America.'' The League is now said to have among its members several hundred active ministers of all denominations in the different states of the Union, besides a large number of laymen. It publishes two papers, the *Christian Socialist*, the *Christian Bugle*, and a monthly magazine entitled *The Beacon*, and does active and systematic work in the propaganda of socialism. The objects of the League are stated to be as follows: ''To carry to churches and other religious organizations the message of socialism; to show the necessity of socialism to a complete realization of the teachings of Jesus; to end the class struggle by establishing industrial and political democracy, and to hasten the reign of justice and brotherhood upon earth.''

Within the last few years the socialist movement has become fully acclimatized on American soil. According to the recent Socialist Party census already alluded to, over 71 per cent. of the members are native citizens of the United States. On the whole it is safe to assert that the socialist movement is to-day as much ''American'' as any other social and reform movement in the country.

VI.—PROBLEMS AND PROSPECTS OF AMERICAN SOCIALISM

THE socialist movement in this country has thus made substantial gains within the last decade. It has begun to penetrate the broad masses of American workingmen, has enlisted the support of many persons in other classes, and has spread to all parts of the country. But with all that the progress of socialism in the United States has even within that period, been slower than in almost any other civilized country. The difficulties which beset the path of the American socialists are varied and many. Some of them have been indicated in previous chapters.

Altho the modern or "capitalist" system of production is at present probably more highly developed in the United States than in any other country, the development is of comparatively recent date. Only one generation ago agriculture was the main industry of the country while manufacture was conducted on a comparatively small scale. This condition, together with the relative prosperity of the country generally, operated to retard the formation of a permanent wage-working class, the existence of which is essential to the growth of the modern socialist movement.

The subsequent development of a permanent class of industrial workers gave rise to a powerful trade-union movement and the earlier birth and superior strength of that movement had the effect of making the organized workers of the United States more conservative than the workers in European countries.

Another obstacle has been the political system of the country. Paradoxical as it may seem, our very democracy has militated against the immediate success of socialism. The tremendous number of our elective offices, with their great powers and patronage, have made the politics of our country a matter of extraordinary importance. The political campaigns of the United States exceed those of all other countries in intensity and dimensions. Politics has become as much an industry with us as railroading or manufacturing. It is conducted by professionals for their private gain, on a large scale and with a lavish outlay of capital. Our political campaigns are more often struggles of individuals for office than contests of masses over principles. Perhaps nowhere in the world is there less political idealism and more political corruption.

This situation has bred in the mind of the average American, including the American workingman, a deep-seated feeling of indifference, even contempt, for politics, which is anything but conducive to the development of a radical movement for political reform.

The difficulties of all such reform movements are still more aggravated by the so-called "two-party" system in American politics. Ever since the creation of the republic the contest for political power has been waged between two, and only two, dominant parties. New political parties, so-called "third parties," have appeared in the arena from time to time, but not one of them has developed any appreciable strength and stability. As a rule they have, after a more or less tempestuous career, been absorbed by one of the old parties. The "two-party" system thus sanctioned by tradition, is now largely continued by design. The dominant political parties, the Republican and Democratic, are in the nature of political trusts. Together they control all the offices and "patronage" of the country, and almost the entire press and other organs of public expression. They have the backing of the great industrial and financial interests and the support of large armies of trained and specialized political workers. They divide all political "spoils" among themselves, mostly by methods of struggle and conquest, and sometimes by voluntary apportionment. The task of a new party to replace either of them or to gain a permanent and important footing alongside of them is thus from the outset a very difficult one.

But what makes it still more difficult is the system of "party tickets" in elections. The popular elections in most other countries are limited to the choice of members of local legislatures or parliament. The elections are by

districts and the ticket of each party is, as a rule, limited
to one candidate for each district. Each electoral campaign is thus conducted on the merits of the given district,
and is in no way dependent upon conditions in other districts. In an electoral district largely made up of radicals
the voters may, therefore, enter the contest with the expectation of victory regardless of the more conservative
sentiments in other districts or in the country at large.
In the United States the offices to be filled in each general
election are many in number and varied in character, and
still they are so closely linked together on the electoral
ticket, that they appear to the ordinary voter as one in-
separable group, to be voted for or against in bulk. Local,
state and national elections are most frequently held together, and the ticket handed to the voter sometimes
contains the names not only of candidates for the state
legislature or congress, but also for all local and state
officers and even for President of the United States. And
since a new party rarely seems to have the chance or
prospect of electing its candidate for governor of a state
or president of the country, the voter is inclined in advance to consider its entire ticket as hopeless. The fear
of "throwing away" the vote is thus a peculiar product
of American politics, and it requires a voter of exceptional
strength of conviction to overcome it.

Another and perhaps not less serious obstacle to the
growth of political socialism in the United States, is our
system of state autonomy. The main socialist program,
as well as the most important immediate reforms advocated
by the socialists, can be realized only on a national scale.
In every other country it is always some concrete demand
addrest to the national legislature, the parliament, which
unites the masses of the population into one solid reform
or revolutionary movement. In the United States, where
the powers and scope of the national government are
exceedingly limited, and the most vital industrial and
social problems of the country are left to be dealt with
by the 46 different and independent legislatures of our

States, general social reform movements have to traverse a much more difficult road.

Nor are the ethnic conditions of the country very favorable to the growth of socialism. According to the last census returns there are over ten millions of foreign born persons in the United States. These represent practically all the nations and races of the world, with the most diversified languages, habits and culture. By far the greater part of them are workers, and they are, of necessity, a factor of greater importance for the socialist movement than they would be for a reform movement of the middle classes. The Socialist Party in the United States is compelled to address the workers of the country in more than twenty different languages and to adjust its organization and methods of propaganda to the conditions and habits of more than twenty different races. The presence of about nine millions of negroes, mostly workers, with special racial and social conditions, raises another very serious problem for the socialist movement in this country. All these factors indicate but do not exhaust the peculiar difficulties of American socialism. Will these difficulties prove insurmountable?

The entire history of socialism militates against such a conclusion. The socialist movement is not a peculiarly American experiment. It is a feature of universal modern social development, an established factor in contemporary civilization. The movement has taken root in all advanced countries of the globe. It has thus far successfully overcome the most diversified obstacles, and prospered under the most variegated political, social and ethnic conditions. It has grown large in the Russian autocracy, Prussian bureaucracy, British democracy and the French republic. In Germany its growth was stimulated by the early struggles of the workers for universal suffrage and greater political freedom; in England it was hastened by the notorious Taff-Vale decision; in Russia it was temporarily suppressed by government persecution; in Austria it was retarded by racial divisions; in each country it has confronted a different constellation of circumstances and has had a different course of development. Its progress has been rapid or slow, even or irregular, according to the special conditions of each country, but progress there has been in all countries, and very decided progress in the long run. For socialism is primarily and mainly a product of modern industrial conditions. It appeared with the appearance of these conditions and it is growing with their growth. The present or "capitalist" mode of production makes necessary the rise of a permanent, large and growing wage-working class, engaged in an ever fiercer struggle for existence and consciously or instinctively forced into organized resistance against the employing classes. This resistance uniformly assumes the form of an economic and political struggle of the working class, for paltry benefits at first, for more radical reforms subsequently, and ultimately for the complete abolition of the oppressive industrial system. This is the logic of war and the history of all struggles of the masses.

In the United States, more than anywhere else, the industrial development is irresistibly preparing the ground for a large and vigorous socialist movement. The industries of the country are rapidly concentrating in the hands of an ever diminishing number of powerful financial concerns. The trusts, monopolies and gigantic industrial combinations are coming to be the ruling factors in the life of the nation, industrial, political and spiritual, and the masses of the people are sinking into a condition of ever greater dependence. The number of propertyless wage earners is on the increase; their material existence is growing more precarious, and the spirit of dissatisfaction and revolt is developing among them. The relations between the classes of producers and the employing classes are marked by intense, though not always conscious, class-antagonism and by overt class struggles. Within the last few years the organized workers of the United States have been assailed with unusual severity by the organized capitalists, the government, the state and national legislatures, and particularly by the courts of the country. The effects of these concerted attacks have served to demonstrate to many workers that the present methods and form of organization of the American trade unions are antiquated and lacking in efficiency. The trade unions are beginning to revise their methods of warfare. They have, within the last few years, made considerable advance in the direction of greater organic and interdependent industrial organization and they have entered the field of politics as a class. True, their steps in both directions have been uncertain, groping and even faulty, but they are nevertheless steps in the right direction. A few more defeats in industrial struggles, a few more adverse court decisions, a few more political disappointments, and the organized workers of the United States will be forced into a solid industrial and political class organization, working in close harmony and cooperation with the socialist movement.

Similarly hopeful for the progress of socialism is the mental attitude of the unorganized workers and of the masses of the population generally. The phenomenal political strength developed from time to time by the sporadic reform movements is a strong indication of the popular dissatisfaction with existing conditions. These movements are, as a rule, very indefinite in their aims and superficial in their programs. They attract the masses by their general radicalism and the promise of a small measure of immediate relief. From their very nature they are bound to be ineffective and short-lived, and their disappointed adherents become peculiarly susceptible to the appeals of socialism.

Thus the conditions for the growth of a powerful socialist movement in this country are rapidly maturing and the rate of that growth will largely depend upon the ability of the socialists to take advantage of these conditions and to win the confidence and support of the discontented masses and especially of the organized workers.

A tactful policy and energetic work on the part of the organized socialists, in the direction indicated, may largely accelerate the progress of the movement; unwise methods or lack of action may retard it somewhat. American socialism has not as yet evolved definite and settled policies and methods. The movement is largely in the making, but the more recent phases of its development tend to indicate that it is beginning to solve its problems and to overcome its obstacles. Slow as has been the progress of political socialism in this country, it has made larger gains within the last ten years than within all the thirty or forty years preceding that period. The vote and the enrolled membership of the Socialist Party have grown almost five fold, and the socialists have gained an important political standing in some sections of the country. Furthermore, there is every reason to believe that the latent political strength of socialism is much larger than the socialist vote would indicate. There is a considerable contingent of American voters who would undoubtedly support socialist candidates if they thought they could be elected. Wherever the Socialist Party has once demonstrated its ability to carry an election, as, for instance, in Wisconsin, it has usually maintained and steadily strengthened its position. In the present state of social and industrial ferment any important event in the politics or in the labor movement of the country, may give the Socialist Party its first real opportunity at the polls, and establish it as a permanent and important factor in American politics.

Nor are the political achievements of socialism the sole, or even most important, test of the growth of the movement. In its present phase, socialism in this country is primarily an educational movement, and as such it has made its greatest gains within recent years. It has succeeded in dispelling many of the grosser popular prejudices against the movement, and has created a more enlightened, tolerant and sympathetic attitude towards its general aims and methods. Many of the measures of industrial, social and political reform, originally advocated exclusively by the socialists, are gradually being forced into the platforms of other parties and organizations. The socialist program has become one of the favorite topics of discussion in books, in the periodical press, and on our public platforms. Socialism is at last beginning to get a hearing before the people, and the people of the United States move fast when once they are set in motion.

APPENDIX

APPENDIX

PRINCIPLES

HUMAN life depends upon food, clothing and shelter. Only with these assured are freedom, culture and higher human development possible. To produce food, clothing or shelter, land and machinery are needed. Land alone does not satisfy human needs. Human labor creates machinery and applies it to the land for the production of raw materials and food. Whoever has control of land and machinery controls human labor, and with it human life and liberty.

Today the machinery and the land used for industrial purposes are owned by a rapidly decreasing minority. So long as machinery is simple and easily handled by one man, its owner cannot dominate the sources of life of others. But when machinery becomes more complex and expensive, and requires for its effective operation the organized effort of many workers, its influence reaches over wide circles of life. The owners of such machinery become the dominant class.

In proportion as the number of such machine owners compared to all other classes decreases, their power in the nation and in the world increases. They bring ever larger masses of working people under their control, reducing them to the point where muscle and brain are their only productive property. Millions of formerly self-employing workers thus become the helpless wage slaves of the industrial masters.

As the economic power of the ruling class grows it becomes less useful in the life of the nation. All the useful work of the nation falls upon the shoulders of the class whose only property is its manual and mental labor power—the wage workers—or of the class who have but little land and little effective machinery outside of their labor power—the small traders and small farmers. The ruling minority is steadily becoming useless and parasitic.

A bitter struggle over the division of the products of labor is waged between the exploiting propertied classes on the one hand and the exploited propertyless class on the other. In this struggle the wage working class cannot expect adequate relief from any reform of the present order at the hands of the dominant class.

The wage workers are therefore the most determined and irreconcilable antagonists of the ruling class. They suffer most from the curse of class rule. The fact that a few capitalists are permitted to control all the country's industrial resources and social tools for their individual profit, and to make the production of the necessaries of life the object of competitive private enterprise and speculation is at the bottom of all the social evils of our time.

In spite of the organization of trusts, pools and combinations, the capitalists are powerless to regulate production for social ends. Industries are largely conducted in a planless manner. Thru periods of feverish activity the strength and health of the workers are mercilessly used up, and during periods of enforced idleness the workers are frequently reduced to starvation.

The climaxes of this system of production are the regularly recurring industrial depressions and crises which paralyze the nation every fifteen or twenty years.

The capitalist class, in its mad race for profits, is bound to exploit the workers to the very limit of their endurance and to sacrifice their physical, moral and mental welfare to its own insatiable greed. Capitalism keeps the masses of workingmen in poverty, destitution, physical exhaustion and ignorance. It drags their wives from their homes to the mill and factory. It snatches their children from the playgrounds and schools and grinds their slender bodies and unformed minds into cold dollars. It disfigures, maims and kills hundreds of thousands of workingmen annually in mines, on railroads and in factories. It drives millions of workers into the ranks of the unemployed and forces large numbers of them into beggary, vagrancy and all forms of crime and vice.

To maintain their rule over their fellow men the capitalists must keep in their pay all organs of the public powers, public mind and public conscience. They control the dominant parties, and thru them, the elected public officials. They select the executives, bribe the legislatures and corrupt the courts of justice. They own and censor the press. They dominate the educational institutions. They own the nation politically and intellectually just as they own it industrially.

The struggle between wage workers and capitalists grows ever fiercer, and has now become the only vital issue before the American people. The wageworking class, therefore, has the most direct interest in abolishing the capitalist system. But in abolishing the present system, the workingmen will free not only their own class, but also all other classes of modern society: the small farmer, who is to-day exploited by large capital more indirectly but not less effectively than is the wage laborer; the small manufacturer and trader, who is engaged in a desperate and losing struggle for economic independence in the face of the all-conquering power of concentrated capital; and even the capitalist himself, who is the slave of his wealth rather than its master. The struggle of the working class against the capitalist class, while it is a class struggle, is thus at the same time a struggle for the abolition of all classes and class privileges.

The private ownership of the land and means of production used for exploitation, is the rock upon which class rule is built; political government is its indispensable instrument. The wageworkers cannot be freed from exploitation without conquering the political power and substituting collective for private ownership of the land and means of production used for exploitation.

The basis for such transformation is rapidly developing within present capitalist society. The factory system, with its complex machinery and minute division of labor, is rapidly destroying all vestiges of individual production in manufacture. Modern production is already very largely a collective and social process. The great trusts and monopolies, which have sprung up in recent years, have organized the work and management of the principal industries on a national scale, and have fitted them for collective use and operation.

There can be no absolute private title to land. All private titles, whether called fee simple or otherwise, are and must be subordinate to the public title. The Socialist Party strives to prevent land from being used for the purpose of exploitation and speculation. It demands the collective possession, control or management of land to whatever extent may be necessary to attain that end. It is not opposed to the occupation and possession of land by those using it in a useful and bona fide manner without exploitation.

The Socialist Party is primarily an economic and political movement. It is not concerned with matters of religious belief.

In the struggle for freedom the interests of all modern workers are identical. The struggle is not only national, but international. It embraces the world and will be carried to ultimate victory by the united workers of the world.

To unite the workers of the nation and their allies and sympathizers of all other classes to this end, is the mission of the Socialist Party. In this battle for freedom the Socialist Party does not strive to substitute working class rule for capitalist class rule, but by working class victory, to free all humanity from class rule and to realize the international brotherhood of man.

PLATFORM FOR 1908

THE Socialist Party, in national convention assembled, again declares itself as the party of the working class, and appeals for the support of all workers of the United States and of all citizens who sympathize with the great and just cause of labor.

We are at this moment in the midst of one of those industrial breakdowns that periodically paralyze the life of the nation. The much-boasted era of our national prosperity has been followed by one of general misery. Factories, mills and mines are closed. Millions of men, ready, willing and able to provide the nation with all the necessaries and comforts of life are forced into idleness and starvation.

Within recent years the trust and monopolies have attained an enormous and menacing development. They have acquired the power to dictate the terms upon which we shall be allowed to live. The trusts fix the prices of our bread, meat and sugar, of our coal, oil and clothing, of our raw material and machinery, of all the necessities of life.

The present desperate condition of the workers has been made the opportunity for a renewed onslaught on organized labor. The highest courts of the country have within the last year rendered decision after decision depriving the workers of rights which they had won by generations of struggle.

The attempt to destroy the Western Federation of Miners, altho defeated by the solidarity of organized labor and the socialist movement, revealed the existence of a far-reaching and unscrupulous conspiracy by the ruling class against the organization of labor.

In their efforts to take the lives of the leaders of the miners the conspirators violated State laws and the federal constitution in a manner seldom equaled even in a country so completely dominated by the profit-seeking class as is the United States.

The congress of the United States has shown its contempt for the interests of labor as plainly and unmistakably as have the other branches of government. The laws for which the labor organizations have continually petitioned have failed to pass. Laws ostensibly enacted for the benefit of labor have been distorted against labor.

The working class of the United States cannot expect any remedy for its wrongs from the present ruling class or from the dominant parties. So long as a small number of individuals are permitted to control the sources of the nation's wealth for their private profit in competition with each other and for the exploitation of their fellowmen, industrial depressions are bound to occur at certain intervals. No currency reforms or other legislative measures proposed by capitalist reformers can avail against these fatal results of utter anarchy in production.

Individual competition leads inevitably to combinations and trusts. No amount of government regulation, or of publicity, or of restrictive legislation will arrest the natural course of modern industrial development.

While our courts, legislatures and executive offices remain in the hands of the ruling classes and their agents, the government will be used in the interest of these classes as against the toilers.

Political parties are but the expression of economic class interests. The Republican, the Democratic, and the so-called "Independence" parties and all parties other than the Socialist Party, are financed, directed and controlled by the representatives of different groups of the ruling class.

In the maintenance of class government both the Democratic and Republican parties have been equally guilty. The Republican Party has had control of the national government and has been directly and actively responsible for these wrongs. The Democratic Party, while saved from direct responsibility by its political impotence, has shown itself equally subservient to the aims of the capitalist class whenever and wherever it has been in power.

INDEX

INDEX

A

"Alarm, The," 221, 226
Allen, John, 85, 100
Allen, William, 97
Alliance Internationale, 162
Alphadelphia Phalanx, 107
Altpeter, 238
Amana Community, 37–40
"American Fabian, The," 293
American Federation of Labor,
269–276, 312, 321, 323, 326–
331, 332, 333
"American Federationist," 328,
329
American Institute of Christian
Sociology, 292
"American Labor Union Jour-
nal," 312
American Railway Union, 284
Anarchism and Socialism com-
pared, 209–212
Anarchism, definitions of, 197,
209–212
Anarchism in the United States,
213–217
Anarchist methods of propagan-
da, 211–212
Anarchists, Chicago, 221–229
Anarchist view of society, 209–
210
Ante-bellum period, 141, 143–
155
"Appeal to Reason, The," 301,
353
"Arbeiterstimme, Die," 191
"Arbeiter Union, Die," 170, 171
"Arbeiter-Zeitung, Die," official
organ of the International in
the United States, 182, 186
"Arbeiter-Zeitung" of Milwau-
kee, 247
Artley, S., 238
Aurora, 40–42
Aveling, Edward, 230
Aveling, Eleanor Marx, 230

B

Bachmann, M., 213–214
Bakounin, Michael, 162, 163, 212
Barlow, Francis Channing, 98
Barnes, J. M., 276, 305, 350
Bauemeler, Joseph, 35, 36, 130
Beesly, Professor, 158
Belding, Dr. Lemuel C., 104
Bellamy, E., 288, 289
Benham, G. B., 305
Berger, V. L., 302, 303, 305
Bethel, 40–42
Beust, Dr., 155
Bimeler, Levy, 37
Bishop, O. A., 241
Black, Captain, 228
Bliss, W. D. P., 292, 293
Bloomfield Association, 105
Borland, W. P., 302
Braun, Charles, 191
Brisbane, Albert, 72, 79–82, 85,
86, 87, 88, 89, 91, 92, 99, 105
Brook Farm, 83, 89, 95–101
Brotherhood of the Cooperative
Commonwealth, 301
Buck's Stove and Range Co. case,
328, 329
Buffalo Strike, 282–283
"Bulletin of the Socialist Labor
Party," 217
Butler, B. F., 174, 243, 246
Butscher, W., 305

C

"Cabaliste," in the philosophy of
Fourierism, 73
Cabet Etienne, 26, 109–113, 116,
118, 119
"Call, The," 354
Cameron, A. C., 173
Carey, J. F., 303, 305
Carl, C., 177, 186
Carnegie, A., 280
Central Federated Union, 261

381

A CATALOGUE OF SELECTED DOVER BOOKS
IN ALL FIELDS OF INTEREST

A CATALOGUE OF SELECTED DOVER BOOKS
IN ALL FIELDS OF INTEREST

AMERICA'S OLD MASTERS, James T. Flexner. Four men emerged unexpectedly from provincial 18th century America to leadership in European art: Benjamin West, J. S. Copley, C. R. Peale, Gilbert Stuart. Brilliant coverage of lives and contributions. Revised, 1967 edition. 69 plates. 365pp. of text.

21806-6 Paperbound $2.75

FIRST FLOWERS OF OUR WILDERNESS: AMERICAN PAINTING, THE COLONIAL PERIOD, James T. Flexner. Painters, and regional painting traditions from earliest Colonial times up to the emergence of Copley, West and Peale Sr., Foster, Gustavus Hesselius, Feke, John Smibert and many anonymous painters in the primitive manner. Engaging presentation, with 162 illustrations. xxii + 368pp.

22180-6 Paperbound $3.50

THE LIGHT OF DISTANT SKIES: AMERICAN PAINTING, 1760-1835, James T. Flexner. The great generation of early American painters goes to Europe to learn and to teach: West, Copley, Gilbert Stuart and others. Allston, Trumbull, Morse; also contemporary American painters—primitives, derivatives, academics—who remained in America. 102 illustrations. xiii + 306pp. 22179-2 Paperbound $3.00

A HISTORY OF THE RISE AND PROGRESS OF THE ARTS OF DESIGN IN THE UNITED STATES, William Dunlap. Much the richest mine of information on early American painters, sculptors, architects, engravers, miniaturists, etc. The only source of information for scores of artists, the major primary source for many others. Unabridged reprint of rare original 1834 edition, with new introduction by James T. Flexner, and 394 new illustrations. Edited by Rita Weiss. 6⅝ x 9⅝.

21695-0, 21696-9, 21697-7 Three volumes, Paperbound $13.50

EPOCHS OF CHINESE AND JAPANESE ART, Ernest F. Fenollosa. From primitive Chinese art to the 20th century, thorough history, explanation of every important art period and form, including Japanese woodcuts; main stress on China and Japan, but Tibet, Korea also included. Still unexcelled for its detailed, rich coverage of cultural background, aesthetic elements, diffusion studies, particularly of the historical period. 2nd, 1913 edition. 242 illustrations. lii + 439pp. of text.

20364-6, 20365-4 Two volumes, Paperbound $5.00

THE GENTLE ART OF MAKING ENEMIES, James A. M. Whistler. Greatest wit of his day deflates Oscar Wilde, Ruskin, Swinburne; strikes back at inane critics, exhibitions, art journalism; aesthetics of impressionist revolution in most striking form. Highly readable classic by great painter. Reproduction of edition designed by Whistler. Introduction by Alfred Werner. xxxvi + 334pp.

21875-9 Paperbound $2.25

VISUAL ILLUSIONS: THEIR CAUSES, CHARACTERISTICS, AND APPLICATIONS, Matthew Luckiesh. Thorough description and discussion of optical illusion, geometric and perspective, particularly; size and shape distortions, illusions of color, of motion; natural illusions; use of illusion in art and magic, industry, etc. Most useful today with op art, also for classical art. Scores of effects illustrated. Introduction by William H. Ittleson. 100 illustrations. xxi + 252pp.

21530-X Paperbound $1.50

A HANDBOOK OF ANATOMY FOR ART STUDENTS, Arthur Thomson. Thorough, virtually exhaustive coverage of skeletal structure, musculature, etc. Full text, supplemented by anatomical diagrams and drawings and by photographs of undraped figures. Unique in its comparison of male and female forms, pointing out differences of contour, texture, form. 211 figures, 40 drawings, 86 photographs. xx + 459pp. 5⅜ x 8⅜.

21163-0 Paperbound $3.00

150 MASTERPIECES OF DRAWING, Selected by Anthony Toney. Full page reproductions of drawings from the early 16th to the end of the 18th century, all beautifully reproduced: Rembrandt, Michelangelo, Dürer, Fragonard, Urs, Graf, Wouwerman, many others. First-rate browsing book, model book for artists. xviii + 150pp. 8⅜ x 11¼.

21032-4 Paperbound $2.00

THE LATER WORK OF AUBREY BEARDSLEY, Aubrey Beardsley. Exotic, erotic, ironic masterpieces in full maturity: Comedy Ballet, Venus and Tannhauser, Pierrot, Lysistrata, Rape of the Lock, Savoy material, Ali Baba, Volpone, etc. This material revolutionized the art world, and is still powerful, fresh, brilliant. With *The Early Work,* all Beardsley's finest work. 174 plates, 2 in color. xiv + 176pp. 8⅛ x 11.

21817-1 Paperbound $2.75

DRAWINGS OF REMBRANDT, Rembrandt van Rijn. Complete reproduction of fabulously rare edition by Lippmann and Hofstede de Groot, completely reedited, updated, improved by Prof. Seymour Slive, Fogg Museum. Portraits, Biblical sketches, landscapes, Oriental types, nudes, episodes from classical mythology—All Rembrandt's fertile genius. Also selection of drawings by his pupils and followers. "Stunning volumes," *Saturday Review.* 550 illustrations. lxxviii + 552pp. 9⅛ x 12¼.

21485-0, 21486-9 Two volumes, Paperbound $6.50

THE DISASTERS OF WAR, Francisco Goya. One of the masterpieces of Western civilization—83 etchings that record Goya's shattering, bitter reaction to the Napoleonic war that swept through Spain after the insurrection of 1808 and to war in general. Reprint of the first edition, with three additional plates from Boston's Museum of Fine Arts. All plates facsimile size. Introduction by Philip Hofer, Fogg Museum. v + 97pp. 9⅜ x 8¼.

21872-4 Paperbound $1.75

GRAPHIC WORKS OF ODILON REDON. Largest collection of Redon's graphic works ever assembled: 172 lithographs, 28 etchings and engravings, 9 drawings. These include some of his most famous works. All the plates from *Odilon Redon: oeuvre graphique complet,* plus additional plates. New introduction and caption translations by Alfred Werner. 209 illustrations. xxvii + 209pp. 9⅛ x 12¼.

21966-8 Paperbound $4.00

A History of Costume, Carl Köhler. Definitive history, based on surviving pieces of clothing primarily, and paintings, statues, etc. secondarily. Highly readable text, supplemented by 594 illustrations of costumes of the ancient Mediterranean peoples, Greece and Rome, the Teutonic prehistoric period; costumes of the Middle Ages, Renaissance, Baroque, 18th and 19th centuries. Clear, measured patterns are provided for many clothing articles. Approach is practical throughout. Enlarged by Emma von Sichart. 464pp. 21030-8 Paperbound $3.00

Oriental Rugs, Antique and Modern, Walter A. Hawley. A complete and authoritative treatise on the Oriental rug—where they are made, by whom and how, designs and symbols, characteristics in detail of the six major groups, how to distinguish them and how to buy them. Detailed technical data is provided on periods, weaves, warps, wefts, textures, sides, ends and knots, although no technical background is required for an understanding. 11 color plates, 80 halftones, 4 maps. vi + 320pp. $6\frac{1}{8}$ x $9\frac{1}{8}$. 22366-3 Paperbound $5.00

Ten Books on Architecture, Vitruvius. By any standards the most important book on architecture ever written. Early Roman discussion of aesthetics of building, construction methods, orders, sites, and every other aspect of architecture has inspired, instructed architecture for about 2,000 years. Stands behind Palladio, Michelangelo, Bramante, Wren, countless others. Definitive Morris H. Morgan translation. 68 illustrations. xii + 331pp. 20645-9 Paperbound $2.50

The Four Books of Architecture, Andrea Palladio. Translated into every major Western European language in the two centuries following its publication in 1570, this has been one of the most influential books in the history of architecture. Complete reprint of the 1738 Isaac Ware edition. New introduction by Adolf Placzek, Columbia Univ. 216 plates. xxii + 110pp. of text. $9\frac{1}{2}$ x $12\frac{3}{4}$.
21308-0 Clothbound $10.00

Sticks and Stones: A Study of American Architecture and Civilization, Lewis Mumford. One of the great classics of American cultural history. American architecture from the medieval-inspired earliest forms to the early 20th century; evolution of structure and style, and reciprocal influences on environment. 21 photographic illustrations. 238pp. 20202-X Paperbound $2.00

The American Builder's Companion, Asher Benjamin. The most widely used early 19th century architectural style and source book, for colonial up into Greek Revival periods. Extensive development of geometry of carpentering, construction of sashes, frames, doors, stairs; plans and elevations of domestic and other buildings. Hundreds of thousands of houses were built according to this book, now invaluable to historians, architects, restorers, etc. 1827 edition. 59 plates. 114pp. $7\frac{7}{8}$ x $10\frac{3}{4}$.
22236-5 Paperbound $3.00

Dutch Houses in the Hudson Valley Before 1776, Helen Wilkinson Reynolds. The standard survey of the Dutch colonial house and outbuildings, with constructional features, decoration, and local history associated with individual homesteads. Introduction by Franklin D. Roosevelt. Map. 150 illustrations. 469pp. $6\frac{5}{8}$ x $9\frac{1}{4}$. 21469-9 Paperbound $3.50

THE ARCHITECTURE OF COUNTRY HOUSES, Andrew J. Downing. Together with Vaux's *Villas and Cottages* this is the basic book for Hudson River Gothic architecture of the middle Victorian period. Full, sound discussions of general aspects of housing, architecture, style, decoration, furnishing, together with scores of detailed house plans, illustrations of specific buildings, accompanied by full text. Perhaps the most influential single American architectural book. 1850 edition. Introduction by J. Stewart Johnson. 321 figures, 34 architectural designs. xvi + 560pp.

22003-6 Paperbound $3.50

LOST EXAMPLES OF COLONIAL ARCHITECTURE, John Mead Howells. Full-page photographs of buildings that have disappeared or been so altered as to be denatured, including many designed by major early American architects. 245 plates. xvii + 248pp. 7⅞ x 10¾. 21143-6 Paperbound $3.00

DOMESTIC ARCHITECTURE OF THE AMERICAN COLONIES AND OF THE EARLY REPUBLIC, Fiske Kimball. Foremost architect and restorer of Williamsburg and Monticello covers nearly 200 homes between 1620-1825. Architectural details, construction, style features, special fixtures, floor plans, etc. Generally considered finest work in its area. 219 illustrations of houses, doorways, windows, capital mantels. xx + 314pp. 7⅞ x 10¾. 21743-4 Paperbound $3.50

EARLY AMERICAN ROOMS: 1650-1858, edited by Russell Hawes Kettell. Tour of 12 rooms, each representative of a different era in American history and each furnished, decorated, designed and occupied in the style of the era. 72 plans and elevations, 8-page color section, etc., show fabrics, wall papers, arrangements, etc. Full descriptive text. xvii + 200pp. of text. 8⅜ x 11¼.

21633-0 Paperbound $4.00

THE FITZWILLIAM VIRGINAL BOOK, edited by J. Fuller Maitland and W. B. Squire. Full modern printing of famous early 17th-century ms. volume of 300 works by Morley, Byrd, Bull, Gibbons, etc. For piano or other modern keyboard instrument; easy to read format. xxxvi + 938pp. 8⅜ x 11.

21068-5, 21069-3 Two volumes, Paperbound $8.00

HARPSICHORD MUSIC, Johann Sebastian Bach. Bach Gesellschaft edition. A rich selection of Bach's masterpieces for the harpsichord: the six English Suites, six French Suites, the six Partitas (Clavierübung part I), the Goldberg Variations (Clavierübung part IV), the fifteen Two-Part Inventions and the fifteen Three-Part Sinfonias. Clearly reproduced on large sheets with ample margins; eminently playable. vi + 312pp. 8⅛ x 11. 22360-4 Paperbound $5.00

THE MUSIC OF BACH: AN INTRODUCTION, Charles Sanford Terry. A fine, nontechnical introduction to Bach's music, both instrumental and vocal. Covers organ music, chamber music, passion music, other types. Analyzes themes, developments, innovations. x + 114pp. 21075-8 Paperbound $1.25

BEETHOVEN AND HIS NINE SYMPHONIES, Sir George Grove. Noted British musicologist provides best history, analysis, commentary on symphonies. Very thorough, rigorously accurate; necessary to both advanced student and amateur music lover. 436 musical passages. vii + 407 pp. 20334-4 Paperbound $2.25

JOHANN SEBASTIAN BACH, Philipp Spitta. One of the great classics of musicology, this definitive analysis of Bach's music (and life) has never been surpassed. Lucid, nontechnical analyses of hundreds of pieces (30 pages devoted to St. Matthew Passion, 26 to B Minor Mass). Also includes major analysis of 18th-century music. 450 musical examples. 40-page musical supplement. Total of xx + 1799pp.

(EUK) 22278-0, 22279-9 Two volumes, Clothbound $15.00

MOZART AND HIS PIANO CONCERTOS, Cuthbert Girdlestone. The only full-length study of an important area of Mozart's creativity. Provides detailed analyses of all 23 concertos, traces inspirational sources. 417 musical examples. Second edition. 509pp. (USO) 21271-8 Paperbound $2.50

THE PERFECT WAGNERITE: A COMMENTARY ON THE NIBLUNG'S RING, George Bernard Shaw. Brilliant and still relevant criticism in remarkable essays on Wagner's Ring cycle, Shaw's ideas on political and social ideology behind the plots, role of Leitmotifs, vocal requisites, etc. Prefaces. xxi + 136pp.

21707-8 Paperbound $1.50

DON GIOVANNI, W. A. Mozart. Complete libretto, modern English translation; biographies of composer and librettist; accounts of early performances and critical reaction. Lavishly illustrated. All the material you need to understand and appreciate this great work. Dover Opera Guide and Libretto Series; translated and introduced by Ellen Bleiler. 92 illustrations. 209pp.

21134-7 Paperbound $1.50

HIGH FIDELITY SYSTEMS: A LAYMAN'S GUIDE, Roy F. Allison. All the basic information you need for setting up your own audio system: high fidelity and stereo record players, tape records, F.M. Connections, adjusting tone arm, cartridge, checking needle alignment, positioning speakers, phasing speakers, adjusting hums, trouble-shooting, maintenance, and similar topics. Enlarged 1965 edition. More than 50 charts, diagrams, photos. iv + 91pp. 21514-8 Paperbound $1.25

REPRODUCTION OF SOUND, Edgar Villchur. Thorough coverage for laymen of high fidelity systems, reproducing systems in general, needles, amplifiers, preamps, loudspeakers, feedback, explaining physical background. "A rare talent for making technicalities vividly comprehensible," R. Darrell, *High Fidelity.* 69 figures. iv + 92pp. 21515-6 Paperbound $1.00

HEAR ME TALKIN' TO YA: THE STORY OF JAZZ AS TOLD BY THE MEN WHO MADE IT, Nat Shapiro and Nat Hentoff. Louis Armstrong, Fats Waller, Jo Jones, Clarence Williams, Billy Holiday, Duke Ellington, Jelly Roll Morton and dozens of other jazz greats tell how it was in Chicago's South Side, New Orleans, depression Harlem and the modern West Coast as jazz was born and grew. xvi + 429pp.

21726-4 Paperbound $2.00

FABLES OF AESOP, translated by Sir Roger L'Estrange. A reproduction of the very rare 1931 Paris edition; a selection of the most interesting fables, together with 50 imaginative drawings by Alexander Calder. v + 128pp. 6½x9¼.

21780-9 Paperbound $1.25

AGAINST THE GRAIN (A REBOURS), Joris K. Huysmans. Filled with weird images, evidences of a bizarre imagination, exotic experiments with hallucinatory drugs, rich tastes and smells and the diversions of its sybarite hero Duc Jean des Esseintes, this classic novel pushed 19th-century literary decadence to its limits. Full unabridged edition. Do not confuse this with abridged editions generally sold. Introduction by Havelock Ellis. xlix + 206pp. 22190-3 Paperbound $2.00

VARIORUM SHAKESPEARE: HAMLET. Edited by Horace H. Furness; a landmark of American scholarship. Exhaustive footnotes and appendices treat all doubtful words and phrases, as well as suggested critical emendations throughout the play's history. First volume contains editor's own text, collated with all Quartos and Folios. Second volume contains full first Quarto, translations of Shakespeare's sources (Belleforest, and Saxo Grammaticus), Der Bestrafte Brudermord, and many essays on critical and historical points of interest by major authorities of past and present. Includes details of staging and costuming over the years. By far the best edition available for serious students of Shakespeare. Total of xx + 905pp. 21004-9, 21005-7, 2 volumes, Paperbound $5.25

A LIFE OF WILLIAM SHAKESPEARE, Sir Sidney Lee. This is the standard life of Shakespeare, summarizing everything known about Shakespeare and his plays. Incredibly rich in material, broad in coverage, clear and judicious, it has served thousands as the best introduction to Shakespeare. 1931 edition. 9 plates. xxix + 792pp. (USO) 21967-4 Paperbound $3.75

MASTERS OF THE DRAMA, John Gassner. Most comprehensive history of the drama in print, covering every tradition from Greeks to modern Europe and America, including India, Far East, etc. Covers more than 800 dramatists, 2000 plays, with biographical material, plot summaries, theatre history, criticism, etc. "Best of its kind in English," New Republic. 77 illustrations. xxii + 890pp. 20100-7 Clothbound $7.50

THE EVOLUTION OF THE ENGLISH LANGUAGE, George McKnight. The growth of English, from the 14th century to the present. Unusual, non-technical account presents basic information in very interesting form: sound shifts, change in grammar and syntax, vocabulary growth, similar topics. Abundantly illustrated with quotations. Formerly Modern English in the Making. xii + 590pp. 21932-1 Paperbound $3.50

AN ETYMOLOGICAL DICTIONARY OF MODERN ENGLISH, Ernest Weekley. Fullest, richest work of its sort, by foremost British lexicographer. Detailed word histories, including many colloquial and archaic words; extensive quotations. Do not confuse this with the Concise Etymological Dictionary, which is much abridged. Total of xxvii + 830pp. $6\frac{1}{2}$ x $9\frac{1}{4}$. 21873-2, 21874-0 Two volumes, Paperbound $5.50

FLATLAND: A ROMANCE OF MANY DIMENSIONS, E. A. Abbott. Classic of science-fiction explores ramifications of life in a two-dimensional world, and what happens when a three-dimensional being intrudes. Amusing reading, but also useful as introduction to thought about hyperspace. Introduction by Banesh Hoffmann. 16 illustrations. xx + 103pp. 20001-9 Paperbound $1.00

POEMS OF ANNE BRADSTREET, edited with an introduction by Robert Hutchinson. A new selection of poems by America's first poet and perhaps the first significant woman poet in the English language. 48 poems display her development in works of considerable variety—love poems, domestic poems, religious meditations, formal elegies, "quaternions," etc. Notes, bibliography. viii + 222pp.
22160-1 Paperbound $2.00

THREE GOTHIC NOVELS: THE CASTLE OF OTRANTO BY HORACE WALPOLE; VATHEK BY WILLIAM BECKFORD; THE VAMPYRE BY JOHN POLIDORI, WITH FRAGMENT OF A NOVEL BY LORD BYRON, edited by E. F. Bleiler. The first Gothic novel, by Walpole; the finest Oriental tale in English, by Beckford; powerful Romantic supernatural story in versions by Polidori and Byron. All extremely important in history of literature; all still exciting, packed with supernatural thrills, ghosts, haunted castles, magic, etc. xl + 291pp.
21232-7 Paperbound $2.00

THE BEST TALES OF HOFFMANN, E. T. A. Hoffmann. 10 of Hoffmann's most important stories, in modern re-editings of standard translations: Nutcracker and the King of Mice, Signor Formica, Automata, The Sandman, Rath Krespel, The Golden Flowerpot, Master Martin the Cooper, The Mines of Falun, The King's Betrothed, A New Year's Eve Adventure. 7 illustrations by Hoffmann. Edited by E. F. Bleiler. xxxix + 419pp.
21793-0 Paperbound $2.25

GHOST AND HORROR STORIES OF AMBROSE BIERCE, Ambrose Bierce. 23 strikingly modern stories of the horrors latent in the human mind: The Eyes of the Panther, The Damned Thing, An Occurrence at Owl Creek Bridge, An Inhabitant of Carcosa, etc., plus the dream-essay, Visions of the Night. Edited by E. F. Bleiler. xxii + 199pp.
20767-6 Paperbound $1.50

BEST GHOST STORIES OF J. S. LEFANU, J. Sheridan LeFanu. Finest stories by Victorian master often considered greatest supernatural writer of all. Carmilla, Green Tea, The Haunted Baronet, The Familiar, and 12 others. Most never before available in the U. S. A. Edited by E. F. Bleiler. 8 illustrations from Victorian publications. xvii + 467pp.
20415-4 Paperbound $2.50

THE TIME STREAM, THE GREATEST ADVENTURE, AND THE PURPLE SAPPHIRE— THREE SCIENCE FICTION NOVELS, John Taine (Eric Temple Bell). Great American mathematician was also foremost science fiction novelist of the 1920's. *The Time Stream,* one of all-time classics, uses concepts of circular time; *The Greatest Adventure,* incredibly ancient biological experiments from Antarctica threaten to escape; *The Purple Sapphire,* superscience, lost races in Central Tibet, survivors of the Great Race. 4 illustrations by Frank R. Paul. v + 532pp.
21180-0 Paperbound $2.50

SEVEN SCIENCE FICTION NOVELS, H. G. Wells. The standard collection of the great novels. Complete, unabridged. *First Men in the Moon, Island of Dr. Moreau, War of the Worlds, Food of the Gods, Invisible Man, Time Machine, In the Days of the Comet.* Not only science fiction fans, but every educated person owes it to himself to read these novels. 1015pp.
20264-X Clothbound $5.00

THE PHILOSOPHY OF THE UPANISHADS, Paul Deussen. Clear, detailed statement of upanishadic system of thought, generally considered among best available. History of these works, full exposition of system emergent from them, parallel concepts in the West. Translated by A. S. Geden. xiv + 429pp.

21616-0 Paperbound $3.00

LANGUAGE, TRUTH AND LOGIC, Alfred J. Ayer. Famous, remarkably clear introduction to the Vienna and Cambridge schools of Logical Positivism; function of philosophy, elimination of metaphysical thought, nature of analysis, similar topics. "Wish I had written it myself," Bertrand Russell. 2nd, 1946 edition. 160pp.

20010-8 Paperbound $1.35

THE GUIDE FOR THE PERPLEXED, Moses Maimonides. Great classic of medieval Judaism, major attempt to reconcile revealed religion (Pentateuch, commentaries) and Aristotelian philosophy. Enormously important in all Western thought. Unabridged Friedländer translation. 50-page introduction. lix + 414pp.

(USO) 20351-4 Paperbound $2.50

OCCULT AND SUPERNATURAL PHENOMENA, D. H. Rawcliffe. Full, serious study of the most persistent delusions of mankind: crystal gazing, mediumistic trance, stigmata, lycanthropy, fire walking, dowsing, telepathy, ghosts, ESP, etc., and their relation to common forms of abnormal psychology. Formerly *Illusions and Delusions of the Supernatural and the Occult.* iii + 551pp. 20503-7 Paperbound $3.50

THE EGYPTIAN BOOK OF THE DEAD: THE PAPYRUS OF ANI, E. A. Wallis Budge. Full hieroglyphic text, interlinear transliteration of sounds, word for word translation, then smooth, connected translation; Theban recension. Basic work in Ancient Egyptian civilization; now even more significant than ever for historical importance, dilation of consciousness, etc. clvi + 377pp. 6½ x 9¼.

21866-X Paperbound $3.75

PSYCHOLOGY OF MUSIC, Carl E. Seashore. Basic, thorough survey of everything known about psychology of music up to 1940's; essential reading for psychologists, musicologists. Physical acoustics; auditory apparatus; relationship of physical sound to perceived sound; role of the mind in sorting, altering, suppressing, creating sound sensations; musical learning, testing for ability, absolute pitch, other topics. Records of Caruso, Menuhin analyzed. 88 figures. xix + 408pp.

21851-1 Paperbound $2.75

THE I CHING (THE BOOK OF CHANGES), translated by James Legge. Complete translated text plus appendices by Confucius, of perhaps the most penetrating divination book ever compiled. Indispensable to all study of early Oriental civilizations. 3 plates. xxiii + 448pp. 21062-6 Paperbound $2.75

THE UPANISHADS, translated by Max Müller. Twelve classical upanishads: Chandogya, Kena, Aitareya, Kaushitaki, Isa, Katha, Mundaka, Taittiriyaka, Brhadaranyaka, Svetasvatara, Prasna, Maitriyana. 160-page introduction, analysis by Prof. Müller. Total of 826pp. 20398-0, 20399-9 Two volumes, Paperbound $5.00

JIM WHITEWOLF: THE LIFE OF A KIOWA APACHE INDIAN, Charles S. Brant, editor. Spans transition between native life and acculturation period, 1880 on. Kiowa culture, personal life pattern, religion and the supernatural, the Ghost Dance, breakdown in the White Man's world, similar material. 1 map. xii + 144pp.
22015-X Paperbound $1.75

THE NATIVE TRIBES OF CENTRAL AUSTRALIA, Baldwin Spencer and F. J. Gillen. Basic book in anthropology, devoted to full coverage of the Arunta and Warramunga tribes; the source for knowledge about kinship systems, material and social culture, religion, etc. Still unsurpassed. 121 photographs, 89 drawings. xviii + 669pp.
21775-2 Paperbound $5.00

MALAY MAGIC, Walter W. Skeat. Classic (1900); still the definitive work on the folklore and popular religion of the Malay peninsula. Describes marriage rites, birth spirits and ceremonies, medicine, dances, games, war and weapons, etc. Extensive quotes from original sources, many magic charms translated into English. 35 illustrations. Preface by Charles Otto Blagden. xxiv + 685pp.
21760-4 Paperbound $3.50

HEAVENS ON EARTH: UTOPIAN COMMUNITIES IN AMERICA, 1680-1880, Mark Holloway. The finest nontechnical account of American utopias, from the early Woman in the Wilderness, Ephrata, Rappites to the enormous mid 19th-century efflorescence; Shakers, New Harmony, Equity Stores, Fourier's Phalanxes, Oneida, Amana, Fruitlands, etc. "Entertaining and very instructive." *Times Literary Supplement.* 15 illustrations. 246pp.
21593-8 Paperbound $2.00

LONDON LABOUR AND THE LONDON POOR, Henry Mayhew. Earliest (c. 1850) sociological study in English, describing myriad subcultures of London poor. Particularly remarkable for the thousands of pages of direct testimony taken from the lips of London prostitutes, thieves, beggars, street sellers, chimney-sweepers, street-musicians, "mudlarks," "pure-finders," rag-gatherers, "running-patterers," dock laborers, cab-men, and hundreds of others, quoted directly in this massive work. An extraordinarily vital picture of London emerges. 110 illustrations. Total of lxxvi + 1951pp. 6⅝ x 10.
21934-8, 21935-6, 21936-4, 21937-2 Four volumes, Paperbound $14.00

HISTORY OF THE LATER ROMAN EMPIRE, J. B. Bury. Eloquent, detailed reconstruction of Western and Byzantine Roman Empire by a major historian, from the death of Theodosius I (395 A.D.) to the death of Justinian (565). Extensive quotations from contemporary sources; full coverage of important Roman and foreign figures of the time. xxxiv + 965pp. 21829-5 Record, book, album. Monaural. $2.75

AN INTELLECTUAL AND CULTURAL HISTORY OF THE WESTERN WORLD, Harry Elmer Barnes. Monumental study, tracing the development of the accomplishments that make up human culture. Every aspect of man's achievement surveyed from its origins in the Paleolithic to the present day (1964); social structures, ideas, economic systems, art, literature, technology, mathematics, the sciences, medicine, religion, jurisprudence, etc. Evaluations of the contributions of scores of great men. 1964 edition, revised and edited by scholars in the many fields represented. Total of xxix + 1381pp. 21275-0, 21276-9, 21277-7 Three volumes, Paperbound $7.75

MATHEMATICAL PUZZLES FOR BEGINNERS AND ENTHUSIASTS, Geoffrey Mott-Smith. 189 puzzles from easy to difficult—involving arithmetic, logic, algebra, properties of digits, probability, etc.—for enjoyment and mental stimulus. Explanation of mathematical principles behind the puzzles. 135 illustrations. viii + 248pp.

20198-8 Paperbound $1.25

PAPER FOLDING FOR BEGINNERS, William D. Murray and Francis J. Rigney. Easiest book on the market, clearest instructions on making interesting, beautiful origami. Sail boats, cups, roosters, frogs that move legs, bonbon boxes, standing birds, etc. 40 projects; more than 275 diagrams and photographs. 94pp.

20713-7 Paperbound $1.00

TRICKS AND GAMES ON THE POOL TABLE, Fred Herrmann. 79 tricks and games— some solitaires, some for two or more players, some competitive games—to entertain you between formal games. Mystifying shots and throws, unusual caroms, tricks involving such props as cork, coins, a hat, etc. Formerly *Fun on the Pool Table*. 77 figures. 95pp.

21814-7 Paperbound $1.00

HAND SHADOWS TO BE THROWN UPON THE WALL: A SERIES OF NOVEL AND AMUSING FIGURES FORMED BY THE HAND, Henry Bursill. Delightful picturebook from great-grandfather's day shows how to make 18 different hand shadows: a bird that flies, duck that quacks, dog that wags his tail, camel, goose, deer, boy, turtle, etc. Only book of its sort. vi + 33pp. 6½ x 9¼.

21779-5 Paperbound $1.00

WHITTLING AND WOODCARVING, E. J. Tangerman. 18th printing of best book on market. "If you can cut a potato you can carve" toys and puzzles, chains, chessmen, caricatures, masks, frames, woodcut blocks, surface patterns, much more. Information on tools, woods, techniques. Also goes into serious wood sculpture from Middle Ages to present, East and West. 464 photos, figures. x + 293pp.

20965-2 Paperbound $2.00

HISTORY OF PHILOSOPHY, Julián Marias. Possibly the clearest, most easily followed, best planned, most useful one-volume history of philosophy on the market; neither skimpy nor overfull. Full details on system of every major philosopher and dozens of less important thinkers from pre-Socratics up to Existentialism and later. Strong on many European figures usually omitted. Has gone through dozens of editions in Europe. 1966 edition, translated by Stanley Appelbaum and Clarence Strowbridge. xviii + 505pp.

21739-6 Paperbound $2.75

YOGA: A SCIENTIFIC EVALUATION, Kovoor T. Behanan. Scientific but non-technical study of physiological results of yoga exercises; done under auspices of Yale U. Relations to Indian thought, to psychoanalysis, etc. 16 photos. xxiii + 270pp.

20505-3 Paperbound $2.50

Prices subject to change without notice.
Available at your book dealer or write for free catalogue to Dept. GI, Dover Publications, Inc., 180 Varick St., N. Y., N. Y. 10014. Dover publishes more than 150 books each year on science, elementary and advanced mathematics, biology, music, art, literary history, social sciences and other areas.

5027